Mortality, Immortality and Other Life Strategies

Mortality, Immortality and Other Life Strategies

ZYGMUNT BAUMAN

Stanford University Press
Stanford, California
1992

Stanford University Press
Stanford, California
© 1992 Zygmunt Bauman
Originating publisher: Polity Press, Cambridge,
   in association with Blackwell Publishers, Oxford
First published in the U.S.A. by
   Stanford University Press, 1992
Printed in Great Britain
Cloth ISBN 0-8047-2163-7
Paper ISBN 0-8047-2164-5
LC 92-64405
This book is printed on acid free paper.

Contents

Judith Adler, Jean Briggs and Robert Paine took the trouble of reading through parts of the manuscript. If only I had the ability to absorb and give justice to the perceptive comments and insights they generously shared with me.

   I am deeply grateful to Anthony Giddens for his thorough reading of the text and penetrating critique.

   Once more, I thank David Roberts for his editorial wisdom, patience and dedication.

About this Book

This is not a study in the *sociology of death and dying*; not a book about the ways we treat people about to die and commemorate those already dead, the way we mourn the beloved and cope with the agony of bereavement, the rituals we devise to prevent the dead from disappearing from the world of living too fast or without a trace – and make their disappearance painless. The number and quality of studies dedicated to that large and important section of our daily life has been growing at a breath-taking pace in the last forty years or so (that is, since death emerged from that protracted conspiracy of silence in which it sunk towards the end of the nineteenth century and which, as Geoffrey Gorer pointedly observed, made all mention of death smack of pornography). The sociology of death and dying has grown by now into a fully fledged branch of social science, armed with everything an academic discipline needs to insure its own survival – a body of literature of its own, a network of university addresses, journals and conferences. This book draws from this achievement rather than adding to it. But the subject-matter of this book is not death or the 'handling of death' as a separate, though large, area of social life and a specific, though ample set of socially sustained patterns of behaviour.

Neither is this a study of the changing *vision* of death: of the images of death and its aftermath, of either the 'other world' or the void that opens once life closes – of that *mentalité collective* which shapes and is in turn shaped by our shifting attitudes to human mortality. After Philippe Ariès and Michel Vovelle (and without the benefit of their supreme historiographic skills) it would be indeed arrogant for this author to think of adding anything of substance to the grand historical canvas already painted.

The prime subject-matter of this book is not those aspects of human mentality, of the practices it supports and of the practices by which it is supported, which openly and explicitly address themselves to the facts and concepts of death and mortality. On the contrary, the immodest intention

1

of this book is to unpack, and to open up to investigation, the presence of death (i.e. of the conscious or repressed knowledge of mortality) in human institutions, rituals and beliefs which, on the face of it, explicitly and self-consciously, serve tasks and functions altogether different, unrelated to the preoccupations normally scrutinized in studies dedicated to the 'history of death and dying'.

We all 'know' very well what death is; that is, until we are asked to give a precise account of what we know – to define death as we 'understand' it. Then the trouble starts. It transpires that it is ultimately impossible to define death, though attempts to define it – to master it (albeit intellectually), to assign it its proper place and keep it there – will never stop. It is impossible to define death, as death stands for the final void, for that non-existence which, absurdly, gives existence to all being. Death is the absolute *other* of being, an *unimaginable* other, hovering beyond the reach of communication; whenever being speaks of that other, it finds itself speaking, through a negative metaphor, of itself. The sentences in this paragraph are, after all, also, without exception, metaphors: death is not like other 'others' – those others which the ego is free to fill with meaning, and in the course of this meaning-bestowing act to constitute and to subordinate.

Death cannot be perceived; still less visualized or 'represented'. As we know from Husserl, all perception is *intentional*; an activity of the perceiving subject, it reaches beyond that subject, it grasps *something beyond* the subject, it simultaneously calls into being an 'object' that belongs to a world which can in principle be shared, and anchors itself in it. But there is no 'something' which is death; nothing in which the stretched intention of the subject struggling for perception would rest, where it could cast its anchor. Death is an absolute *nothing* and 'absolute nothing' makes no sense – we know that 'there is nothing' only when *we can perceive* the absence of perception; every 'nothing' is a faced, perceived, contemplated nothing, and so no 'nothing' can be absolute – an unqualified nothing. But death is the cessation of the very 'acting subject', and with it, *the end* of all perception. Such an end of perception is one state of affairs the perceiving subject cannot conjure up: it cannot 'blot itself out' of the perception and still wish the perception to be. (As Husserl would say, there is no *noesis*, the act of cognition, without *noema*, the objects to be known – and vice versa.) Faced with such impossibility, the perceiving subject may only delude itself with a play of metaphors, which conceals rather than reveals what is to be perceived, and in the end belies the state of non-perception which death would be. Failing that, the knowing subject must admit its impotence and throw in the towel.

This is why the frequently suggested exit from the quandary ('I cannot visualize my own death, but I do observe death of others. I know that all people die, and thus, so to speak, I "know death" by proxy, and I know death is unavoidable, and I have a clear idea of mortality.') would not really do. The death of others is an event in the world of objects 'out there', which I perceive as any other event or object. It is *my* death, and my death only, which is not an event of that 'knowable' world of objects. The death of others does not affect the continuity of my perception. The death of others is painful and shattering precisely because it does not do it. I may dread the death of another more than my own; I may shout, with total sincerity, that I would rather die myself than live through the death of a beloved other – but this is precisely for my knowledge that *after* that death *I would have to face* a particular nothing, a void which the departure of the beloved other would create, a void which I do not want to perceive but which, stubbornly and to my horror, will be fully and clearly perceivable. What I cannot truly grasp is an altogether different state – a void or fullness *without me to tell it as such*. It is my death that cannot be narrated, that is to remain unspeakable. I am not able to experience it, and once I go through it, I shall not be around to tell the story.

In the light of the above, it is really curious why our own death fills us with horror. I will not be here when it will have come, I will not *experience* it when it comes and I most certainly do not experience it now, before its coming – so why should I worry, and why should I worry *now*? This impeccably logical – reasoning has been attributed to Epicurus, and it has lost none of its logic since antiquity. And yet, for all its undeniable wisdom, rational elegance and assumed power of persuasion, generation after generation failed to derive from it much succour. Though it is obviously correct, it sounds and feels fraudulent; it seems to pass by our real worry, to be curiously remote, indeed unrelated to all we think and feel about our death and all that makes us fear it so dreadfully. How can we explain this baffling incapacity of reason to placate the anguish? Why does philosophy so abominably fail to console? What follows is but a tentative answer to this question which stands little chance of ever being answered conclusively.

Humans are the only creatures who not only know, but also know that they know – and cannot 'unknow' their knowledge. In particular, they cannot 'unknow' the knowledge of their mortality. Once humans tasted of the Tree of Knowledge, the taste could not be forgotten, it could only be *not remembered* – for a while, with attention shifting to other impressions. Once learned, knowledge that death may not be escaped cannot be forgotten – it can only *not be thought about* for a while, with attention shifting to other concerns. Knowledge has, so to speak, an olfactory rather than a visual or audial quality; odours, like knowledge, cannot be undone, they can be only 'made unfelt' by being suppressed by yet stronger odours.

One can say that culture, another 'human only' quality, has been from the start a device for such a suppression. This is not to imply that all the creative drive of human culture stems from the conspiracy 'to forget death' – indeed, once set in motion, cultural inventiveness acquired its own momentum and like most other parts or aspects of culture 'develops because it develops'. But this is to imply that, were there no need to make life worth living while it is known that, in Schopenhauer's words, life is but a short-term loan from death, there hardly would be any culture. Death (more exactly, knowledge of mortality) is not the root of everything there is in culture; after all, culture is precisely about *transcendence*, about *going beyond* what is given and found before the creative imagination of culture set to work; culture is after that permanence and durability which life, by itself, so sorely misses. But death (more exactly, awareness of mortality) is the ultimate condition of cultural creativity as such. It makes permanence into a task, into an urgent task, into a paramount task – a fount and a measure of all tasks – and so it makes culture, that huge and never stopping factory of permanence.

The curious ineffectuality of Epicurus' logic is the direct outcome of culture's success. One may say that culture 'overfulfilled the plan'; it has 'overdone it'. (Yet, in all fairness, it could not do it at all without over-doing . . .) Epicurus' dictum would perhaps sound more convincing were we confronted with death in its 'raw state' – just a cessation of biological life, of eating, defecating, copulating. Thanks to culture, however, this is dazzlingly not the case. We have gone far beyond what we now call – with more than a hint of disdain – 'animal existence'. Eating and defecating and copulating will stop when life stops, but neither is the real 'life content'. What occupies most of our time (that is, if only we have time left after satisfying our 'animal' needs), what we are taught to consider the most important and most worthy thing in life, does not have to stop when our metabolism grinds to a halt, not the day after, not ever. And to make them last, to prevent them from stopping, from 'going to the grave with us', is the mission which culture made into our responsibility. Culture's 'over-doing' rebounds daily as our own individual inadequacy. Whatever we do for what we believe to be our responsibility, is unlikely to be enough. Death, when it comes, will brutally interrupt our work before our task is done, our mission accomplished. This is why we have every reason to be worried about death now, when we are still very much alive and when death remains but a remote and abstract prospect.

And so we beget kinship trees – offspring we care for and want to help around rough corners of the future; will they be able to negotiate them once they are bereaved? We build businesses of which we shall never be able to say that they are, finally, secure against competitors or that they do not need to expand any further. We 'make money', and the more money we have made, the stronger are we compelled to make still more. We dedicate our emotions and efforts to institutions or groups whose fate we wish to follow through, now and in the infinite future, and which we want to assist in what we hope will be a never-ending string of successes. We become collectors – of antiques, paintings, stamps, impressions or memories – knowing only too well that our collections will be never complete and 'finished', and that their incompleteness is the most exciting of the satisfactions they bring. We become creators – and can the 'life work' of an artist, a painter, a writer ever be brought to its 'natural' end? We develop a passion for knowledge, for consuming it, for adding to it – and each new discovery shows only how much remains to be learned. Whatever task we embrace seems to possess the same vexing quality: it sticks beyond the probable reach of our *biological lives* – of our task-performing, things-doing capacity. To make the plight still worse, this irritating feature of the tasks that give 'true content' to our lives cannot be cured. It is, after all, precisely because of that feature that the tasks in question are capable of giving life meaning which *transcends* life's biological limitations and allows us to live, to enjoy life, and to stretch ourselves to make life more enjoyable still – and all this despite what we know about the limitations, the endemic brevity and ultimate futility of life's efforts. If for one reason or another culture's suggestions lose some or all of this quality, or without losing that quality cease to be viable proposals – life loses its meaning and death becomes the only cure for the anguish and misery it itself caused in the first place. Durkheim's 'anomic suicide' comes when culture ceases to allure and seduce.

Transcendence is what, everything having been said and done, culture is about. Culture is about expanding temporal and spatial boundaries of being, with a view to dismantling them altogether. Their expansion and effacement of boundaries are partly independent, partly interpenetrating endeavours, and culture's ways and means in pursuing them are partly specialized, partly overlapping.

The first activity of culture relates to *survival* – pushing back the moment of death, extending the life-span, increasing life expectation and thus life's content-absorbing capacity; making death a matter of concern, a significant event – lifting the event of death above the level of the mundane, the ordinary, the natural; directly or indirectly (yet still more importantly), making the job of death somewhat more difficult. Commenting on Camus, Maurice Blanchot points out that 'to give death certain kind of purity was always the task of culture: to render it authentic, personal, proper ... Instinctively, we feel the danger in searching for the human limits at too low a level . . . at a point at which existence appears – through the suffering, misery and frustration – so denuded of "value" that death finds itself rehabilitated and the violence justified'. At that bottom level, where it resides until processed and ennobled by the labours of culture, death 'attracts no horror, not even an interest'. It may well be 'something as unimportant as chopping a cabbage head or drinking a glass of water'.[1]

The second relates to *immortality* – surviving, so to speak, beyond death, denying the moment of death its final say, and thus taking off some of its sinister and horrifying significance: 'He died, but his work lives on.'; 'She will always remain in our memory forever.' Though separate, the two activities depend on each other. Obviously, there is no dreaming of immortality unless survival is secure. But, on the other hand, it is the culture-endorsed assignment of life-transcending, immortal value to certain human acts and attainment that creates the potential of 'life expansion'.

'How many people will find it worth while living once they don't have to die?' asked, rhetorically, Elias Canetti. The question is rhetorical, since it has been asked in order to elicit an answer deemed to be obvious: not many, perhaps none. But the question is rhetorical also for another, more seminal reason: we all *have* to die, and we *know* it. It is here that the most sinister, and the most creative, paradox of the human predicament is rooted: the fact of having to die condemns *a priori* all survival efforts to ultimate failure, while the knowledge of having to die may well dwarf and make futile, pompous and absurd even the most grandiose of human projects. If 'meaning' is the product of intention, if action is meaningful in as far as it is purpose-oriented – then what is the meaning of life? This question, and the stubborn necessity and relentless urge to *ask it*, is the curse of the human condition and the source of interminable agony. But it is also life's mind-boggling chance. There is a void to be filled; a void which in no way limits the range of contents with which it can be filled. Purposes and meanings are not 'given'; therefore, purpose can be chosen, meaning can be created *ab nihilo*.

The woe of mortality makes humans God-like. It is because we know that we must *die* that we are so busy *making* life. It is because we are

---

[1]Maurice Blanchot, *L'Entretien infini* (Paris: Gallimard, 1969), pp. 269–70.

aware of mortality that we preserve the past and create the future. Mortality is ours without asking – but *im*mortality is something we must build ourselves. Immortality is not a mere absence of death; it is *defiance* and denial of death. It is 'meaningful' only because there is death, that implacable reality which is to be defied. There would be no immortality without mortality. Without mortality, no history, no culture – no humanity. Mortality 'created' the opportunity: all the rest has been created by beings aware that they are mortal. Mortality gave the chance; the human way of life is the outcome of that chance having been, and being, taken up.

Thus death makes its presence in human life weighty and tangible not necessarily (and not mainly!) in those selected places and times where it appears *under its own name*. True, death is the explicit target of many of the things we do and think of. There are hospitals and hospices, graveyards and crematoria, funerals and obituaries, rituals of remembrance and of mourning, special treatments meted out for the bereaved and the orphaned. If this were the end of the story, if death called just for one more repertory of specialized functions, there would be little indeed to set it apart from so many other 'objective circumstances' of the human condition. This is not, however, the case. The impact of death is at its most powerful (and creative) when death *does not appear under its own name*; in areas and times which are not explicitly dedicated to it; precisely where we manage to live *as if* death was not or did not matter, when we do not remember about mortality and are not put off or vexed by the thoughts of the ultimate futility of life.

Such a life – life forgetful of death, life lived as meaningful and worth living, life alive with purposes instead of being crushed and incapacitated by purposelessness – is a formidable *human* achievement. The totality of social organization, the whole of human culture (not certain functionally specialized institutions, nor certain functionally specialized cultural precepts) co-operate to make this achievement possible. They do not openly admit that this is so; they do not admit that most things we do (and are socially determined and culturally trained to believe that we do them for altogether different reasons) serve in the end the 'purpose of all purposes' – making possible a meaningful life in a world which 'by itself' is devoid of meaning. They cannot admit it, as admitting it would detract from the effectiveness of the achievement which consists mostly in forgetting its true reasons. The emancipation from mortality practised by social organization or promised by culture is bound to remain forever precarious and in the end illusory: thought must conjure up on its own what reality would neither supply nor permit. For this feat to be plausible, a volume of daring is needed which will be sufficient only if courage is unselfconscious of its futility. Memory of illegitimate birth must be erased if noble life is to be practised at ease.

Human culture is, on the one hand, a gigantic (and spectacularly successful) ongoing effort to give meaning to human life; on the other hand, it is an obstinate (and somewhat less successful) effort to suppress the awareness of the irreparably surrogate, and brittle, character of such meaning. The first effort would be lamentably ineffective without the constant support of the second.

This book is an attempt to lay bare this work of culture. It has, on the whole, a character of a detectivistic adventure. (And thus, owing to the nature of all detection, it is bound to rely on conjecture as much as it does on the unassailable power of deduction, and much as it would wish to rely on the hard evidence of induction.) With certain predictable qualifications, one could perhaps describe the method applied in this book as that of the 'psychoanalysis' of the 'collective unconscious' concealed in, but also analytically recoverable from, culturally created and sustained life. The analysis rests on a hypothesis – a *heuristic assumption* – that the analyzed social institutions and 'cultural solutions' are sediments of the processes which had been set in motion by the fact of human mortality and motivated by the need to cope with the issues that fact posits; as well as by the parallel need to repress the awareness of the true motives of such arrangements. This book is an attempt to find out in what respect, if any, our understanding of socio-cultural institutions may be deepened by making the above assumption and exploring its consequences.

The social institutions and cultural patterns subjected to analysis in this book would seldom be found in studies dedicated to the problematic of death and dying. Most such studies start from the point to which our culture has already brought us. They take not just the form, but the very presence of 'social realities' for granted, and stop short of penetrating the 'made-up' nature of cultural products. They therefore accept as unproblematic the confinement of death (or rather of its still protruding and visible, unassimilitated, resistant to all cultural processing, 'hard leftovers') to explicitly, purposefully designated enclaves and functions; they concur with the culturally accomplished reduction of the *issue* of mortality to the series of named, publicly recognized *problems* of the dying and the bereaved. Most certainly, such investigative practices are fully legitimate in addition to being scholarly respectable; in fact, one cannot easily imagine how the enormous inventory of variable yet invariably ingenious treatments accorded by different cultures in different historical periods to the problems posited by death could have been put together – meticulously and convincingly as they are – were it not for the deliberate narrowing of focus that marks such investigative practices.

And yet something quite crucial has been left out in the result, and is bound to remain undiscussed as long as the focus remains as it is: namely, the 'mortality connection' of such aspects of life as the cultures in question did manage to wrench out of the deadly embrace and then cover all mention of the provenance by a sort of unwritten Official Secrets act. As far as these aspects of social life are concerned, the suppression of the memory of their erstwhile 'mortality connections' is a necessary condition of their emancipation. It is precisely such aspects of social existence that have been chosen as the main subject-matter of this book; and thus the mystery of 'by-passing' or forcefully suppressing their links with the issue of mortality constitutes a major problem for this study.

I propose that the fact of human mortality, and the necessity to live with the constant awareness of that fact, go a long way toward accounting for many a crucial aspect of social and cultural organization of all known societies; and that most, perhaps all, known cultures can be better understood (or at least understood differently, in a novel way) if conceived of as alternative ways in which that primary trait of human existence – *the fact of mortality and the knowledge of it* – is dealt with and processed, so that it may turn from the condition of impossibility of meaningful life into the major source of life's meaning. At the end of such process death, a fact of nature, a biological phenomenon, re-emerges as a cultural artefact, and in this culturally processed form offers the primary building material for social institutions and behavioural patterns crucial to the reproduction of societies in their distinctive forms.

In other words, mortality and *immortality* (as well as their imagined opposition, itself construed as a cultural reality through patterned thoughts and practices) become approved and practised *life strategies*. All human societies deploy them in one form or another, but cultures may play up or play down the significance of death-avoidance concerns in the conduct of life (Ariès wrote profusely of the 'taming' or 'domesticating' of death in pre-modern societies; death-avoidance, re-forged into daily concern with health and obsessive worry about death-carrying agents, becomes on the contrary the most salient feature of modern life.) They also offer formulae for defusing the horror of death through hopes, and sometimes institutional guarantees, of immortality. The latter may be posited as either a collective destiny or an individual achievement. In the first case, it serves as a major means of social division and surfaces spectacularly in the phenomenon of tribalism and tribal enmity. In the second case, it serves as a major vehicle of social stratification, supplies the core content of distinction and privilege as well as the main bait for status-seeking efforts and a coveted stake in positional strife.

The first three chapters of the book consider in general terms (one is tempted to say existential terms) this universal and permanent role of mortality in the process of social structuration and the setting of cultural agenda. The last two chapters, on the other hand, face the fact that the concrete ways of tackling that universal role of mortality change over time and are culturally specific; a circumstance which will be shown to have far-reaching consequences for society as a whole – determining to a large extent its overall character, also in aspects ostensibly unconnected, or related only obliquely, to the phenomena of death and dying.

Two types of strategies (which *contemporary* society, not without a contradiction, tries to deploy *simultaneously* – the circumstance that makes even more futile the barren efforts to draw, or to efface, the *time-boundary* between the 'modern' and 'postmodern' eras) come under a closer scrutiny: the *modern* type, with its characteristic drive to 'decon-struct' *mortality* (i.e. to dissolve the issue of the struggle against death in an ever growing and never exhausted set of battles against particular diseases and other threats to life; and to move death from its past position of the ultimate yet remote horizon of life-span right into the centre of daily life, thereby filling the latter with the defences against non-ultimate, relatively smaller and thus in principle 'soluble' problems of health hazards), and the *postmodern*, with its effort to 'deconstruct' *immortality* (i.e. to substitute notoriety for historical memory, and disappearance for final – irreversible – death, and to transform life into an unstoppable, daily rehearsal of universal 'mortality' of things and of the effacement of opposition between the transient and the durable).

To sum up: in its intention at least, this book is not a contribution to the specialized discipline of sociology of death, dying and bereavement, but rather to sociological theory in general. An attempt is made here to trace the cognitive profits which may be gained from the interpretation of major socio-cultural processes as both *arising from* (triggered by) the prominence of death in the human existential condition, and *deploying* that prominence as the principal building material in the socio-cultural organization of historically specific forms of practical human existence. What this book offers is a perspective from which to view anew, from an uncommon yet crucial angle, the apparently familiar topics of social and cultural life.

This book is an exercise in *sociological hermeneutics*. The meaning of social institutions and collectively pursued patterns of conduct is sought through considering them as members of such sets of strategies as are, in a sense, pre-selected and made realistic (available for choosing and possible to deploy) in given social figurations. In this instance, sociological hermeneutics demands that the continuous and changing aspects of life strategies alike be traced back to the social figurations they serve (in a dialectic process of reciprocal determination) – and forward, to the patterns of daily life in which they find expression.

In all or most interpretations – those exercises in comprehension, in 'making sense' – the interpreted phenomena may be ascribed more system-like cohesiveness than they in fact demonstrate. What is in real life an agonizingly confused, contradictory and often incoherent state of affairs, may be portrayed as endowed with simple and regular features. A special effort has been made here to avoid this danger, to refuse the temptation to represent the analyzed life strategies and their behavioural consequences as more coherent and less ambiguous than they indeed are. And yet strategies had to be offered 'identities' to separate them and distinguish from their alternatives, and hence little could be done to prevent them from appearing more self-contained and complete than they have ever been or can be. Any reading of this book ought to be done with this proviso in mind. We do not live, after all, once in a pre-modern, once in a modern, once in postmodern world. All three 'worlds' are but abstract idealizations of mutually incoherent aspects of the single life process which we all try our best to make as coherent as we can manage. Idealizations are no more (but no less either) than sediments, and also indispensable tools, of those efforts.

1

Living with Death

Unlike other animals, we not only know; we *know that we know*. We are aware of being aware, conscious of 'having' consciousness, of being conscious. Our knowledge is itself an object of knowledge: we can gaze at our thoughts 'the same way' we look at our hands or feet and at the 'things' which surround our bodies not being part of them. Our knowledge shares in the existential, inalienable, defining quality of *things*: it cannot be (except in fantasy) *wished away*, that is annihilated by the sheer exertion of will. 'It is there', stubbornly, relentlessly, 'permanently' in the sense that it lasts longer than our active awareness of its presence, and that its 'staying there' is not synchronized with our look. We know that we can look at it again and again, that we will find it in place the moment we focus our alertness on the right point – turn our eyes (our attention) in the right direction. (When the thought we are looking for, and know 'to be there', cannot 'be found' at the moment, we call the failure 'lapse of memory'; we explain the difficulty in the same fashion in which we think of the absence of other things we expected to find in a certain place but did not – like a lost pen or a pair of glasses: we do not suppose that the things ceased to exist, only that they have been moved, or that we could not locate them as we have been looking in the wrong direction.) When our knowledge is hard to bear with, our only escape is to treat it the way we treat things that offend us: we sweep such things away, put them at a distance from which their stench or repulsive sight is less likely to affect us; we hide them. Offensive thoughts must be *suppressed*. Failing that, they must be prettified or otherwise disguised, so that their ugly look would not vex us. But as with all things, escape is seldom complete and conclusive. We must not suspend our vigilance; we must keep trying – and we know it.

There is hardly a thought more offensive than that of death; or, rather, of the inevitability of dying; of the transience of our being-in-the-world. After all, this part of our knowledge defies, radically and irrevocably, our intellectual faculties. Death is the ultimate defeat of reason, since reason cannot 'think' death – not what we *know* death to be like; the thought of death is – and is bound to remain – a *contradiction in terms*. 'Neither my birth nor my death can appear to me as *my* experiences', observed Merleau-Ponty. 'I can only grasp myself as "already born" and "still living" – grasping my birth and death only as pre-personal horizons.' Sigmund Freud is of a similar view: 'It is indeed impossible to imagine our own death; and whenever we attempt to do so we can perceive that we are in fact still present as spectators.' Edgar Morin concluded in his pioneering study of the anthropological status of death that 'the idea of death is an idea without content'; or, to put it another way, it is 'the hollowest of the hollow ideas', since its content 'is unthinkable, inexplicable, a conceptual *je ne sais quoi*'. The horror of death is the horror of void, of the ultimate absence, of 'non-being'. The conscience of death is, and is bound to remain, *traumatic*.[1]

---

[1] Maurice Merleau-Ponty, *Phenomenologie de la perception*, quoted after Robert Jay Lifton, 'On Death and Death Symbolism', in: *The Phenomenon of Death: Faces of Mortality*, ed. Edith Wyschogrod (New York: Harper & Row, 1973), p. 93; Sigmund Freud, 'Thoughts for the Times on War and Death', in *Complete Psychological Works*, vol. 14 (London: Hogarth, 1957), p. 289; Edgar Morin, *L'Homme et la Mort* (Paris: Seuil, 1970), pp. 29–30. In the preface to the second edition of the book (published originally in 1951), Morin suggests that the knowledge of death is a much more decisive break between human modality and animal existence than tool-production, brain or language: all such normally pinpointed 'human-only' characteristics are either metaphors or extensions of the work of biological evolution and mechanisms of survival that evolution made available to animal species. Not so our knowledge of death. 'Death – that is, the refusal to die, the myths of survival, of resurrection, of immortality – what do they tell us about specifically human quality, and the universally biological quality? Is there any continuity in this break?' (pp. 7–8).

Arthur Schopenhauer insists that 'without death there would hardly have been any philosophizing'. *All* religious and philosophical systems (Schopenhauer would add, were the word part of his vocabulary, all *culture*) are 'primarily an antidote to the certainty of death which reflecting reason produces from its own resources'. (*The World as Will and Representation*, trans. E.F.J. Payne (New York: Dover, 1966), p. 463.) This, in Schopenhauer's view, is the case, one would suppose, precisely because 'a man to his astonishment all at once becomes conscious of existing after having been in a state of non-existence for many thousands of years, when, presently again, he returns to a state of non-existence for an equally long time. This cannot possibly be true, says the heart.' (*Essays of Schopenhauer*, trans. Rudolf Dircks (London: Walter Scott, n.d.), pp. 54–5).

Knowledge that cannot be believed

And there are more than enough reasons for the consciousness of mortality to be traumatic. First and foremost, thinking about death defies thought itself. The nature of thought is its non-confinement, its 'untiedness' to time and space: its ability to reach into the time which is no more or the time that has not yet been, to visualize places that eyes cannot see nor fingers touch. In all such times and places, however, the thought that conjures them up remains present; they 'exist' only in and through its act of 'conjuring up'. The one thing thought cannot grasp is *its own* non-existence: it cannot conceive of a time or place that does not contain it anymore, as all conceiving includes it – thought, the thinking capacity – as the 'conceiving power'. (This incapacity of thought to imagine its own non-being had been perversely presented by Descartes as the world-sustaining potency of thought: we think, *therefore* we exist; our act of thinking is the one and only existence we cannot doubt, an existence by which all other certainties are to be measured.) Because of this organic incapacity of thought it simply cannot occur to us that our consciousness – so obvious, so pervasive, so ubiquitous – may, like other things, cease to be. Thought's power is, one may say, born of weakness: thought seems all-powerful because certain thoughts cannot be thought and thus are 'blotted out' by default rather than by design. Most importantly and crucially, the thought that cannot be thought and thus may well escape scrutiny is the thought of non-existence of thought. The resulting cosy self-confidence of thought, so comforting and so desirable, would be foolproof, if it were not for the knowledge of death. Death is, after all, precisely the unthinkable: a state without thought; one we cannot visualize – even construe conceptually. But death *is*, is *real*, and we know it.

There are, of course, other things we know of, without being able to visualize and 'understand' them. The spatial and temporary *infinity* of the universe is the classic case: indeed, it is a mind-boggling state of affairs for the very reason that its alternative – the temporal or spatial *confinement* of the universe – can be visualized no better. This is frightening enough: a spectacular insight into the irreparable disjointment between mind and body, between what the mind can *think* and what the body can *'see'*, directly or metaphorically. But thought's quandary brought up by the reality of death reaches deeper than that. The predicament that death reveals is still more radically frightening. One can, after all, think of existence without stars and galaxies, without matter even; one cannot think, however, of an *existence without thought*. So death – an unadorned death, death in all its stark, uncompromised bluntness, a death that would induce consciousness to stop – is the *ultimate absurdity*, while being at the same time the *ultimate truth*! Death reveals that truth and absurdity are one ... We cannot think of death otherwise than of an event of which we (who, as we know, have ceased to be) are witnesses; events at which we (we, thinking and seeing foundations of all experience) are present in that relentless, obstinate fashion that is the constitutive mark of awareness. Whenever we 'imagine' ourselves as dead, we are irremovably present in the picture as those who do the imagining: our living consciousness looks at our dead bodies. Death does not just defy imagination: death is the archetypal *contradiction in terms*, The non-being of matter is difficult, nay impossible, to *imagine*; to imagine the non-existence of mind is downright impossible. Such a non-being may be thought only in its denial. The very act of thinking death is already its denial. Our thoughts of death, to be at all thinkable, must already be processed, artificed, tinkered with, interpreted away from their pristine absurdity. As La Rochefoucauld used to say, one cannot look *directly* at either the sun or death.

Also in yet another respect death blatantly defies the power of reason: reason's power is to be a guide to good choice, but death is not a matter of choice. Death is the scandal, the ultimate humiliation of reason. It saps the trust in reason and the security that reason promises. It loudly declares reason's lie. It inspires fear that undermines and ultimately defeats reason's offer of confidence. Reason cannot exculpate itself of this ignominy. It can only try a cover-up. And it does. Since the discovery of death (and the state of having discovered death is the defining, and distinctive, feature of humanity) human societies have kept designing elaborate subterfuges, hoping that they would be allowed to forget about the scandal; failing that, hoping that they could afford not to think about it; failing that, they forbade speaking of it. According to Ernest Becker, 'all culture, all man's creative life-ways, are in some basic part of them a fabricated protest against natural reality, a denial of the truth of human condition, and an attempt to forget the pathetic creature that man is ... Society itself is a codified hero system, which means that the society everywhere is a living myth of the significance of human life, a defiant creation of meaning.'[2]

---

[2] Ernest Becker, *The Denial of Death* (New York: Free Press, 1973), pp. 33, 7. According to Becker, the essential incongruity of human predicament makes human existence irreparably *heroic*: an incessant struggle to transcend what in principle cannot be transcended. 'The fact is that this is what society is and always has been: a symbolic action system, a structure of statuses and roles, customs and rules of behaviour, designed to serve as a vehicle for earthly heroism.' (p. 4) 'But the truth about the need for heroism is not easy for anyone to admit'; in most men heroics 'is disguised as they humbly and complainingly follow out the roles that

Death is the ultimate defeat of reason, as it exposes the absurdity that lies at the foundation of reason's logic and the void that underpins – indeed, nourishes – reason's audacity and self-confidence. There is little reason can do about this defeat, and the fashion in which it tries to extricate itself from rout only adds to its humiliation. In Charles W. Wahl's words, death 'does not yield to science and to rationality', and thus 'we are perforce impelled to employ the heavy artillery of defence, namely, a recourse to magic and irrationality'.

We tend to lie (to cover up the silence we would be sunk in, hopelessly, were we ready or able to speak what we know but do not wish to remember) whenever we speak of death; we lie whenever we refer to the event of death as 'passing on', and to the dead as the 'departed'. Yet the lie is not conscious, because 'at bottom', as Freud states, 'no one believes in his own death', and our unconscious 'behaves as if it were immortal'.[3]

---

society provides for their heroics and try to earn their promotions within the system: wearing the standard uniforms – but allowing themselves to stick out, but ever so little and so safely, with a little ribbon or a red boutonniere, but not with head and shoulders.' (p. 6) Within society, 'man cuts out for himself a manageable world ... He accepts the cultural programming that turns his nose where he is supposed to look ... He learns not to expose himself, not to stand out; he learns to embed himself in other-power, both of concrete persons and of things and cultural commands; the result is that he comes to exist in the imagined infallibility of the world around him. He doesn't have to have fears when his feet are solidly mired and his life mapped out in a ready-made maze.' (p. 23)

The shared understanding of death which we owe to the string of modern philosophers and novelists from Kierkegaard through Tolstoy and Nietzsche to Sartre has been usefully summarized by Peter Koestenbaum: 'Death is not an experience but either a felt anticipation or a sorrowful loss. In any event, death is an influential self-concept. And it is this certainty about our eventual death and that of all other human beings that is the key to understanding our human nature ... Death – our own and that of others – explains what it means to be human (searching for meaning, immortality, freedom, love, and individuality) far better than psychological principles of sex and aggression, the biological instincts of survival and procreation, the utilitarian theories of happiness and approbation, or the religious ukase of God's will. *The anticipation of our death reveals to us who we are.*' (*Is There and Answer to Death?* (Englewood Cliffs: Prentice-Hall, 1976), p. 7.)

[3] Cf. Wahl's 'The Fear of Death', in *Death and Identity*, ed. Robert Fulton (New York: John Wiley & Sons, 1965), p. 57. Wahl insists that our thoughts of death, whether emotionally coloured or detached, are as a rule 'once removed', mediated by the preceding symbolic activity. 'When we fear death intensely and unremittingly, we fear instead, often, some of the unconscious irrational symbolic equivalences of death.' (p. 66) Freud's words are quoted from 'Thoughts for the Times of War and Death', in *The Penguin Freud Library*, vol. 12, ed. Albert Dickson, trans. under the general editorship of James Strachey, (Harmondsworth, 1991), pp. 77, 85.

One would, however, add to Freud's observation that we need not strain ourselves in order *not to believe* in death; there is no active effort of denial behind the disbelief – it is the facing the opposite of disbelief which takes effort. If not prompted or prodded, we fall back easily into the state of consciousness from which the thought of our own death (that is, of the terminal point of that state of consciousness) is simply absent. That effortless, 'natural' state, from which we do not emerge unless a force is applied, seems for this reason misnamed; the prefix 'dis-' in *dis*-belief suggests a 'marked' member of the opposition, while it is its opposite (that is, the belief in one's own death), that is contrived and construed as the extraordinary disruption of 'normality'. The constitutive order of beliefs reverses, so to speak, the order of the conceptual work of reason. When *thinking* about being and non-being, we try hard (and, usually, in vain) to construe nothingness as the absence of existence. Logically, non-being is the 'marked' member of the opposition. Psychology, however, defies logic, and with *beliefs* (and non-beliefs) concerning death it is the other way round: the non-belief, the assumption of the non-being of death is the benchmark against which we assess the credibility of its opposite – the reality of personal death, one's own death. It is the *belief* in non-death (misnamed as 'disbelief in death') which is 'given', self-evident, taken for granted.

Through the work of belief the imaginary masks as the truth, while the true is detoxicated or banished from consciousness. We live *as if* we were not going to die. By all standards, this is a remarkable achievement, a triumph of will over reason. Looking at the effortlessness with which that formidable feat is attained daily by most of us, one doubts whether it has been secured with individual resources alone. More powerful forces must have been at work. The disbelief must have been permitted, sanctioned, legalized beforehand, so that wan individual faculties of understanding are seldom tested by the need to argue, to substantiate, to convince, to ward off counter-proofs – a hopeless task in the best of circumstances. As it were, disbelief performs its protective service reasonably well only as long as it stays unexamined and is not looked at closely and attentively. Disbelief is too counterfactual, too illogical, too absurd to survive a superficial scrutiny, let alone an inquisitive one. Thus, it is in the end fortunate that the 'problem' which disbelief attempts to blot out is hardly a problem in the first place. Problems are defined by having solutions; this one does not. Discovery of the absence of a solution is the ultimate source of horror. What the social sanction of disbelief amounts to is permission not to look, and to refrain from asking for reasons.

Notoriously, societies are arrangements that permit humans to live with weaknesses that would otherwise render life impossible. Perhaps most crucial of such arrangements is one that conceals the ultimate absurdity of the *conscious* existence of *mortal* beings; failing the concealment, one that defuses the potentially poisonous effects of its unconcealed, known presence. (Let us note, that – as in their other benefactory functions – societies strive here to cope with the consequences of their own deeds. After all, our 'knowing that we know', and thus being aware of death's absurdity, we owe to living in society: to being animals with *language,* that product as well as existential foundation of the self-same society that later struggles to repair the damage it has done.)

The existential ambivalence of being

As individuals, we know that our individual bodies are mortal, though – as we have seen above – the fact of possessing such knowledge suggests that our minds are not, not in the same way at any rate: the thought can slight time and reach beyond the confines of bodily mortality. But thanks to this uncanny 'extemporality' of thought we also know that the opposite is true: while my own, individual thinking will in all probability grind to a halt at the moment of my death, with the demise of my individual body bodily existence will not really end. It will continue, much as it started before the appearance of my body and before the beginning of my own thinking, before my 'entering the world'. It will continue in the form of the bodily presence of other people. My personal existence is surrounded on both sides by the existence of predecessors and successors. Surrounded, yet not anchored, not rooted, not bound: why has my personal existence been squeezed in this particular place and not in any of the countless others I know of or am able to imagine? No one perhaps expressed more fully that fundamental puzzle of personal existence, that mind-boggling accidentality, contingency of being, than Pascal (*Pensée* 205):[4]

> When I consider the short duration of my life, swallowed up in eternity past and to come, the little space that I fill, and even can see, engulfed in the infinite immensity of spaces of which I am ignorant and which know me not, I am terrified, and am astonished at being here rather than there; for there is no reason why here rather than there, why now rather than then.

Neither the beginning nor the end are absolute. Not just the spirit, but

---

[4] Quoted after *The Modern Vision of Death*, ed. Nathan A. Scott, Jr. (Richmond: John Knox Press, 1967), p. 12.

the body as well are, so to speak, irreparably torn between mortality and immortality: doomed to cessation in one respect, each is destined to last in another. Neither is straightforward, both are ambivalent where they are most vulnerable: in reasons, or the absence of reason, of being where they are. It is this ambivalence with which societies play. Ambivalence of being is a waste-product of society; but at the same time the ineradicable ambivalence of existence supplies the raw material from which social organizations are woven and cultures are sculpted.

According to Freud, to be exact, that ambivalence precedes society: it is in place before society starts its work. In humans, that unique species in which the capacity and the necessity to learn has almost totally displaced and replaced the natural equipment for life, Freud recognized just two instincts: that of life and that of death.[5] All instincts, Freud insists, are conservative: in-built drives pressing to return to equilibrium, urging 'towards the restoration of an earlier state of things'. But the 'earlier state of things', 'the initial state' from which they once departed and to which instincts prompt them to return, is for all living organisms the same: the state of inorganic matter. It is for this reason that 'the aim of all life is death'. Death, the return to the inanimate state of inorganic matter, is the goal to which all life tends and to which it eventually arrives on its own and in its own time, unless disturbed by outside pressures.[6] And yet the *status quo ante* entailed not only the non existence of the *organism*. It entailed as well the existence of the *species*. For the conservative function to be duly performed, the death instinct must be supplemented by the instinct of life: *thanatos* by *libido*, death-drive by the sex-drive. Between themselves, the two in-born instincts meet and satisfy, so to speak, nature's requirements. In some non-humanly 'objective' nature's perspective, they collaborate closely in bringing about a joint yet cohesive accomplishment

---

[5] Sigmund Freud, 'Beyond the Pleasure Principle', in *The Penguin Freud Library*, vol. 11, ed. Angela Richards, trans. under the general editorship of James Strachey (Harmondsworth, 1991), pp. 310–26.

[6] 'In one of the Vedic Upanishads', writes Arthur Schopenhauer, admittedly one of Freud's major inspirations, 'the *natural length* of human life is put down at one hundred years. And I believe this to be right. I have observed, as a matter of fact, that it is only people who exceed the age of ninety who attain *euthanasia* – who die, that is to say, of no disease, apoplexy or convulsion, and pass away without agony of any sort; nay, who sometimes even show no pallor, but expire generally in a sitting attitude, and often after a meal – or, I may say, simply cease to live rather than die. To come to one's end before the age of ninety, means to die of disease, in other words, prematurely.' (*Counsels and Maxims* [Aphorismen zur Lebensweisheit], trans. T. Bailey-Saunders (London: Swan Sonneschein, 1892), p. 159.)

which can be thought of as the preservation and continuation of the species. Not so in human, all-too-human perspective of individual exist-ence: here they are at odds with each other, send contradictory signals and press in opposite directions. What was elsewhere complementarity turns here into conflict. The functional *cohesion* of nature rebounds as *ambivalence* of human life.

The instinct of life, as defined by nature, is aimed at the least reliable, the most ephemeral, the most evidently mortal side of the human indi-vidual – the physical body. It is through human bodies that the species perpetuates itself, invariably at the expense of non-perpetuation of each single body that contributes to the collective effect of reproduction. So it is the body that, in order to perform its creative/self-annihilating role, becomes the object of *libido*, of sexual desire; yet it does so while never ceasing to be but a temporary suspension of nothingness, a 'detour' from the 'normal', inorganic state of matter. Its other, non-sexual activities (its physiological dependency on an inanimate environment, its constant engagement in metabolism) are a reminder of its transience, of senesc-ence as the natural product of youth, of the raw meat barely concealed under just a few millimetres of the epidermis. (That beauty that allures libido and excites imagination of its poetic troubadours is, indeed, no more than 'skin deep', a veneer of appearance that hides the repulsive truth of mortal flesh.) The same body that is the inexhaustible source of libidinal joy cannot cease being the ultimate embodiment of death's terror: 'nature mocks us, and poets live in torture'.[7]

In 'Beyond the Pleasure Principle', the acclaimed, breakthrough study published in 1920, Freud noted (not without a dose of bewilderment) that the opposition between life and death instincts seems to penetrate the

---

[7] Becker, *The Denial of Death*, p. 34. 'The strangest and most repugnant' thing about 'the fleshy casing' of the human person is 'that it aches and bleeds and will decay and die' (p. 26). Charles Baudelaire's *Les Fleurs du mal* is the masterpiece arising from this horror: a desperate and heroic attempt to take a stock of, and face point-blank the inseparable wedlock of life and death. 'O lure of Nothingness so well tricked out!' is Baudelaire's anguished cry. Female beauty, the most sublime of life's creations? 'For all your skill with powder and with musk/ each of you stinks to heaven – or hell – of death!' 'And you will come to this offence,/ this horrible decay,/ you, the light of my life, the sun/ and moon and stars of my love!' And thus 'The abyss that is your bed', and 'Lethe runs between your lips'. Life cannot be purified of the lethal admixture, and love at its most sublime moments cannot forget its mortality – 'Nothing can withstand the Irreparable –/ its termites undermine/ our soul, pathetic citadel, until/ the ruined tower falls./ Nothing can withstand the Irreparable!' (Here quoted in Michael Mazur's translation (London: Pan Books, 1982.)

inside of relationships that 'logically' should stand apart, each one fully guided and structured by one (and one only) of the two great instinctual adversaries. Amazingly, object-love seems to be shot through with attitudinal ambivalence. Most astonishingly of all, it includes, alongside the expected love (affection), also hate (aggressiveness) – an attitude 'evidently' out of place, a posture that inside the context of love may be seen only as logically incongruous. 'If only we could succeed in relating these two polarities to each other and in deriving one from the other!' – Freud muses wistfully on his discovery. The attempt to do just that follows the orthodox line of thought: the aggressive posture and hateful aversion found in object-love are phenomena which – once pushed to the extreme – turn into a sadistic perversion; in a less condensed, attenuated form however, they are necessary, fully functional tools of Eros: 'During the oral stage of organization of the libido, the act of obtaining erotic mastery over an object coincides with that object's destruction; . . . at the stage of genital primacy, it takes on, for the purposes of reproduction, the function of overpowering the sexual object to the extent necessary for carrying out the sexual act'.[8]

Three years later, in 'The Ego and the Id', an essay which in the opinion of many commentators was the last, most comprehensive and conclusive of Freud's numerous restatements of psychoanalytical theory, interpretation undergoes a subtle shift: functionality of the otherwise incongruous mixture is no more postulated. Instead, we read that *ambivalence* is 'a fundamental phenomenon', probably representing 'an instinctual fusion that has not been completed'; the reader is left to surmise, quite legitimately, that the fusion *cannot* be completed: the permanent co-presence of Eros and Thanatos casts a gigantic shadow of ambivalence on all human existence. 'Continuance of life' and 'the striving towards death' are inseparably linked; 'life itself would be a conflict and compromise between these two trends'.[9] Note that this is not a conflict resolved, but a compromise – always short of full satisfaction, forever provisional, fragile and 'until further notice'. . .

Others – Freud's disciples and successors – spelled out what the life in that shadow is like. (Let us repeat: what is at stake is *conscious* life, life with the knowledge of the 'package deal' that once and for all made death the ultimate destination of all and any life-supporting and life-promoting acts). Having done that, many came to the conclusion that it is not so much

---

[8] Freud, 'Beyond the Pleasure Principle', p. 327.

[9] Sigmund Freud, 'The Ego and the Id', in: *The Penguin Freud Library*, vol.11, pp. 380–90.

'nature's decree', however incongruous, that bears direct responsibility for the torments of ambivalence (as Freud, in his obsessive search for 'scientific' grounds for his theory, more than once and more than tentatively implied). Nature's way of pursuing collective perpetuity of the species through individual mortality of its members appears incongruous only when *known*; incongruity, after all, is not a feature of unthinking 'reality', but of its conscious, logic-seeking models. Incongruity is 'just' the defeat of the mind's own Thanatos-like drive towards that stable tranquillity which only the cohesion, the absence of contradiction, can bring. It is this conscious presence of man in the unthinking world that exposes 'the ways of nature' as incongruous. The awareness of incongruity rebounds as irreparable ambivalence of contingent existence. 'Man's nature', Erich Fromm insists, 'cannot be defined in terms of a specific quality, such as love, hate, reason, good or evil, but only in terms of fundamental *contradictions* that characterize human existence.'

> Self-awareness, reason, and imagination have disrupted the 'harmony' that characterizes animal existence. Their emergence has made man into an anomaly, the freak of the universe. He is part of nature, subject to her physical laws and unable to change them, yet he transcends nature; he is set apart while being a part; he is homeless, yet chained to the home he shares with all creatures. Cast into this world as an accidental place and time, he is forced out of it accidentally and against his will. Being aware of himself, he realizes his powerlessness and the limitations of his existence. He is never free from the dichotomy of his existence: he cannot rid himself of his mind, even if he would want to; he cannot rid himself of his body as long as he is alive – and his body makes him want to be alive.[10]

These contradictions are truly existential (the French would say anthropological). The socially sustained awareness only laid them bare and re-forged into the painful knowledge of ambivalence or subconscious anguish. They had been decreed by nature before human culture would have a chance to discover them and thus become obliged to interfere. It was left to culture to improvise what nature failed to supply – but whatever tunes culture would compose, it had to patch them together out of the sounds nature had already supplied. Nature, so to speak, *determined the indetermination* of man; it was the task of culture – a task in no way freely chosen – to solidify the contingent, to entrench the rootless, to give the powerless an impression of power, to hide uncontrived absurdity behind

[10] Erich Fromm, *The Anatomy of Human Destructiveness* (Harmondsworth: Penguin Books, 1977), p. 302ff.

contrived meanings. And culture did what it had to do – with such dedication and self-abandon, and with so spectacular (though far from satisfactory) effects, that Hegel could in good conscience sum up history as a record of 'what man does with death', and W.B. Yeats could inform his readers that it was man who 'created death'.

The effort to conceal or, short of concealing, to temper and defuse the pivotal absurdity of human predicament, occupied such a strategic place in the work of culture that a growing amount of historians follow Hegel's insight and assert that one could grasp the essence of history's drama through recording the consecutive changes in the imagery of death and in the ways humans cope with death and dying. The transformations of attitudes to death and connected practices cannot be conclusively explained causally (after all, each one is just a palliative, a pseudo-solution to a lasting need, which sooner or later must be disavowed as it inexorably runs out of credible normative potential), but they may in their turn serve as an explanation of wider shifts – those affecting *total cultures*, saturated as they are with the evasive yet mighty substance of 'sensibilities'. Ideas and rites of death would therefore occupy the status of 'prime facts', reflecting the primacy of individual mortality among the constituents of the human predicament.

Accepted (particularly by French historians)[11] a few decades ago, this view continues to represent hopes and methodological postulates rather than an empirically confirmed truth. As far as the handling of mortality goes, 'total cultures' appear curiously and uncharacteristically tolerant to quite heterogenous attitudes (though each seems to have an attitudinal complex favoured, extolled and practised with greater or lesser vigour by its spiritual elite). Human reactions to death are ostensibly too complex and perhaps also too stubborn to be successfully channelled by any culture in a universally acceptable fashion. Culture would never be permitted to stop trying to achieve just that, but all attempts seem to have arrived thus far fairly short of convincing success. According to Joachim Whaley's summary of historians' unnerving experience with their coveted, yet elusive goal, 'attitudes to death in all ages are characterized by the most diverse emotions – fear, sorrow, anger, despair, resentment, resignation,

---

[11] Compare, for instance, the following bold programmatic declarations: 'Le poids de la mortalité se reflète dans l'accueil fait à la vie'; 'on a pu dire que toute société se jauge ou s'apprécie, d'une certaine façon, à son système de la mort'. (Michel Vovelle, *La Mort et l'Occident: de 1300 à nos jours* (Paris: Gallimard, 1983), pp. 7–8.)

defiance, pity, avarice, triumph, helplessness';[12] a mixed bunch, indeed, of affects that must make any effort of 'standardization' – a very tall order. In view of the enormity of the task, socially managed efforts to resolve the inherent ambivalence of the mortal/immortal existence of the individual/species (a uniquely *human* ambivalence for the uniquely human quality of self-awareness) were but a series of just partly successful, yet ultimately unsatisfactory expedients.

Coping with ambivalence: a brief survey of expedients

The most universally and continuously practised expedient has been the spatial separation between life and death through the exclusion of the dead – making the dead 'cease to exist'. Cemeteries, Baudrillard suggests, were the first ghettos;[13] the archetypal ghettos, the patterns for all ghettos to come. However they differ in ritual, all funerals are acts of exclusion. They proclaim the dead abnormal, dangerous, those to be shunned. They expel the dead from the company of the normal, the innocuous – those to be associated with. But they do more than that. Through applying to the dead the same technique of separation as they do to the carriers of infectious diseases or contagious malpractices, they cast the dead among the manageable threats that lose their potency if kept at a distance. Thus they try hard to keep them at a distance: forcing them to remain there, begging and bribing them to do so, or currying their favours if the banishment cannot be fully trusted. Better still, the dead, like the ill, insane or the criminal, are put in trust, into 'the care of licensed professionals'[14] and thus are supposed to disappear not only from sight, but from mind. The self-deceit is all too visible, though; the dead cannot be buried in the past, as their lot is the future of all those living in the present. As sites of confinement, cemeteries are not half as secure as leprosaria, lunatic asylums or prisons. Haunted houses and haunted lives testify to the porousness of cemetery walls.

---

[12] Joachim Whaley, *Mirrors of Mortality: Studies in the Social History of Death* (London: Europa Publications, 1981), p. 9. Edgar Morin comes to a similar conclusion from a different standpoint: 'no society, including our own, has known as yet an absolute victory – be it immortality, or a demystified conscience of death, or the horror of death, or a victory over the horror of death'. With the war perpetually inconclusive, 'the individual never reaches stability and keeps moving from forgetting death to the horror of death, and from that horror to seeking death-risks'. (*L'Homme et la mort*, pp. 34, 73.)

[13] Cf. Jean Baudrillard, *L'Échange symbolique et la mort* (Paris: Gallimard, 1976), pp. 195ff.

[14] Ray S. Anderson, *Theology, Death and Dying* (Oxford: Blackwell, 1986), p. 16.

Another common expedient is to deny the substance of death – its finality. One can do it in many ways, but two essential patterns have emerged over the centuries.

The first can be interpreted as a sort of metaphorical permutation of natural order: the finitude of the individual earthly presence does not count for much, as it is not the proper criterion of longevity, indeed the immortality, of being. Being as such does not come to a stop with the disappearance of individuals; as a matter of fact, the change-over of individuals, each with his contribution to make, is exactly what guarantees the permanence of existence. A most critical example of such a pattern (one that went furthest towards dissolving the identity of each given individual sojourn on earth, having effaced the gravity and significance of the individual life's end by redefining it as a stage in continuity, rather than a radical rupture) was the Hinduist privatization of death, lavishly compensated for by the collectivization of immortality: the acceptance of the permanence of being ('that which is can never cease to be'),[15] made life and death into exchangeable forms of eternal being, into stages whose duration does not matter in view of the perpetuity of existence. The Judaist stratagem has been, in a sense, a somewhat humbler, less radical variety of the same strategy – different in trying to bring closer home that 'being' which is eternal. In this case, the perpetuity has been ascribed to the special relationship – the covenant   between Jewish people and God. Personal death does not matter much as long as the conversation of God with His people – God's revelation to the Jews and the Jews' service to God – goes on.[16]

---

[15] Quoted from the *Bhagavad-Gita* by James R. Carse, *Death and Existence: a Conceptual Theory of Human Mortality* (New York: John Wiley, 1980), p. 133.

[16] The narrowly tribal ambitions of the Judaist conception of covenant were not uncontested from within. An underground and for a long time officially suppressed, yet nevertheless philosophically and intellectually powerful strand in Judaism insisted for many centuries on the universal, species-wide function of Jewish communion with God. This strand, dubbed by the rabbinic officialdom as mystical, gathering in force after the Spanish expulsion, connected the notions of Diaspora and redemption 'with the central question of the essence of the universe', and insisted on the universal meaning of Jewish exile. It 'managed to elaborate a system which transformed the exile of the people of Israel into an exile of the whole world, and the redemption of their people into a universal, cosmic redemption'. (Cf. Gershon Scholem, *The Messianic Idea in Judaism* (London: Allen & Unwin, 1971), p. 43.) The *tikkun* – repairing of the vessels broken at the moment of world's creation – was to be a cosmic event, the Jewish exile was a concentrated symbol of exile of God from the world it created, and its end will signal 'a permanent, blissful state of communion' between *every creature* and God, with the cosmic harmony restored once for all. (Cf. Gershon Scholem, *Kabbalah* (New York: Quadrangle, 1974), pp. 142–3, 165.)

At the other end of the spectrum remain the strategies that insist, against the odds, on the chance of individual continuous existence beyond the point of biological death. One will survive the death of the body through the immortality of the soul, whose reward or punishment that starts with the moment of bodily death will retrospectively render meaning to the life that ended; this was the Christian solution. As the decay of the physical body of the dead were too evident and unexceptional to be refuted, the preservation of the body could not be entertained in any but a miraculous form (the idea is entertained again in our time, in the form of the miraculously potent science and technology – as 'cryonics' – the artificially induced hibernation 'until such time when the medicine for the now terminal disease will have been found'). But the preservation of the soul could be postulated without fear of empirical refutation, and one would never know for sure whether the postulate is truthful or not; the care of the soul's unending future would then take precedence over the worry about the flesh destined for putrefaction. Hopefully, the experts attending to the soul's future would also take precedence over the specialists caring for the body's present. One can think of the Hellenic tradition, articulated in the Platonian rendition of Socrates' teachings, as of an earlier, secular version of the same, though a rather aristocratic version, not meant nor fit for a popular consumption and thus unusable as a foundation for a universal Church. Franz Borkenau laid bare the contrast between the two essential strategies taking the Jewish and the Hellenic stratagems as their prototypical specimens (and thus considering it as another aspect of the Athens/Jerusalem controversy):

> The particular Jewish solution of the problem . . . was the transference of immortality from the individual to the community. The parallel Hellenic solution was the extolling of the individual's undying glory, the hero surviving death through fame.[17]

Of modern totalitarianisms, in their nationalistic, class or racist forms, one can think as of attempts to bring together the most promising aspects

---

[17] Franz Borkenau, 'The Concept of Death', in *Death and Identity*, ed. Robert Fulton (New York: John Wiley & Sons, 1965), p. 48. Let us note that the Hellenic tradition was not as homogenous and straightforward as Borkenau would suggest. Particularly in the Socrates/Plato rendition, it may be depicted as a variety of 'collectivist' strategies (though, indeed, devising a collectivism fit only for an elitist use): Hinduist eternal being and Judaist immortal community of chosen people are here replaced by the extemporal truth of the philosophers as their, in many respects, functional equivalent: being of ideas transcends the span of individual life, and the privilege of sages is to partake of that eternity.

of both strategies: to combine the assumption of the collectivized immortality of the *folk* with the promise of perpetual presence of individual heroes in folk memory. The battle-cries of modern versions of tribalism – 'For the Homeland', 'For the glory of our Nation', 'For our beloved Leader' – are but thinly disguised metaphors for the species' way of securing survival through the extinction of its members, yet they attempt to render meaningful (indeed, noble and desirable) what unless culturally processed would appear an unalloyed absurdity. These battle-cries call for the surrender of individual life, suggesting that personal death would somehow enhance and revitalize the life collectively and thus in a roundabout way would secure the perpetual existence of the dead through the nation, the race, or a party which, having gratefully absorbed the sacrifice, will be the victims' lasting accomplishment. From other forms of 'collectivized immortality' the tribal/totalitarian ideologies differ in one important respect: they actively *demand* sacrifice of life and *glorify* death 'for the cause'. Only apparently they are descriptive. The ostensible description contains a *prescription* as its pivotal ingredient. The narrative disguised as a story of necessity is in fact an invocation of a duty. From an apparently neutral statement – 'I learnt that life is a cruel struggle, and has no other object but the preservation of the species. The individual can disappear, provided there are other men to replace him.' – there is but a step (all too often taken) to the declaration that 'If I can accept a divine Commandment, it's this one: "Thou shalt preserve the species". The life of the individual must not be set at too high a price. If the individual were important in the eyes of nature, nature would take care to preserve him. Amongst the millions of eggs a fly lays, very few are hatched out – and yet the race of flies thrives'.[18]

What if religious and tribal versions of transcendence fail, lose popular-

---

[18] *Hitler's Table Talk, 1941–1944* (London: Oxford University Press, 1988). The quoted – frank, 'from the heart', over-the-dinner musings – cannot be dismissed as merely expressions of Hitler's private aberration. The call to self-abandonment, indeed self-annihilation, for the sake of preserving a cause higher and nobler than one's own existence has been heard in many quarters, as a rule with the same awesome and sinister mobilizing impact. A recent case has been succinctly presented by Hans Magnus Enzensberger: 'Ce qui enthousiasmait les Allemands, ce n'était pas seulement la levée de l'interdit de tuer mais plus encore la perspective d'être tués eux-mêmes. Des millions d'Arabes expriment aujourd'hui le souhait de mourir pour Saddam. "Notre peuple veut respirer le gaz de Saddam Hussein", a déclaré Assad el-Tamini, un prédicateur palestinien de Jordanie. Cette continuité prouve que nous ne sommes pas confrontés à un phénomène allemand, ou arabe, mais à un phénomène anthropologique.' ('Adolf Hitler réincarné', *Liberation*, 11 February 1991, p. 16.)

ity, miss earthly powers willing and capable of promoting practices that
lend those versions credibility and at least an appearance of realism? The
love relationship seems to be transcendence's last shelter. According to
Otto Rank, the modern person's dependency on the love partner 'is the
result of the loss of spiritual ideologies'. Bereaved by God and His secular
emulators, the modern person 'needs *somebody*, some "individual ideology of justification", to replace the declining collective ideologies'.[19] Love
takes over at the point where God and the Despot-with-a-Mission left. Not
that love is born of modern bereavement. But it is the modern predicament, one which emerged in the wake of the bankruptcy of tested old
policies of survival, that has burdened love with new load which it was
never before called to carry.

It is now the partner in love that is expected to offer the space for
transcendence, *to be* the transcendence. He or she must be a mirror in
which my fantasy looks real; my fantasy is to become real by the very fact
of being reflected. My own self, confined as it is by the mortality of its own
bodily carapace, is to acquire a vicarious immortality by sundering its
private bond and being set free. It has to gain a new, unbound and more
credible existence within the trans-individual 'universe of two'. I may
dream that, in the process, mortality of the self is defeated by the sheer
feat of abandoning the hopelessly mortal individual body. But the new
anchorage of survival is another body and another self, entangled much
as my own in the mutual conflict from which only subterfuges pretend to
offer an exit. Itself afloat, it can hardly hold the anchor fast.

'We want an object that reflects a truly ideal image of ourselves. But no
human object can do this . . . No human relationship can bear the burden
of godhood' – so sums up Ernest Becker the fate of love.[20] Hence the
anguish particularly acute in our own times: just when all other hopes of
transcendence have lost much of their lustre, and the functional importance of love has accordingly risen to unprecedented heights, its carrying
capacity seems to have fallen drastically. The heightened expectations have
multiplied the likelihood of failure. Defeats do not necessarily expose the
lie ensconced at the bottom of the love strategy. They only gestate – in
the partners – impatience and restlessness, the breathless search for the

[19] Otto Rank, *Modern Education: A Critique of its Fundamental Ideas* (New York: Knopf, 1932), p. 232.
[20] Becker, *The Denial of Death*, p. 166. According to Schopenhauer: 'Why, then, is a lover so absolutely devoted to every look and turn of his beloved . . . ? Because the *immortal* part of him is yearning for her; it is only the *mortal* part of him that longs for everything else.' (*Essays of Schopenhauer*, p. 207.)

'true partner' who must, just must, be waiting round the corner. The consequence is the endemic brittleness of the 'universes of two': the couples break at the first hurdle, as the partners prefer a brand new, yet unexplored and not discredited track to the chores of negotiating the already revealed obstacles of the old one.

Terminal dangers surround the love relationship on both sides. My bid for the confirmation of the self my partner may reject – or accept with such reservations to which I am not prepared to consent. But even if my bid has been assented to in full, the acceptance may fail to bring the expected satisfaction. It may not carry the degree of reassurance I sought. After all, my stakes in *immortality* have been invested in another *mortal* creature, and this latter fact cannot be concealed for long by even the most passionate deification of the partner. Unlike God or anointed despot, my partner in love has a distinct disadvantage of being constantly within the field of my vision, of being watched by me at close quarters also in situations which make brutally obvious the truth of his or her bodily mortality. The despot fails as an object of survival policy once he publicly reveals the absence of supra-human potency – showing cowardice or indecision, being outmanoeuvred or losing a battle; for a partner in love, it is enough to be human in humanity's endemic, irreparable duality. And since it is precisely the partner's human duality that makes him or her fit to be an object of love, it cannot be reduced or left outside; it cannot but be drawn into the love relationship in its terrifying totality.

These inner contradictions of love as a policy of survival are nowhere as protruding as in the case of erotic relationship, where spiritual and sexual intimacy feed and reinforce each other (or are presumed to). In its natural function, sexual procreation is a method through which the species preserves its immortality at *the expense of the mortality* of its individual members. The cunning of the species leaves its indelible stamp, and for this reason erotic partnership is, deep down, unfit for the role of the vehicle of individual transcendence of death. Sexual intimacy can bear exaggerated hopes only at the cost of extreme inner tension. In modern practice, the disappointment (or the subconscious desire to ward it off) leads to the playing down or even total rejection of 'spiritual investment' in sexual relationship, and a pronounced tendency to divest sexual inter-course of the last vestiges of spiritual union. The absolute and the transcendent are no longer sought in the sexual partner; what is expected from the partner is at best the willingness and ability to arouse and stimulate the 'perfect performance' – and thus reconfirm the value of the self in a roundabout fashion, by allowing it to stretch to the fantasized about limits (which, in *fantasy*, always transcend the *genuine* limits in a symbolic rehearsal of the transcendence as such). The love relationship turns then to be another form of self-assertion, that obsessive (because never satisfied) urge to make the notoriously incredible – the personal power to overpower death – credible; or, at least, to evict from consciousness the knowledge of its futility. A transcendence strategy falling upon itself, aiming back at its point of emergence, is a logical next step. The recoiling of the urge to transcendence back onto the effort of personal survival is both the cause and the outcome of dashed sexual hopes: of the sexual prowess of the ego drifting into the centre of expectation, and sexual intimacy reduced to the role of an occasion for its release and display.

But the weight ascribed to the display of sexual prowess can be seen also from another perspective. As if replicating the contrast between extemporal mind and transient body, the centre of gravity moves from transcendence as an achieved (and once achieved, constant) state to the transcendence as a momentary event – a performance. When seen in such a way, erotic love reduced to sexual self-assertion appears to be a specimen of a new type of mortality-effacing strategy: one that differs sharply from the policies considered so far, and (perhaps due to this difference) shows an amazing capacity for expansion. What is involved here is an attempt not just to find compensation for the temporal fragility of bodily existence, but arrogantly belie the ultimate limits of the body by breaking, successively, its *currently* encountered, *specific* limitations (personally or vicariously; here lies the secret of the fascination carried by the record-breaking performance of sportspersons, admired for their symbolic significance as victories over the natural constraints and experienced as acts committed on behalf of the species as a whole). The task of escaping the mortality of the body, which would immediately reveal its futility if faced point-blank, as a consciously articulated purpose, is never allowed to be encountered in its awesome totality. It is split instead into a never ending series of concrete challenges, reduced to a *manageable* size, that is to situations which allow for credibility of success. The time dimension of transcendence is turning here into a spatial issue: stretching the *span of life* is turned into the effort to stretch the *capacity to live*. Time all but disappears: it has been reduced and flattened out of existence, subjected to a process that 'narrows the present down to a chaos of evanescent events'.[21] What matters amidst such chaos is that the body, the only stable point of reference, lives permanently in the current moment and the current moment only, carefully avoiding to look beyond the

---

[21] Harry Redner, *In the Beginning was the Deed*, (University of California Press, 1982), p. 280.

present; what draws all attention, leaving no room for other concerns, is not what the body is bent on accomplishing in the future, but 'bodily fitness', body as multi-purpose instrument; ready for all challenge, and indifferent to the nature of any task it may confront.

The mortal roots of culture's immortality

There would probably be no culture were humans unaware of their mortality; culture is an elaborate counter-mnemotechnic device to forget what they are aware of. Culture would be useless if not for the devouring need of forgetting; there would be no transcending were there nothing to be transcended. In the light of mortality, all meanings of life look pallid, wan, insubstantial. This light must be extinguished, if only for a time and an occasion, for life meanings to appear solid and reliable. Thus the constant risk of death – the risk always *knowable* even if flushed down into the murky depths of the subconscious – is, arguably, the very foundation of culture. As Simmel argued, the knowledge of death is the very force that prises apart life and its contents: it is thus the selfsame force that permits the 'objectification' of life contents, rendering them immune to the vagaries of life, stronger than life – indeed, as immortal as life is mortal. By proxy, that force may give life itself an extemporal flavour: a *meaning* that cancels out the absurdity of its transience. A temporal life acquires an extemporal value, and so the cumulative accomplishment of culture can be born. In Edgar Morin's words,

> The unavoidable continuity of the death risk has acquired in the course of history also a total cultural and anthropological meaning: the risk of death is human adventure as such. Without the risk, everything would be too facile, therefore useless, therefore impossible. Life, action, success, not only individual but collective as well, would be no more than limp jokes. Culture has no meaning outside the life-and-death struggle against nature, bestiality and barbarity, waged simultaneously outside and inside the human person.[22]

In the City of the Immortals, Jorge Luis Borges tells us, 'a hundred or so irregular niches . . . furrowed the mountain and the valley. In the sand

---

[22] Morin, *L'Homme et la mort*, p. 273. Of the same, Elias Canetti, with that serene Pascal-like scepticism against which culture, to do its job, must defend itself tooth and nail: 'Culture is concocted from the vanities of its promoters. It is a dangerous love potion, distracting us from death. The purest expression of culture is an Egyptian tomb, where everything lies about futilely, utensils, adornments, food, pictures, sculpture, prayers, and yet the dead man is not alive.' (*The Human Province*, trans. Joachim Neugroschel (London: Deutsch, 1985), p. 22.)

there were shallow pits; from these miserable holes (and from the niches) naked, grey-skinned, scraggly bearded men emerged. I thought I recognized them: they belonged to the bestial breed of the troglodytes . . .' The troglodytes, apparently, knew not the art of writing; neither would they speak. Only after prolonged (and vain) effort to usher a troglodyte into the mysteries of human language did the visitor discover that his reluctant disciple was Homer; Homer who has been admitted to the City of the Immortals and came to know that he would never die. Once he learned of his immortality, it became clear to him that 'if we postulate an infinite period of time, with infinite circumstances and changes, the impossible thing is not to compose the *Odyssey*, at least once'. Thus the composition of the *Odyssey* that *cannot not be* loses its lustre; the composition is no more a unique event, and thus not an act of heroism; it is useless as a vehicle of self-assertion. 'Everything among the mortals has the value of the irretrievable and the perilous. Among the Immortals, on the other hand, every act (and every thought) is the echo of others that preceded it in the past, with no visible beginning, or the faithful passage of others that in the future will repeat it to a vertiginous degree . . . Nothing can happen only once, nothing is preciously precarious.'[23]

Let us observe that the Immortals conjured up by the power of Borges' imagination all had a mortal past; they came to disdain struggle for the unique (and that disdain had a beginning; that beginning was an *event*, and as such had already organized the infinity as a time flow) because they *ceased* to be mortals for whom such a struggle was the content of life. Borges's Immortals construed themselves out of the *negation* (defeat, annulment) of mortality. Even the reason they offered for the contempt they felt for all action or mental effort (namely, that neither of them can be unique, and therefore none is worthy of trouble) was a tribute to their mortal past. In all probability, the contempt itself, let alone the effort to legitimize it, would stay beyond their reach, were they not to experience

---

[23] Jorge Luis Borges, 'The Immortal' in *Labyrinths: Selected Stories and Other Writings*, ed. Donald A. Yates and James E. Irby (Harmonsworth: Penguin Books, 1970), pp. 138, 145, 146. Immortality of Borges's Immortals was *received* (through drinking from the river of immortality) – and they knew it. James P. Carse suggests that 'death, perceived as discontinuity, is not that which robs life of its meaning, but that which makes life's meaningfulness possible.' (*Death and Existence*, p. 9.) I propose that there is a conjunction (indeed, a causal link) where Carse sees an alternative and an opposition. The perception of death makes life meaningfulness possible – nay, unavoidable – precisely because it makes life first empty of meaning, and thus leaves it to the humans to conjure up any meaning that could fill the void.

once the risk of death, were they not made aware of the possibility of mortality, were they immortals (and aware of being immortal, if that was at all logically possible) 'from the beginning' (would there be a beginning then?). Whatever contents the visitor found in their existence, came from the suppression, repeal, invalidation or rejection of the substance moulded of the past fear of mortality; they derived their substance from that ancient fear which they had left behind (and could now speak about only negatively, in terms of 'no more is', 'no more does', 'no more has') ... The conception that if circumstances are infinite, deeds and thoughts are *worthless* – is itself a product of finite existence, of life injected with the known inevitability of death. It could make sense only to those who remembered that their circumstances were once finite and thereby *precious*; to those capable to grasp the significance of values, once born of finitude.

The genuine immortals would not be aware that they are *not mortal*. For this very reason they elude our imagination, however much we strain it and however large the pool of allegorical skills we summon to our assistance. Their experience (that is, *if* there was an experience) could not be narrated in our language, which was itself begotten of the premonition of finitude and accommodated itself to the service of finite experience. As to human mortals, they are aware that they are *not immortal*; this is what gives measure to time, makes every moment both fearful and precious, transforms being into action and existence into a purpose and a task. We can only imagine the absolute as a denial of the local and temporal we know – and we can only work for the absolute since we wish to escape the locality and temporality of our predicament.

The game of survival

Inescapably, as Elias Canetti wrote,[24] man is a *survivor*: 'the most elementary and obvious form of success is to remain alive'. We are not just alive; at every moment we are *still* alive. Success is always an 'until further notice' success; it is never final. It must be repeated over and over again. The effort can never grind to a halt. Survival is a lifelong task. Its energizing, creative potential in never exhausted. Whatever is left of it will be just locked up, in one felt swoop, at the moment of death.

Canetti insists that survival is not identical with the old and trivial notion

---

[24] Elias Canetti, *Crowds and Power*, trans. Carol Stewart (Harmondsworth: Penguin Books, 1973), pp. 290, 291.

of 'self-preservation'. The idea of self-preservation, sometimes conceived of as an instinct, sometimes as a rational choice, hides or beautifies the gruesome truth of survival. Survival is targeted on others, not on the self. Though we never live through our own death, we do live through the deaths of the others, and their death gives meaning to our success: we have not died, *we* are *still* alive. Thus 'the desire for a long life which plays such a large part in most cultures really means that most people want to survive their contemporaries. They know that many die early and they want a different fate for themselves.' I would not conceive of my own performance as a success if it were not for the fact that performances of others proved unsuccessful; I can only measure my own performance against those other performances. I want to know what I should do to escape or to postpone the others' lot – to *outlive* others. Others die of smoking; perhaps if I don't smoke, I'd survive them?

At the radical extreme of survival, says Canetti, looms murder: 'He wants to kill so that he can survive others; he wants to stay alive so as not to have others surviving him.' This wish can be silenced, even denied, indignantly, by consciousness – but it cannot be really effaced: 'Only survival at a distance in time is wholly innocent.'[25] The cynicism with which the wish of survival is inevitably, though self-ashamedly, infused, comes blatantly into the open during war – that socially sanctioned, legitimate murder: the declared purpose is then 'to limit our casualties', and anyone knows, even if refrains from spelling it out, that the price of that limiting is multiplying the dead on the other side of the battleline. 'Kill, so that you and your beloved shalt not be killed.' Declaration of war means suspension of the guilt and shame that the wish of survival spawns at 'normal' times. That normally carefully concealed wish now emerges from hiding, dressed as the noble mission of fighting evil empires or disarming the enemies of mankind, be they carriers of disease that saps the civilized life or spoilers of harmonious world order. It shapes itself up as liberation, restoration of order, or crusade; it ends up as genocide. The survivor's 'most fantastic triumphs have taken place in our own time, among people who set great store by the idea of humanity . . . The survivor is mankind's worst evil, its curse and perhaps its doom.'[26] War is, admittedly, an extreme case – but, Canetti insists, it shows in a spectacular way

---

[25] Canetti, *Crowds and Power*, pp. 293, 292. It is plausible that it is precisely the suppressed presence of the true meaning of survival that adds to the already considerable difficulty we experience when addressing the dying.

[26] Canetti, *Crowds and Power*, p. 544. Canetti goes on to suggest that the danger of the survivor has been if anything increasing, and reaching a totally new scale: thanks to the new technology of action and the new means the action can use, 'a single individual can easily destroy a good part of mankind. To bring this about

what is always there, though hidden; survival is never wholly innocent when re-forged into action.

This is a dramatic, tragic vision of the inner tendency *of survival*. One wonders to what extent this tendency is truly *inner* (or innate); one is entitled to suspect that the destructive edge of survival is sharpened (and even more probably directed) by the socially organized setting in which the activity of survival takes place. It is this setting that may (or may not) arrange the survival as a zero-sum game, and then split the habitat into a part that is threatening and has to be subdued or better still annihilated, and another part whose well-being enhances the chance of my own survival; this is what most societies have been doing all along, and continue to do. Like other in-built qualities of the human predicament, the impulse of survival is the stuff of which societies are patched together. Even though this impulse is not the society's creation, it is keenly, skilfully and on the whole effectively manipulated by society; it is, as a rule, *socially managed* – in a way that for one reason or another is deemed useful. It is deployed to build and preserve boundaries of states, nations, races, classes. It is invoked, explicitly or tacitly, whenever hostility is to be directed, but also whenever loyalty to the cause and group solidarity are called for. It is not just, and not necessarily destructive in its application. But if it can be put effectively to non-destructive uses, it is because of its destructive potential.

One of such uses can be traced back to what Norman O. Brown dubbed the *Oedipal project*.[27] 'The project of becoming God – in Spinoza's terms,

---

he can use technical means he does not understand; he can himself remain completely hidden; and he does not even have to run any personal risk in the process . . . Seen in retrospect, history appears innocent and almost comfortable.' (pp. 544–5) Against the looming danger, Canetti can draw little hope from past experience: 'Hitherto the only answer to man's passionate desire for survival has been a creative solitude which earns immortality for itself; and this, by definition, can be the solution only for a few.' (p. 545) Mortality, and its obtrusive companion, survival, are the twin keys to Canetti's historiosophy: 'The efforts of individuals to ward off death gave rise to the monstrous structure of power. Countless deaths were demanded for the survival of one individual. The resulting confusion is known as history.' (Canetti, *The Human Province*, p. 280.) Indeed, for most of the time history has been written as a chronicle of survivors; as a record of the battles won by princes so that they could outlive, even if for a time, their rivals for the survival; the hard core of all fame.

[27] Cf. Norman O. Brown, *Life against Death: The Psychoanalytical Meaning of History* (New York: Viking Books, 1959), pp. 118ff. Brown undertook to correct Freud's concept of Oedipal complex, purifying it of the narrowly sexual content; or, rather, reversing the order of interpretation and representing the sexual aspects of the Oedipal crisis as derivatives, or manifestations, of an actively embraced project, aimed in the first place at mastery and control.

causa sui.' The Oedipal project is a flight from infantile dependency, a wish to become 'the father of himself'. This stage in development always arrives, and once it arrives it is invariably directed against the parents, the true embodiment of dependency – and this whatever the parents do and however they behave. The Oedipal project is a drive to emancipation that cannot be achieved unless the bond of dependency is broken. However, the deepest, the ultimate dependency is that on one's own mortal body – that ultimate limit of autonomy; for this reason the battle cannot be won. Oedipal project is just a first 'trial skirmish' in a long series of battles doomed to defeat (though the hubbub of successive skirmishes silences for a while, perhaps a long while, the thought of the final debacle). The *causa sui* project stays unfulfilled, and as long as it is unfulfilled it generates the energy needed to wage ever new battles. It also needs ever new battlefields and war strategies, so that the struggle may continue while each successive engagement is lost. The tragic paradox is that the undeclared purpose of the struggle is gaining exclusive mastery over one's own body (and thus, by proxy, surviving its unsurvivable mortality). The dream of survival constitutes the body as the most important of targets, as own body is the mortal side of the self, and – with its procreative function – is also the instrument through which individual immortality has been expropriated by the species. The body is the 'natural enemy' of survival, and the only *uncontrived* enemy. A paradox indeed – and the seat of perhaps the deepest and most hopeless of ambivalences: in the struggle aimed at the survival of the body, the would-be survivors meet the selfsame body as the arch-enemy.

But let us note that even in the 'struggle of liberation' targeted against one's own body it is always the socially set framework of dependence that injects meaning into the experience of the lack of mastery. These battlefronts are, like all others, socially drawn. And it is the selfsame society which has articulated the aims of the struggle and drawn the battlelines, that also supplies the weapons and the strategies with which the battles can be fought. It is therefore on this interface that the survival impulse of the developing individual meets and merges with the self-perpetuating processes of sociality. Society, in other respects the hostile field of competitors against which one's own survival can be measured and hopefully asserted, appears simultaneously as the armoury of survival's weapons, trusty ally, source of succour, encouragement, and hope. Society fares no better than the body: it also emerges from the existential predicament as a monster of ambivalence: half-friend, half-enemy – the *object* and the *means* of the struggle.

The impulse of survival renders both the body and society ambivalent.

Yet all ambivalence it spawns seem to pale into insignificance when compared to its own. Survival is torn apart by a contradiction no amount of lies may assuage; an inner split resulting in a constant outpouring of guilt which can be no more placated than its source can be drained. Philippe Ariès[28] suggested that the spectres of 'la mort de Moi' (self-death) and 'la mort de Toi' (Thou-death) were crystallization points of two successive (respectively, eighteenth-century, Enlightenment, and nineteenth-century Romanticism), and to an extent mutually exclusive, attitudes towards death. We may surmise instead that the two terrors are just twin aspects of the hopelessly ambivalent sentiment gestated and sustained by the impulse of survival at all ages of human existence. My own survival, as we have seen before, cannot be savoured otherwise than as a macabre privilege over the others, less fortunate. Yet these others may be, and more often than not are, the very meaning of my existence – the uppermost value which makes my life worth living; the very sense of being alive: life is communicating with others, being with others, acting for others and being addressed, wanted, lifted into importance by the need of others and by the bid they make for my attention and sympathy.

The death of others may be a benchmark for my own survival success, but it is the life of others which made that success desirable in the first place, as well as is making it now worthy of effort. After all, I want to survive mostly because the thought of all that communication, intercourse, loving, being loved – all that grinding suddenly to a halt is so unbearable. My desire to survive is all the stronger the richer and more satisfying is that experience of being with others. The world without my seeing it or fantasizing it is unimaginable; but the image of a world emptied of others, a world that testifies to my ultimate triumph as a survivor, is unbearable. (The 'sole survivor's' plight is no less a nightmare than death; after all, it shows what death is about, it is a mirror-image of death; moreover, only if reflected in that imaginary mirror can death be visualized in all its brutal truth.) More immediately, the exit of every person that inhabits my life and stands between sense and senselessness, fullness and void, impoverishes that life of mine which feeds and in turn feeds on the drive to survival. Is not survival, therefore, a self-destructive and self-defeating impulse? Is not it the case that it can fulfil itself only in its defeat?

The core of all callousness, cruelty and brutality, the survival impulse

---

[28] Cf. Philippe Ariès, *Western Attitudes toward Death: From the Middle Ages to the Present*, trans. Patricia M. Ranum (Baltimore, Johns Hopkins University Press, 1974); Philippe Ariès, *L'Homme devant la mort* (Paris: Seuil, 1977); also Vovelle, *La Mort et l'Occident*.

seems also to be the fount of sociability. It is neither selfish nor selfless; or perhaps it is both, and cannot but be both at the same time. In a tormented, self-immolating and painful way it implements the order of nature: it seals the bond between individual self-preservation effort and the survival of the species. By mobilizing the emotional and rational faculties of individuals, its practice fulfils and reinforces the logical and pragmatic interdependence between perpetuity of the species and the temporal existence of its members. Its innate ambivalence has itself a survival value.

It is an ambivalence all the same, and an acute one with that. One would expect therefore a drive to separate the inseparable – a favourite point of entry for all societal managerial skills and ambitions; a stuff from which all man-made, 'cultured', contrived social order is made. Making distinctions, discriminating, setting apart, classifying, is culture's foremost mark, craft and *tour de force*. In its intentions (though hardly ever in its practical accomplishments) culture is a war of attrition declared on ambivalence. Its promise is to separate the grain from the chaff in all their incarnations – be they called truth and falsehood, beauty and ugliness, friends and enemies, or good and evil. Its job is to see that the world is well mapped and well marked, so that confusion will have little chance to arise. Its ambition is to make the world hospitable by eliminating the torments of choice where no fully satisfying choice seems available. Its struggle – futile yet unstoppable – is to cut the ambivalent human predicament into a multitude of logically and pragmatically unequivocal situations.

Obviously, the poignantly ambivalent survival impulse is the prime candidate for such treatment. Individual survival makes no sense and offers no allurement without survival of others; but then such others as are needed for survival to remain attractive and to make sense may be – should be – separated from the rest of the others who are not. This is exactly what society, through its 'culturing' effort, achieves – or at least tries hard to achieve. 'The others' are divided into those who support, and those who threaten survival. The uncompromising, overwhelming self-assertion of the *species* is split into more palatable and easier-to-manage *tribal* interests. The 'inside' and the 'outside' are thereby created and carefully demarcated. Inside – unity, co-operation and mutual love. Outside – wilderness, vigilance and fight. My tribe is to be spared all casualties at all costs. Among the costs (or are they costs at all? Are they not, to be frank, gains?), the most indispensable of all is 'collateral damage' inflicted on the enemy tribe once it has been appointed 'the target' and, as targets are meant to be, is 'hit' and 'neutralized'. My tribe's survival has been offered what it demands: a measure of callous self-love and a measure of loving co-operation with others. Only such others as are earmarked for love, and the others selected for callous treatment, are no more the same others. In Reinhold Niebuhr's words, tribal patriotism 'transmutes individual unselfishness into national egoism'.[29] Murders which the survival impulse clamours for are no more clouded with the sorrow with which *la mort de Toi* tends to inject the survivor. The killed is not *Tu*, and so the murder is not a murder. The haunting contradiction of *human* survival has been resolved.

The resolution is greatly helped by the ingenious game of universality and particularity: by the uncanny talent of particularity to dress up as universality. Most instances of collectivized survival succeeded in what Régis Debray described as 'melting the meanness of chauvinism with the generosity of messianism'.[30] Universality, the code-name for unbound inclusion, is deployed as a tool of *exclusion*. Once the cause in the service of which the survival impulse is mobilized (the cause that ennobles survival exertions, legitimizes them, cleans them of the gnawing suspicion of selfishness, immorality, a sociality) has been proclaimed universal, nothing is left outside; or, rather, whatever has been left outside is now non-entity: it does not count, it has no value left, its destruction is not counted among the costs of survival. At best, the leftovers are waste to be disposed of for the sake of the health and sanity of that which has been marked for survival. If the leftovers had feelings and gumption, they would, surely, rejoice in their destruction, which has been sealed as a necessary and *universally* beneficent event the moment the boundaries of universality closed outside their abode. They would sing merrily on the way to the sewage gutters.

---

[29] Reinhold Niebuhr, *Moral Man and Immoral Society: A Study in Ethics and Politics* (New York: Scribner & Sons, 1948), p. 91. Niehbuhr considers that nation - the most conspicuous and effective among the 'collectivizers' - as a 'final vent for the expression of individual egoism' (p. 95). One recalls Canetti's observation: 'If you had to face one another naked, you would have a hard time slaughtering. The murderous uniforms.' (*The Human Province*, p. 12.)

[30] Régis Debray, *Le Scribe: genèse du politique* (Paris: Grasset, 1980), p. 127. Debray concentrates on a most vivid example of post-revolutionary France. There, much like many years later in the Communist 'homeland of mankind' or American 'world capital of freedom', group egoism never appeared under its own name. Instead, it paraded as the torch-carrier, avant-garde, spokesman for, benefactor of all those waiting to be lifted to its own heights. 'Le Français a le privilège de représenter un peuple qui incarne le Peuple.'

Yearning for face, fleeing from face

With leftovers safely out of the way, what remains is the world composed of an inner circle: those special, important Others who constitute my identity; the we-group, the life environment that is life itself. If, as Merleau-Ponty observed, I can grasp myself only as 'already born' or 'still living', it is mostly because I know of life only as of being with others, communicating with others, connecting with others. When I strive to imagine the end of my being, the first thing that comes to my mind (as a notion, not a picture) is, as Robert Jay Lifton found out, the 'severance of the sense of connection'.[31] Connection is more than mere co-presence. Connection is what fills the connected with content – perhaps all the content there is. Connection makes the connected meaningful. One may say it makes the connected *human*, if the humans are distinguished by the *meaningfulness of their being*.

But connections achieve all that only in so far as they make the existence of the connected into *being for each other*, not merely being *with* each other. My continuing being 'makes sense' only in as far as there are others who go on needing me. Beckoning to me, making me attentive to their plight, filling me with the feeling of responsibility for them, they make me unique, irreplaceable, indispensable individual that I am: that entity whose disappearance would make a hole in the universe, create that void which is the source of my terror. Unless 'I am *for*', I am not. The human being is a being with meaning. And being for others is the only meaning present in the human condition 'naturally', from the start, 'matter-of-factly', with the degree of obviousness that borders on invisibility. It is only this kind of 'being for others' which stands between me and the absurd emptiness of contingent existence. Not the *interested* concern, zestful or reluctant readiness to serve for the sake of future rewards or gains in self-respect, but a concern with the Other for the Other's benefit, as in Aristotle's description of friendship as 'wishing another's good for his sake, not for yours',[32] or Max Scheler's account of commiseration: 'to be sorry at another person's sorrow, as being his'.[33]

The corollary of such openness for the other's plight (*disinterested*

---

[31] Robert Jay Lifton, 'On Death and Death Symbolism: The Hiroshima Disaster', in *The Phenomenon of Death: Faces of Mortality*, ed. Edith Wyschogrod (New York: Harper & Row, 1973), p. 103.

[32] *Nichomachean Ethics*, 9.4.1166 A2–4.

[33] Max Scheler, *The Nature of Sympathy*, trans. Peter Heath (London: Routledge, 1954), p. 37.

openness) is an imperative character of the concern in question, i.e. its independence from the qualities of the Other. Thus, by this definition, the kind of friendship dictated, as Plato suggested in *Lysis*, by the usefulness of the object to the subject of affection, by the subject's hope that the befriended object will supply something which the subject lacks and misses[34] does not belong here. (And so neither does Niklas Luhmann's love fall into this category, if it is considered as a credit extended in anticipation of coveted certification of self-identity, or any other 'trans-actional', exchange-conscious varieties or conceptions of love relation-ship.) Gregory Vlastos summed up Plato as a champion of 'spiritualized egocentrism'. By his reading of Plato's discourse of friendship and love, Plato is 'scarcely aware of kindness, tenderness, compassion, concern for the freedom, respect for the integrity of the beloved'.[35] Only such concern with the Other fills the emptiness of contingent existence which is, simultaneously, an *unconcern* with the subject's own comfort, pleasure or welfare. And one that does not call on the Other to justify his right to concern. There is nothing the Other must do, or nothing in particular he should become, to trigger off the concern of the subject. We can find perhaps the fullest description of such concern in the investigations of the greatest moral philosopher of this century, Emmanuel Levinas.

In his first great book, *Existence and Existents* (1947) Levinas finds 'there is' a void, a hollowness, a featureless 'neither being nor nothingness' – something akin to the eery sound coming from an empty shell pressed to the ear; or to indecipherable noise from behind the wall in a strange hotel room; or to insomnia, that intrusion of objective impossibility into being, that depersonalization of consciousness. Prising 'there is' apart and making its parts into objects, *existents*, present or potential objects of possession, makes no breach in the bottomless infinity of 'there is'; nor does it detract from its meaninglessness. Instead, it fastens the self to the existents it craves to dominate, and through them to the non-sense of 'there is'. It does not break the 'rumbling silence' of 'there is'. It does not offer solace for the horror and panic of discovery of the nothingness as the contents, the hard core of being. In the end of the day, as throughout the day, everything remains as it was. If there is an escape from 'there is', it leads not through 'position', but through 'deposition' of the self. Only

[34] Cf. A.W. Price, *Love and Friendship in Plato and Aristotle* (Oxford: Clarendon Press, 1989), pp. 2ff.

[35] Gregory Vlastos, *Platonic Studies* (Princeton: Princeton University Press, 1981), pp. 30–1.

abdication of sovereignty in the face of the Other, responsibility for the Other, stops the meaningless, rumbling clamour of the 'there is'.

Being reduced to the 'is', being without the 'ought', equals solitude. This was the theme of the companion book, *Time and the Other*. Existence is intransitive, without intention and without meaning. It is mine and mine alone. Knowledge and communication would not deliver the self from loneliness. One can *tell about* one's existence, but one cannot *share* it. 'Being with' does not relieve existential solitude. If 'being with' means exchanging and sharing, one can exchange and share everything but the being itself. Thus 'being with', like all other modes or facets of existence, cannot establish true togetherness, true sharing; it cannot sustain a *moral* relationship. It is solely 'being for' which can do this.

The last of Levinas' books, *Otherwise than Being, or Beyond Essence* (1974), concludes the search. Moral relationship is irreducible, it is not a derivative or artefact or effect of anything else. It is neither deducible from being nor provable in knowledge. It is grounded instead in a pre-ontological and pre-intellectual relationship which already contains the 'for'. I being *for* the Other, I bearing *responsibility* for the Other. That 'for' would not be inserted, by whatever effort, into it were it not there from the start.

> The responsibility for the other cannot have begun in my commitment, in my decision. The unlimited responsibility in which I find myself comes from the other side of my freedom, from a 'prior to every memory', an 'ulterior to every accomplishment', from the non-present par excellence, the non original, anarchical, prior to or beyond essence ... It is as though the first movement of responsibility could not consist in awaiting nor even in welcoming the order (which would still be a quasi-activity), but consists in obeying this order before it is formulated.[36]

Responsibility for the Other appears uninvited; it is not let in *knowingly* – it has been neither deliberately conceived, nor accepted with a sigh of resignation. It is there whether I know of it or not. It does not hang on my resolve to take it. Neither does it vanish with my refusal to bear it. 'I am responsible without having taken on responsibility.' I am responsible because of the *proximity* of the Other. Proximity means, indeed, my responsibility. Proximity pregnant with responsibility 'in nowise resembles the intentional relation which in knowledge attaches us to the object – to no matter what object, be it a human object. Proximity does not revert

[36] Emmanuel Levinas, *Otherwise than Being, or Beyond Essence*, trans. Alphonso Linges (The Hague: Martinus Nijhoff, 1981), pp. 10, 13.

to this intentionality; in particular it does not revert to the fact that the Other is known to me.' Proximity does not follow from anything else and has not been heaved into the face-to-face with a lever of enforced coexistence or calculated commonality of interest. In fact, 'the tie with the Other is knotted only of responsibility'. No second bottom, no hidden cause. Particularly, no foundation. Responsibility is 'the essential, primary, and fundamental structure of subjectivity'. Ethics does not follow subjectivity: it is subjectivity that is ethical. In Levinas's description, ethics 'does not supplement a preceding existential base; the very node of the subjective is knotted in ethics understood as responsibility'.[37]

Levinas disqualifies existence and subjectivity as sources of morality – the 'face to face', the seat of moral relationship, of the 'being for', is placed outside the hunting grounds of both. Ethics, insists Levinas, is 'first philosophy'; morality is *prior* to being. (Let us note that since morality is prior to being – the 'ought' *precedes* the 'is' – priority itself is *ethical*, not ontological; priority of morality means that morality is *better* than being, not that morality 'exists' before being and constitutes its *determining cause*.) In Levinas' own words:

> The proximity of one to the other is here conceived outside of ontological categories in which, in different ways, the notion of the *other* also figures, whether as an obstacle to freedom, intelligibility, or perfection, or as a term that confirms a finite being, mortal and uncertain of itself, by recognizing it, or a slave, collaborator or God able to succour.

In all these categories, which between themselves exhaust the alternatives offered by the extant philosophical tradition, 'proximity is conceived ontologically', i.e. it 'remains a distance diminished, an exteriority conjured'.

In opposition to this shared view, Levinas 'sets out to not conceive proximity in function of being'.[38] Proximity, exposure to the Other, responsibility for the other are all 'chosen without assuming the choice'; as such, they 'must have the meaning of a "goodness despite itself", a goodness always older than the choice'.[39] (One invests that 'older', again,

---

[37] Levinas, *Ethics and Infinity*, pp. 97, 95.

[38] Levinas, *Otherwise than Being*, p. 16.

[39] Levinas, *Otherwise than Being*, p. 56–7. The absolute primacy of the ethical, its stubborn, arrogant, obstreperous nature, disrespectful of all existential, cognitive, calculated reasons, is of course Søren Kierkegaard's idea: the ethical 'rests immanently in itself, has nothing outside itself that is its *telos* but is itself the *telos* of everything outside'. (*Fear and Trembling*, trans. Alastair Hannay (Harmondsworth: Penguin Books, 1985), p. 83.)

with ethical sense; 'older' means 'better' – ethical impulse is before the choice has begun, and it is therefore autonomous toward, and immune to all cognitive, calculable criteria, like utility, rationality, agreement with the 'facts of the matter', by which the subsequent choice can, or may claim to, evaluate itself.)

Not the knowledge of the Other, not the shame of being looked at by Him (as Sartre would say), not even my effort to reach Him, to console Him or placate, to disarm or overpower, makes me that unique and irreplaceable being that I am – but the call of responsibility, preconscious obsession, trauma of command which is heard unspoken, which comes pure, bodiless, free of representation, demands submission without authority, consent without argument, duty without law. My uniqueness, my selfness is grounded in my being called upon, and hence being someone no one else can replace. Responsibility is mine, I have been singled out, there is no one else to share my obsession or relieve its burden by taking it upon himself. And since my calling can be none else but mine, my responsibility bears no relief and bars all escape: 'The face of a neighbour signifies for me an unexceptionable responsibility, preceding every free consent, every pact, every contract.'

> Humanity, to which proximity properly so called refers, must ... not be first understood as consciousness ... Proximity does not resolve into the consciousness a being would have of another being that it would judge to be near inasmuch as the other would be under one's eyes or within one's reach, and inasmuch as it would be possible for one to take hold of that being, hold on to it or converse with it, in the reciprocity of handshakes, caresses, struggle, collaboration, commerce, conversation. Consciousness ... would then have already lost proximity properly so called, now surveyed and thematized.[40]

Consciousness of the Other is already a break in proximity. Once *known* and cognized, the Other turns into an object. My consciousness of

---

[40] Levinas, *Otherwise than Being*, pp. 88, 83. In Jacques Derrida's brilliant summary: 'Beneath solidarity, beneath companionship, before *Mitsein*, which would be only a derivative and modified form of the originary relation with the other, Levinas already aims for the face-to-face, the encounter with the face. "Face-to-face without intermediary" and without "communion"...' The 'being together' in Levinas' sense, Derrida concludes, 'precedes or exceeds society, collectivity, community'. But it is such a being together only in as far as it does precedes or exceed society or any structured communion. 'The visage is a face only in the face-to-face.' For this reason, the other of the face-to-face is alone in being able to order 'thou shalt not kill' – 'and thus absolutely limits my power'. (Jacques Derrida, *Writing and Difference*, trans. Alan Bras (London: Routledge, 1978), pp. 90–104.

him begets my mastery over him and his impotence. My responsibility dissolves in his duty to apologize for his presence and argue his case. Now I start asking questions. I am interrogating him and demanding explanations, justifications and 'good reasons': 'What is it to me?' or, 'What is in it for me?' or, 'Where does he get his right to command?' or, 'What have I done to be in debt to him?' I demand legitimation for the command and evidence of my duty. At the end of all this, I may – just may – accept the legitimation and consider the duty justified and proven. And yet the original proximity has been now lost. There is now a distance between us, never to be bridged again. At worst a war, at best a contract and a compromise are now where my responsibility was.

This is, however, not only *his* loss. That responsibility which had made me before the unique being that I was, the one and only, the being at the same time irreplaceable, indisposable and indispensable, is now gone. I have lost my obsession, I am free from that shuddering which overwhelmed me in the face-to-face with the Other, but I have also lost my uniqueness, my calling, my meaningfulness. Once more I am alone with the 'there is', that rumbling silence which can neither be quashed nor made to speak, that terrifying emptiness of contingency that will never be filled, however earnestly – through mastery, possession or knowledge – I try.

Responsibility is *mine* in the strongest of conceivable senses: it 'forgets reciprocity, as in a love that does not expect to be shared'.

> The knot of subjectivity consists in going to the other without concerning oneself with his movement toward me. Or, more exactly, it consists in approaching in such a way that, over and beyond all the reciprocal relations that do not fail to get set up between me and the neighbour, I have always taken one step more toward him – which is possible only if this step is responsibility. In the responsibility which we have for one another, I have always one response more to give, I have to answer for his very responsibility.[41]

Responsibility is my affair, reciprocity is his. My responsibility is unexceptional and unconditional. The Other does not need to 'prove' anything to 'deserve' it. Neither do I bear my responsibility 'in order' to 'earn' his response in kind. There is no aforethought, no anticipation of reward and no calculation of gain in my responsibility. I am responsible for the Other whatever the Other does, I am responsible *before* he does anything at all and *before* I am aware of his doing anything – indeed, of his very capacity

---

[41] Levinas, *Otherwise than Being*, pp. 82, 84.

for doing something. And it is precisely the *otherness* of the Other which burdens me with responsibility. Recognition of community, rationalization of similarity or commonality of interest – all this, if it does come, comes later. I am responsible *before* my responsibility is justified or vindicated.

> The neighbour concerns me before all assumption, all contract consented to or refused ... Here is a relation of kinship outside all biology, 'against all logic'. It is not because the neighbour would be recognized as belonging to the same genus as me that he concerns me. He is precisely *other*. The community with him begins in my obligation to him.[42]

Everything else begins after that obligation. Also the questioning of the obligation: the call for responsibility to show its *reasons*, for the Other to supply evidence of his *entitlement* to my concern. Let us repeat: once the questioning starts, proximity has been already replaced with a distance, and responsibility has lost its unconditionality; the obsession has been replaced by calculation. No effort will restore the pristine unexceptionality of my responsibility. All responsibility grounded in being (unlike one rooted in the otherwise-than-being, in the face-to-face which is the creation, simultaneously, of my uniqueness, my humanity, and *our* community) will forever remain fragile, negotiable, until further notice - ultimately, like the rest of the 'there is', meaningless.

Once the innocence of responsibility has been lost and a distance opens where once proximity was, questions may be and are asked.

> Why does the other concern me? ... Am I my brother's keeper? These questions have meaning only if one has already supposed that the ego is concerned only with itself, is only a concern for itself. In this hypothesis it indeed remains incomprehensible that the absolute outside-of-me, the other, would concern me.[43]

---

[42] Levinas, *Otherwise than Being*, p. 87. One may note a more than contingent similarity between this radical altruism of Levinas's ethic and the unilateral responsibility for the 'dialogical' relationship between I and Thou in Martin Buber (Cf. *I and Thou* (New York: Charles Scribner, 1958).) A dialogue, for Buber, is, however, something to be established and sustained, which may not come to pass at all, which peters out in monologue unless made into a focus of concern and effort. Community between I and Thou, for Buber, originates in dialogue; it stands and falls by the quality of the dialogue; it has to be called into being and sustained; it may be withdrawn from. (Compare, for instance, the profound study of Buber's concept in Maurice Friedman, *Martin Buber: Life and Work, The Early Years, 1978 –1923* (London: Search Press, 1982).) For Levinas, on the other hand, community precedes the dialogue and conditions its very possibility. In the dialogue, proximity of the face-to-face has been already compromised.

[43] Levinas, *Otherwise than Being*, p. 117.

But how come that the self-concern of the self has been supposed? How come that this hypothesis carries credibility which allowed it to hide its hypothetical character so successfully? Unless we are prepared to say that it was simply the matter of the philosophers' collective blindness or folly (that, while busy 'writing footnotes to Plato', we have been, boldly yet hopelessly, smarting under the blow delivered by his false, yet so cogent argument) we can only suppose that the self-concern is more than a mere illusion which can be dispersed through exposing the philosophers' blunder. We must concede that the all-too-evident calculability of together-ness and conditionality of responsibility are more than a figment of philosophical fantasy. We must allow the possibility that in the cold climate of being the pristine proximity does wilt and crumble. It either dies out, or – if resilient – is stored away into that huge warehouse of infamy named 'irrationality' or 'mysticism'. (Civilization, as Hans Peter Duerr pointed out, equates the boundaries drawn 'between itself and the wilderness with a dividing line between reality and illusion'.)[44] In the constructed order of being, nothing is tolerated unless it is able to show itself to be a construct. Something must have happened or must be constantly happening to the groundless, reasonless obsession of proximity in the socially constructed world of human existence. Something fatal. Perhaps also irrevocable.

In our world, Levinas insists, proximity (this of the otherwise-than-being kind, not the one laboriously construed in the fragile (because exclusive and contractual) love relationship, conjured up 'until further notice' in tribal gatherings, or imagined in the countless variants of group therapy) is not completely extinct. It cannot be; however few offshoots show through the thick concrete of social order, the roots must be there somewhere beneath for any life to be sustainable on the top of the lifeless base.

> It is through the condition of being hostage that there can be in the world pity, compassion, pardon and proximity – even the little there is, even the simple 'After you, sir'. The unconditionality of being hostage is not the limit case of solidarity, but the condition of all solidarity.[45]

This may well be the case, yet the 'After you, sir' courtesy cannot but strike us as falling far short of the unconditional self-abandonment, that 'deposition of sovereignty', which the original proximity implied. In the strainer of social order little has remained of that inter-human responsibil-

---

[44] Hans Peter Duerr, *Dreamtime: Concerning the Boundary between Wilderness and Civilization*, trans. Felicitas Goodman (Oxford: Basil Blackwell, 1985), p. 89.
[45] Levinas, *Otherwise than Being*, p. 117.

ity, which is still allowed to retain spontaneity and to be followed without rhyme or reason; indeed, so little that it does not feel right to wonder over the blindness of philosophers. The strainer must have done its job well, as it is excruciatingly difficult to guess the noble origin of the humble leftovers one can see. This job holds the secret of the vanishing act of that ethics which preceded sociality as, simultaneously, its condition and its *better* alterity. It is the absence or paucity, not the presence or possibility, of morality in social life which is to be explored and explained if the secret is to be revealed. This is the practical lesson from Levinas' argument:

> It is extremely important to know if society in the current sense of the term is the result of a limitation of the principle that men are predators of one another, or if to the contrary it results from the limitation of the principle that men are *for* one another. Does the social, with its institutions, universal forms and laws, result from limiting the consequences of the war between men, or from limiting the infinity which opens in the ethical relationship of man to man?[46]

The loneliness of terror

The subtlety of Levinas' argument notwithstanding, the quotidianity of social existence has been set at a considerable distance from that pristine space he has postulated – a space occupied solely by ethical responsibility. The proximity of the face-to-face has been broken and not allowed to heal, if healed it can be. That face-to-face we know (empirically, from experience) is but a hapless though frantic attempt to conjure up what has been lost and is missed. This mock, substitute 'face-to-face' may be 'cool': calculated and circumspectly constructed, and thus stubbornly reminding us of its merely artificial and contingent status. Or it may be 'hot': intense, emotional, yet elusive and ephemeral, never exuding the air of finality, never really certain – and thus awakening us to the inconclusivity and 'cancellability' of all roots-replacing engagements. Indeed, for all we know, 'the social' results 'from limiting the infinity which opens in the ethical relationship of man to man' (though always and everywhere it claims to result from 'limiting the consequences of the war between men'). That infinity has been foreclosed.[47] Instead, it is the void it once filled that has

---

[46] Levinas, *Ethics and Infinity*, p. 80.

[47] Why this has been (must have been?) the case, and universally so, I tried to explain in 'The Social Manipulation of Morality: Moralizing Actors, Adiaphorizing Action', in *Theory, Culture & Society*, vol. 8 (1991).

been reopened. The 'rumbling silence' of the hollowness of 'there is' is the only sound heard – and it is this sound that life bustle strives to stifle, with little or no success. 'Existents', however plentiful and however shiny and fragrant, cannot fill the hole that is the existence which is not 'being for'. The hole is bottomless, and the lifelong exertion can do nothing to fathom its depth.

The reopening of the void is what brings the terror of death right into the centre of life. The 'limiting of infinity which opens in the ethical relationship' lets in another, frightening infinity – that of the emptiness of existence in which life is sunk. The less there is left of the first, the more salient, obtrusive and arrogant is the second.

We have come to see as 'progress' the relentless 'emancipation' of man from 'constraints'. We have learnt (and have been taught) to view the primal human bonds, that *domaine de l'à-peu-près*, the fidelities that claimed 'naturalness' and priority over all wilful action, as oppression. Throughout the modern era political legislators, warriors of free trade and philosophers joined forces in order to free man from that oppression. Bonds were now to be freely chosen, freely entered into and abandoned, drawing all the limiting power they may legitimately claim merely from the contract freely signed by both sides – each one guided in its decisions solely by its understanding of what serves its happiness best. Bonds were now to pass the test of that happiness; or, rather, of the promise of happiness they carry. Most certainly, this was liberation from the many petty slaveries of life. But the liberated have been ushered into new, no less awesome slavery. Life had now little else to define itself by as the movement toward death. With everything that fills it with contents reduced to ephemerality, to the status of 'until further notice', it turns into a long dress rehearsal of non-being.

Life is now a lonely pursuit. Whatever company may be gained must be earned. But even when gained it is not there to stay. It may go much as it has come – tomorrow if not tonight. It is my self, I alone that lasts through life; it is only my self on which the sense of that life can be founded. Once the feat has been accomplished, man has been freed 'from all those historical influences and diversions that ravage his deepest essence' (which is his uncompromising freedom, also freedom from that responsibility that arose from 'being for'); 'the quest of the individual is for his self, for a fixed and unambiguous point of reference'. Simmel commented:

All relations with others are thus ultimately mere stations along the road by which the ego arrives at its self. This is true whether the ego feels itself to be basically identical to these others because it still needs this supporting conviction as it stands alone upon itself and its own powers, or whether it is strong enough to bear the loneliness of its own quality, the multitude being there only so that each individual can use the others as a measure of his incomparability and the individuality of his world.[48]

Once life has been emancipated from all pre-arranged, inalienable responsibility, once this life is not 'for' anybody and anything in particular, once all that there might ever be to it will be there only if laboriously fudged together by my own undetermined and indeterminate labour – everything will abruptly come to a stop the moment that only power behind life, 'the ego', my own self, ceases to be. Loneliness of life results in the loneliness of death (itself being its result). It is because life lost the only sense given to it 'of right' - that of *being for* – that death lost its meaning as well. Its terror cannot be shared. It is, after all, my thoroughly private, self-centred and (in its intention) self-sustained world that will disappear. The most terrifying of the thoughts of that void which would open once I die is that in the end no gaping hole will be left in the universe where once I was. That void will be also private, like my life was. My death will be a non-event. Unless I do something to change all this: to force others *to be for me* as staunchly as I refused to be *for them*, and to be as steadfastly affirmative as I have been dismissive . . .

It is the *loneliness* of terror that wants to be assuaged in the ego's bid for private immortality.

---

[48] 'Freedom and the Individual', in Georg Simmel, *On Individuality and Social Forms*, ed. Donald N. Levine (Chicago: University of Chicago Press, 1971), pp. 220, 223.

2

Bidding for Immortality

Admittedly, death means descent into a depersonalized nothingness. This nothingness is utterly *private*; depersonalization is personal. With the ego's demise, life as such will not grind to a halt – and it is from the imagined perspective of that continuing life that my own future nothingness (again as a social relation) can be, and is, grasped and conceived. Those about to survive me will be spectators of the impending revelation of my nothingness. It is their gaze that will constitute my nothingness. And it is in relation to them that the nothingness ought to be (if this is at all possible) denied. Were it indeed denied, freedom of judgement of those who go on living 'after' would be constrained; their announcement of the ego's descent into nothingness would be prevented, or at least made less credible or final. In their conduct, in their thoughts, in their existence the ego's presence-in-the-world may find its extension. *Individual* demise may be *collectively* annulled. Posterity (which, after all, is by definition more lasting than the ego's own life), is that site where the hope, if not certainty, of the ego's immortality, or at least the ego's longer-than-life existence, can be invested. It is in that site and through its occupants that the 'depersonalized nothingness' will be clinched. Alternatively, it is there and there only that it may – just may – be suspended or declared null and void.

The universal, supra-historical and supra-cultural presence of funeral rites and ritualized commemoration of the dead has been one of the earliest and most striking discoveries of comparative ethnography. No form of human life, however simple, has been found that failed to pattern the treatment of the deceased bodies and their posthumous presence in the memory of the descendants. Indeed, the patterning has been found so universal that discovery of graves and cemeteries is generally accepted by the explorers of prehistory as the proof that a humanoid strain whose life was never observed directly had passed the threshold of humanhood.

Drawing from ample ethnographic and historiographic evidence, Effie

51

Bendann's classic cross-cultural study[1] offers a bewildering array of death customs – burial ceremonies, mourning rites, funeral feasts, as well as behavioural displays of explicit or latent beliefs in the posthumous existence of the dead. In many societies the dead are offered food either as a hoard deposited in the grave, or at regular intervals for months or years after their burial. For instance, in pre-Christian Rome *dies parentales* were celebrated annually (between 13 and 21 February), during which the dead were brought fresh supplies of water, milk, honey and oil.[2] Faithful to the intuitions prevalent at his time, Bendann explained the rites by the *fears of living*, rather than the *dreams of the future dead*: the offerings, he suggested, were motivated mostly by the desire of the living to prevent the ghosts from haunting their lives, to keep the dead away, to placate their malice and stave off the damage they may inflict if unappeased ('the propitiation of the spirit of the departed'). It seems, however, that this explanation does not square well with the litany of profuse commemorative ceremonies that follows.

All explored societies induce their members to engage periodically, if not daily, in acts of collective remembrance – which seem to be aimed at the living rather than at the dead whose memory they kept alive. Ritualization of memory might have had spiritual comfort to the living, rather than the imaginary material comfort of the dead, as its main purpose and achievement. The practising of commemorative rites has an reassuring effect on those who practise them and watch everybody around practising them as well: what they do now to their predecessors will be done to them by their own successors. The remembering of today will themselves, come their time, be remembered. Collective memory will in the future, as it does now, outlast individual life, and the future dead will then, as they do now, go on living in the spirits of those who are not dead yet. What we do unto others will be done unto us. The intense and meticulous attention devoted to institutionalizing the collective memory of the dead seems to service in no small measure the search of the living for some anchorage of their desire of immortality, and an address for possible efforts to fulfil that desire.

Commemorative rites rehearse the non-finality of death. They also represent the continuing existence of community as the pledge to over-

---

[1] Effie Bendann, *Death Customs; An Analytical Study of Burial Rites* (London: Dawsons of Pall Mall, 1969).
[2] Bendann, *Death Customs*, pp. 152ff. Bendann relies here on the authority of W. Warde Fowler, *The Roman Festivals of the Period of the Republic* (London, 1899). In our own times the role of more earthly offerings have been taken over, symbolically, by flowers.

come, at least for a time, the individual transience. They separate the moment of bodily death from that of *social* death, making the second independent of the other and endowing only the second, social, death with the status of finality. While giving form to the dream of immortality, they deploy the dread of mortality in the service of communal cohesion.

Immortality: the great de-equalizer

There is another fascinating insight which can be gleaned from Bendann's study. Societies tried hard to convince their members of social guarantees of immortality. Since these were *social* guarantees, however, they could in principle be socially managed and socially distributed. (And so they were). The promise of immortality turned into a most powerful disciplining effort in the hands of society. Like other socially allocated rewards, immortality could be awarded in larger or smaller quantities, depending on the deads' assumed possession of values whose dominance society wished to secure or perpetuate. The amount of public mourning and the intensity of public manifestations of memory became symbolic expressions of relative social placement at the same time as they were major stakes at the game of domination. Thanks to social rituals, all members were immortal, yet some were clearly more immortal than others. Society promised immortality: but it promised immortality as an interest on mortal life properly lived. Society encourages *individual* bids for immortality. Political economy of immortality, under closer scrutiny, proves to be just another policy of stratification; perhaps the most effective of such policies.

> At Saa, the burial of common people is extremely simple; an inferior person is buried immediately; an ordinary man is buried the day after his death. However, men of rank are not buried for two days. Women sit around the corpse and wail and gather to get a last glimpse at the deceased and to partake of the funeral feast . . .
>
> For a man who has no significant position his friends throw yams and other food upon the roof of the dead man's house in his memory; whereas if a chief dies, they . . . fence round a plot of ground, and place his canoe, his bowls, and weapons there; his friends add their own tributes in his honour, and decorate the fence with leaves and flowers.
>
> In Savo the bodies of commoners are thrown into the sea, while those of chiefs are interred.[3]

---

[3] Bendann, *Death Customs*, p. 197. The rank difference in funeral rites is continued long after the bodies are buried or otherwise disposed of. In Melanesia 'the ghost of a distinguished man is worshipped and is looked upon as very potent

The pattern is repeated everywhere and at all times, in that exuberant variety of forms which is a tribute, simultaneously, to boundless human ingenuity and the constancy of human fears. Commoners die leaving little trace on the surface of earth and but a momentary scar on the minds and hearts of survivors. The hole left by their departure is expected to be filled rapidly; no need to alert the world to the event that is destined to efface itself from memory like a footprint in the sand. Funeral rites and commemorative ceremonies show themselves to be another code in which human inequality is recorded and programmed. The more elaborate, impressive (and, indeed, costly) they are – the more power they have to bind collective attention and coerce it into underwriting and sustaining individual immortality. Struggling to secure selective treatment to his own corpse and life record, the individual may translate his present – mortal only – privilege into the future (hopefully, immortal) one. At the price of conformity to its model of order, society offers the means which individuals may deploy to bind the future they will not be around to supervise and control in person. Giddens's *structuration* capacity extends thereby beyond the actor's death. Thanks to such means, some people may hope to be 'less mortal' than others. Some people would succeed in bending future judgements so that they would deny their demise; the rest will sink into oblivion precisely because they lack or miss the survival entitlements of the first.

With all that, colonization of the future is bound to remain forever disconcertingly provisional and non-definite; the future is, after all, the site of the selfsame uncertainty which has prompted the colonizing thrust in the first place. Denial of nothingness lacks all solidity if anchored in the future; even if addressed to future survivors and prompted by the wish to bind *their* judgements, it could derive its apparent substantiality (indeed, its capacity to comfort and reassure those living at present) only from the roots struck firmly in the 'site of certainty' – the past. Paradoxically, the

---

in its influence since it retains the powers which belonged to it in life, but the ghosts of insignificant persons are regarded with the same indifference as before ... It is significant to note that the great people who are buried on land turn into land ghosts, and the commoners who are sunk into the sea become sea ghosts.' In New Guinea the remnants of great men are at regular intervals ritually re-invigorated, so that continuous existence is maintained: 'the skulls and bones of chiefs, their wives, and other members of their families' are preserved by 'dipping of them into the blood of pigs at great festivals every fifteen or twenty years' (p. 264). (James Frazer interpreted such and similar rites, in our view mistakenly, as a device for propitiating the ghost of the dead chief, rather than as a device for satisfy the current chief's craving for immortality.)

hope of transcending the present and stretching it into the future can be rooted only in making the past last.

That hope lies behind the constant temptation to retrieve the past, never to let it out of living memory – as if to demonstrate in such a roundabout way the non-transience of things; more precisely, the non-transience of *certain* things, relevant to *certain* people, and thus by proxy also the non-transience of the people to whom non-transient things are relevant. The thrust toward differential immortality rebounds as a partisan, necessarily *selective*, retrieval of history. Obversely, the struggle against inequality of immortality chances (against unequal hopes to bind the future) chooses history writing and rewriting as its major battlefield (a struggle essentially akin to that for a more equal distribution of posthumous attention, as in the drive to 'democratize' the use of elaborate graveyard sculptures or the introduction of the cult of fallen soldiers). The war to colonize the imagined future is fought on the territory of imagined past.

Let us sharpen the point still further: immortality is ultimately a *social relation*. Binding history may be hoped to be effective as a warrant for the binding of future only because, and in as far as, other people cannot demonstrate the lasting visibility of their own past (better still: 'have no past of their own'). Differentiality of posthumous fate requires a differential deprivation of history. Long and carefully recorded pedigrees are significant through setting the scions of long and *known* lineages apart from the commoners who cannot trace their ancestors beyond a second or a third generation. Aristocracies, with their long survival record, stand out in a world populated by people without a past. The existence of people with long pedigrees *has been* deeply rooted and solidly entrenched – the fact they find easy to argue in view of the shallow and evanescent presence of all others. The past success in survival augurs well for the cause of immortality. For similar reasons, the splendour of old, inherited riches can be never matched by the glitter of brand-new fortune; the latter exudes the pungent odour of mortality which the former claimed to have dissipated, exorcised and washed away during its long march through past ages.

Private roads to immortality

The difference, the decisive difference, a difference – literally – between life and death, is one between *durability* and *transience* of things that can be possessed or performed. Durable things are not meant for consumption. They are explicitly exempt from consumption; their 'use' for any purpose other than display and a surrogate, symbolic only enjoyment, is perceived as destruction and, unlike the annihilation of other objects, is decreed to be a crime. In his remarkable and eye-opening study of rubbish-production and manipulation, Michael Thompson informs us that 'durable objects ideally last for ever' – they are, indeed, as close as things can come to be immortal; they stand for immortality. The point is, however, that

> those people near the top have the power to make things durable and to make things transient, so they can ensure that their own objects are always durable and that those of others are always transient. They are like a football team whose centre-forward also happens to be the referee; they cannot lose.[4]

However durable they are and however firmly and 'bindingly' they have been established in their privileged status of durability, certain things are irreparably movable; they exist separately from their owners and may be detached from them and appropriated by others. This is, as it were, a prime achievement of the market game. New fortunes may be used to rob the holders of inherited ones of the tokens of their immortality: their castles and their adornments. The adornments now carry immortality by proxy: their acquisition bestows vicarious immortality on the new owners. They are ascribed an *immortal* beauty (or is it the beauty of immortality?). And unlike the pedigrees, they are movable – so that they can service a flexible stratification, a hierarchy with mobility: a game of musical chairs which gives everybody a chance to win a battle in which most must lose. Of the precious ore of time-defying ancestry, charms and mascots of immortality are minted, fit for marketing and available for private acquisition. Aristocracy may have lost the monopoly for immortality; but the scramble for the trappings of its past glory is a posthumous tribute to the astounding success of its formula of transcendence.

One way or the other – with the preferential access to immortality

---

[4] Michael Thompson, *Rubbish Theory: The Creation and Destruction of Value* (London: Oxford University Press, 1979), pp. 113, 9. Not only are the durable things never exposed to the dangers of consumption, like the transient do, they are also safely protected from ever falling into the third category of objects – that of *rubbish*. Thompson pointedly corrects the famous Lord Chesterfield/Mary Douglas observation that 'dirt is a matter out of place', suggesting instead that 'some, and perhaps all, orderly arrangements are hierarchical – not everything in the wrong place is rubbish, it depends on the displacement relative to the values gradient. The Old Master print in the junk shop window may be out of place but it is certainly not rubbish.' (p. 117)

founded in the past which 'no living in the present can change', or in the present power of wealth which makes even the past into a commodity – future chances depend ultimately on present hegemony: that is, on the management of public attention. The stakes on which the hope of immortality is founded must be assured a central place in the way the living universe is charted – a prominent, not-to-be-missed place, a place that attracts acute ('undying'!) interest and is widely accepted as a proper site for public celebration. To be of significance as a tool of the bid for immortality, antiquities must be first made venerable. To assure princes and generals and prime ministers of their immortality, history must be first written in terms of dynasties, battles and legislative acts. Future immortality will grow of today's recordings. Tomorrow's immortals must first get hold of today's archives.

It is ultimately the current socially approved division of things and qualities into *durable* and *transient* which charts the possible roads to immortality (that is, which selects the fashions in which individual thirst for differential immortality may be satiated). One needs to know of one's posthumous presence in the world when still alive – and for this one needs the reassurance of one's contemporaries, a credible, trustworthy assurance. Assurances bear these traits when – and only when – they are backed with authority of one of the two essential types. It may be a promise coming from sources socially defined as experts in 'seeing into the future' or, more generally, in 'knowing how history works'. In most cases, these are history-tellers and history writers; history (as a narrative with an audience, as a text with a readership) is, after all, the very place in which the posthumous life, if there is to be such a life, will have been conducted. Alternatively (in the age of mass democracy in particular) the authority of numbers may be trusted – the power of great numbers to leave an imprint on future events, to force history to reckon and to take note. The more massive today's notoriety, the less likely it seems that it will disappear without trace, and the 'trivial pursuit' type of information populism helps considerably to make such an expectation credible. Whichever of the two authorities is in operation, the purpose is fulfilled: the promise of immortality (though always provisional and until further notice) is granted when it matters – that is, during the lifetime of the mortals.

Thus, we hear repeatedly that one or another of our contemporaries 'has made history'. Some 'make history' automatically, but gaining a position whose incumbents are written down in the 'official records' that make the stuff of which historical narratives are composed. Every prime minister or war commander 'makes history' in this sense, though of course the question of the solidity of historical survival, the splendour of post-humous existence – the size of the accommodation to be allotted in future historical narratives – remains open. The latter depends on the incumbent's pursuits while in the office. A prime minister may hope to enter history in a more impressive fashion than is the case with most prime ministers if, for instance, he becomes a 'longest serving' head of government, or presides over times of particularly high prosperity or particularly disastrous economic collapse. In a different way, but according to the same rules, 'history is made' by footballers, tennis-players, pop-singers, murderers, painters, wine-growers, inventors, film actors, scientists. In all these, as in so many other cases when the socially warranted promise of individual immortality is granted, the same pattern is followed. First, the activity itself must have been assigned a durable significance and thus a 'place in history'. Second, to make the case of immortality stronger and posthumous existence more prominent, a particular excellence must be reached in the fashion in which the activity in question is performed. The evaluation of excellence tends to be formalized or semi-formalized, as in the case of the Academie Française, which grants its members the title of Immortals, or the periodic chess championship competitions, Olympic Games, or institutions of records and record-breaking.

Immortal thoughts, immortal thinkers

We learned from Marx that the ideas of the ruling class are ruling ideas. Yet the ruling class does not rest satisfied with the rule of ideas contemporaneous with its class rule: it also tries (perhaps harder than anything else) to make sure that the rule of its ideas survives its own earthly rule so that the latter may be recorded as immortal and sustained in its immortality for a long time to come. The reasonable degree of certainty that this will indeed be the case when the unknown and essentially uncertain *not-yet* finally arrives, is grounded in the hope of eternality of values which the rule struggles to promote and preserve. As it serves the eternal values, life of the rulers 'transcends mere quotidianity'. The rulers' *biographies* become *history*. Unlike the lives of ordinary mortals, who enter history, if at all, as *statistics* – depersonalized and 'demographized', they will be considered worthy to be carefully recorded, studied, written and taught about, interpreted and reinterpreted. They will escape the lot of transient objects – which, once consumed and used up, disappear from view (and thus from the existence that counts) and dissolve, perhaps forever, in anonymous formlessness of obscurity.

This chance of immortality depends totally on whether the significance of deeds and virtues displayed by the ruling class as the entitlement to rule will be acknowledged by future generations. Promoting such chances amounts once more to the effort of binding the future – and, as in other cases, it must, by nature, be a collective enterprise. For the members of the ruling class to be able to make their individual bids for immortality with any hope of success, the possibility to use the stakes at their disposal in the bidding game must be assured by the future-binding dominance of the class. Errant knights may vie with each other for a more prominent place among the immortals by excelling in individual prowess and cour-age; but the chance of securing a place in the immortal memory of posterity is not of their making. The link between their individual deeds and their immortality is not achieved individually, but collectively. The link will hold as long as the ideas of the warrior class remain ruling ideas; as long as history and poetry and music consider the exertions on the battlefield to be the most suitable topics for epic of lyrical *oeuvres*.

There is one category of humans which is as if 'made for immortality', since it mediates between individual accomplishments and their public memory, so that no one can fulfil his dream of immortality without its assistance. This is the category of professional immortality brokers; those who mint the coins of lasting value, administer their hoards and attach value tags of immortality to the lives destined to last. As Régis Debray put it,

> il y a les mémorables et il y a les préposés à la mémoire. L'éphemère de la domination et son immémorial. Ceux qui laissent leurs noms sur le livre d'or et ceux qui couchent sur papier, argile ou papyrus les noms des premiers.
>
> Les héros et les artisans de la puissance. Les premiers figurent, les seconds structurent. C'est ce petit sphinx discret – qui s'est appelé tour à tour scribe, aède, sophiste, clerc, lettré, intellectuel . . .[5]

A *discreet* sphinx, says Debray. One may say: an invisible one. At the beginning, anonymous and faceless. A mere tool, to be discarded once the job has been done; no match for the durable glitter of the finished product. The product will be put proudly on display for everyone to admire. It will be preserved for posterity in museums and art galleries. But who will remember the tools? To put a tool among their products (say, a clay-spattered potter wheel and a potter's knife among the exquisitely sculpted and delicately encrusted vases) is the surest way to evoke the dirt effect, the shock of a thing 'out of place' (a stratagem used with relish

---

[5] Régis Debray, *Le Scribe: genèse du politique* (Paris: Grasset, 1980), p. 12.

by all artists wishing to *épater le bourgeois*; the only thing they had to do was to remind the viewer of the artisan behind the art).

Yet the 'dirt' of the case happens to be powerful and endowed with truly magic power. It must be, as it has created the durable out of the transient, made the passing into the lasting. Like artisans, who through their artwork allocate immortality of form to the transient raw matter they process – the scribe allocates immortality to mortal lives, endows the events and the deeds with the lasting quality of memorable and remembered tradition. The dirt effect is, therefore, but an outcome of the domination game and a reversal of the genuine hierarchy of power. It is only a matter of time before the truth will out and the real managers of immortality emerge from the oblivion in which the disdain of their powerful clients cast them. It will take a little more time for the scribes to turn into intellectuals (one is tempted to say: into scribes *für sich*), for the managers of the immortality of the great and mighty to claim immortality for their own accomplishments, their own work, the work only they can do – and thus for themselves. It is the thoughts that are immortal, and it is the text that makes them so, and it is the writers of texts that transform the transient into the durable.

Thus, from behind the timelessness of all other things – heroic deeds, long pedigrees, exploits of power – emerges that one power that has the capacity to make them timeless and to preserve them in that state: the extemporal mind, the precondition and the true abode of timeless *tradition* and *continuity* of being. From Plato's immortal ideas to Husserl's dehistoricised subjectivity, philosophers struggled to forge the on-going conversation of those who converse into an entity longer lasting than the lives of the conversationalists – so that the other conversationalists who will come later, after their death, will have to feel addressed by them, as they themselves had been addressed by their predecessors, and obliged to address them back in their own conversations; in this way the eternity of conversation, the immortality of texts in which it has been recorded, will have become reality. It is through the durability of the texts that the future is bound by the present, itself filled with the preserved past; it is through that binding that the texts are durable – immortal. Having tamed the time, so that it can ride securely on its back instead of being trampled under its feet, the ongoing discourse spans distances impassable for 'ordinary' men and women. It sets its participants apart from ordinary – illiterate or numb, historically speaking – mortals; it sets testing conditions of entry into immortality which only the chosen (or self-chosen) few can hope to meet. It plays impeccably the role which all viable policies of immortality are expected to play: it establishes immortality as social relation, as a stratifying vehicle, as the principle of inclusion that draws its potency from its practice of exclusion.

The 'made up' nature of immortality, the fact that it roots are firmly set in the present, did not escape the penetrating insight of Plato:

> The past and the future are created species of time, which we unconsciously but wrongly transfer to the eternal essence; for we say that [the eternal being] 'was', it 'is', it 'will be', but the truth is that 'is' alone is properly attributed to it, and that 'was' and 'will be' are only to be spoken of becoming in time (*Timaeus* 37e–38a)

'Essences' (Plato uses the terms *eidos, ousia, genos, fysis*, variously translated into English as 'idea', 'form', 'essence')[6] are eternal, durable (durability is the 'empirical', tangible, not-so-bewildering form in which 'eternity' may be grasped by reason): they are exempted from the time flow, they cancel the distinction between past and future (that distinction which is a mental extrapolation of ageing, decease, new birth), they *make* eternity an infinitely stretched *present*. Essence is 'in' things, so that it cannot be dismissed as irrelevant to all that fills life and attracts its concerns. Essence is the most important, creative, causal, determining 'inside' of things. But at the same time the essence is *separate*, independent and self-sufficing – not merely 'an element' of things, sharing equally in their transience and temporality. Because of the cancellation of time, the way in which ideas (essences, forms) 'are' is thoroughly distinct from the way in which things are. The essence 'is absolutely and perfectly what it is, independent of all else, changeless, divine' – and thanks to that quality 'more real than the changing animals and things around us'. The senses cannot, obviously, grasp something that is absolute, perfect and above all changeless: whatever senses perceive is protean and transient. Ideas can therefore be grasped solely by *thought* as distinct from senses. Whatever the senses produce shares the fate of the objects of sensual perception: it is bound to be unreliable and temporary, it is no more than an *opinion*. Thought, on the other hand, basks in the sun (sun is the metaphor Plato uses, to great effect, in his metaphor of the cave: the brilliance of the sunlight is too dazzling for ordinary eyes to gaze upon) of durability, permanence, 'reality stronger than existence' of ideas, forms, essences; it produces *knowledge*. 'Opinion is changeable, fallible, irrational, and the result of persuasion; knowledge is enduring, infallible, rational, exact,

---

[6] Cf. A. Wedberg, 'The Theory of Ideas', in *Plato: A Collection of Critical Essays*, vol. I, *Metaphysics and Epistemology*, ed. Gregory Vlastos (London: Macmillan, 1972), pp. 31ff.

clear.'[7] Unlike opinions, immersed in the flow of quotidianity and forever shackled to the cave, where they can eye only the dance of fickle and transient shadows – thoughts are about ideas; thoughts are the documents of encounter with immortality; ideas are eternal – and so are the thoughts, and so are the thinkers.

Knowledge that comes from immersion in timeless ideas is a glimpse of eternity. It washes off the pollution that quotidianity[8] which wears off and condemns to dissolution everything durable. No other human activity can achieve this, each being branded with indelible mark of transience. Care of the body, gymnastics 'is devoted to what becomes and perishes, for it presides over bodily growth and decay', while 'all the arts and crafts' are 'vulgar'. Only 'the turning of a soul round from a day which is like night to a true day – this is the ascent into real being, which we shall say is true philosophy'. Only 'through reason and without any help from the senses', on condition that he 'will not desist until he grasps by thought alone the real nature of good itself', the philosopher may arrive 'at the very end of the world of thought', while all the others, ordinary mortals end up at the opposite pole – 'at the end of the world of sight'. At that end the 'common beliefs of the multitude' reside. 'Sound-fanciers and sight-fanciers, delight in beautiful voices and colours and shapes and all which craftsmen have made from such; but their mind is incapable of seeing and delighting in the beautiful itself.' 'Very few' 'are able to approach the beautiful itself and to see it by itself'. These 'very few' are the philosophers.[9]

These are not merely epistemological propositions. These are also

---

[7] R. Robinson and J.D. Denniston, 'The Philosophical Economy of the Theory of Ideas', in *Metaphysics and Epistemology*, ed. Vlastos, pp. 9–10.

[8] 'Another is the river I seek', said the hero of Borges's *The Immortal*, 'the secret river which cleanses men of death.' He started off on his journey well equipped, with slaves carrying supplies and soldiers guarding the expedition against the hazards of the wilderness. 'Then the desertions began; very shortly afterwards, mutinies.' The closer the secret river of immortality, the more complete was the seeker's loneliness. At the banks of the river he arrived alone. Loneliness as the price of immortality; a price the slaves and the armed horsemen are not prepared to pay. Borges found a truly marvellous metaphor to convey Plato's imagery: ideas as clean as the water of a river no human presence could pollute, and like water refreshing, rejuvenating, invigorating. (Cf. Jorge Luis Borges, 'The Immortal', in *Labyrinths: Selected Stories and Other Writings*, ed. Donald A. Yates and James E. Irby (Harmondsworth: Penguin Books, 1974), pp. 135–7).

[9] All quotations are from W.H.D. Rouse's translation of Plato's *Republic*, in *Great Dialogues of Plato*, ed. Eric H. Warmington and Philip G. Rouse (New York: Mentor Books, 1956), pp. 320, 331, 280, 276.

statements in political science and, above all, in practical politics. At the time of Plato immortality was the lot of the rulers, and rulers alone. Now the rulers face a challenge. To justify their immortality, they have to show credentials: they have to prove that they have visited the land of the durable, that they stood face to face with the ideas as they truly and forever are. They must justify their entitlement to immortality in terms in which only philosophers are past masters. They stand little chance in this game. In as far as the rulers set the archetype of immortality (and made it into their sole property), in as far as rule and immortality had been rendered synonymous, it is the sages, these few who converse with the eternal, who ought to be rulers.

> Since philosophers alone are able to lay hold of the ever same and unchangeable, and those who cannot do so, but keep wandering amid the changeable and manifold are not philosophers, – which ought to be leaders of a city? . . .
>
> The philosophers must become kings in our cities ... It is the proper nature of these to keep hold of true wisdom and to lead in the city, but of others to leave philosophy alone and follow their leader ...
>
> The city shall make public monuments and sacrifices in their honour, as holy spirits, if the Pythian oracle concurs, or else as men happy and divine.[10]

The subsequent, two-and-a-half millennium, history of *les scribes*, and their relentless ascent to the stature of intellectuals, may indeed be seen as a vast footnote to Plato's *Republic*. The libraries written through

---

[10] *Great Dialogues of Plato*, pp. 281, 273, 274, 340. Plato's blunt solution to the intricate relationship between kings and philosophers has re-emerged in modern times in a subtler garb. A more pragmatic solution to the thorny and potentially explosive problem was sought. Thus Kant's rendition of the problem is not a demand of unconditional surrender of kings, but an invitation to negotiate mutually beneficial division of labour: '*Popular enlightenment* is the public instruction of the people upon their duties and rights towards the state to which they belong. Since this concerns only natural rights which can be derived from ordinary common sense, their obvious exponents and interpreters among the people will not be officials appointed by the state, but free teachers of right, i.e. the philosophers. The latter, on account of the very freedom which they allow themselves, are a stumbling-block to the State, whose only wish is to rule; they are accordingly given the appellation of "enlighteners", and decried as a menace to the State. And yet they do not address themselves in familiar tones to the *people* (who themselves take little or no notice of them and their writings), but in *respectful* tones to the State, which is thereby implored to take the rightful needs of the people to heart.' (*Kant's Political Writings*, trans. H.B. Nisbet (Cambridge: Cambridge University Press, 1970), p. 186.) For a fuller discussion of the issue, see my *Legislation and Interpreters* (Cambridge: Polity Press, 1987).

centuries in support of the right of the intellect to, simultaneously, personal immortality and leadership of the mortals, kept on wrapping Plato's original bid in ever new and updated vocabulary, but added virtually nothing to its substance. It is the intellectuals who have been writing history, thus shaping it into tradition and 'our heritage'. Plato's bequest is the most important collective tradition and heritage of the writers. No wonder we have learned to consider the Athenian philosophical revolution as the true beginning of 'our civilization', as our – European, Western – common (and *foundational*) legacy. Men of intellect (and only such men are heard in public, *are* the public) cling fast to it much as the Roman Church held tight to the Edict of Constantine, and for much the same reasons.

Plato's *Republic* has been proved to be one of the most influential and culturally formative books ever written. The author's achievement is truly astonishing. Almost single-handedly, a frame was created for all future discourse; the one 'meta-narrative' that survived all vicissitudes of history and is unlikely ever to lose its attraction and binding power, as it is that meta-narrative which establishes the *raison d'être* of all narrative and all narrators. The bond between immortality, power and knowledge as, simultaneously, the legitimation and the constantly renewed accomplishment of discourse, is that *raison d'être*. And the bond was tied by Plato. A bid was made for the philosophers' right to rule; the bid was justified by reference to the philosophers' sole access to the eternal; and the philosophers' own hope for immortality was firmly grounded in the boldly and uncompromisingly asserted monopoly of that access. The outcome was a divide, simultaneously ontological and social. Social – a divide between the 'multitude' with their 'common beliefs', and 'the few' with their 'knowledge of the eternal'. And ontological – between the transient and the durable, things and ideas, crafts and arts. With the sides located on opposite poles ('the end of sight' versus 'the end of thought'), both divides were likely to remain unbridgeable for most of those affected, with the right of passage allowed in one direction only.

This was to be, for centuries to come, the substance of intellectuals' bid for immortality. Yet centuries had to pass before social conditions emerged in which that bid faced its chance of definitive success.

Within the Hellenic tradition, royalty and philosophy emerged as the two main strategies of survival beyond death, the two principal bids for immortality, the two most frequently trodden ways of binding the future so that it is obliged to retain the present (all other strategies of posthumous existence, either practised by other mortals or recommended to them by the theorists of immortality, were just metaphorical variations, pale reflections of these two). This made kings and philosophers into allies and competitors at the same time. They could join forces to make the victory of each more probable. Or they could have been forced to question each other's rights in case they felt the coveted goods to be scarce.

In their bid for immortality, kings and philosophers were seldom threatened by others. Pascal observed that only such people tend to meditate about death (and thereby about immortality) who do not have to fight for their lives, sweat to gain their daily bread, struggle to bring up their children. 'Eternity', Paul Valéry commented, 'occupies those who have time to lose'. Eternity 'is a form of leisure'.[11] The would-be immortals were, as a rule, members of the leisure classes when still alive. Already that common trait set them apart from the rest of the society. The hope of immortality was preceded by, and founded in, earthly privilege. And it could not be preserved unless privilege was retained. If individual bids for durability were to stand any chance, they would succeed solely thanks to the separation of the temporary sojourn of the bidders' class in the material, bodily world from the transience of the mundane.

The loneliness of immortality

As must be trivially obvious, this entitlement has been theorized by those who are in the habit of theorizing what for the others is, as a rule, a matter of unreflexive practice: by the philosophic centre-forward of the immortals' side. Culture, with its elevation of taste and discretion (that is, the ability to distinguish between the lasting and the temporal, the truly durable and the merely transient) to the rank of the supreme mark of humanity, has been by far the most widely used and the most effective among such theories. According to the perceptive and poignant comment by Pierre Bourdieu,

> the denial of lower, coarse, vulgar, venal, servile – in a word, natural – enjoyment, which constitutes the sacred sphere of culture, implies an affirmation of the superiority of those who can be satisfied with the sublimated, refined, disinterested, gratuitous, distinguished pleasures forever closed to the profane.
>
> ... [since Kant, the basis of 'high aesthetics' was the opposition] between facile pleasure, pleasure reduced to the pleasure of senses, and pure pleasure, pleasure purified of pleasure, which is predisposed to become a

---

[11] Pierre Valery, *Mauvais pensées et autres* (Paris: Galimard, 1943), p. 104.

symbol of moral excellence and a measure of the capacity for sublimation which defines the truly human man. The culture which results from this magical division is sacred. Cultural consecration does indeed confer on the objects, persons and situations it touches, a sort of ontological promotion akin to transubstantiation.[12]

Renunciation of the sensual (redefinition of the sensual as vulgar – unworthy and loathsome) is the pretence of such transubstantiation: it is a declaration of intent to turn ephemeral life, tightly as it is bound to the transient world of sensuality, into personal immortality. 'Durable' is everything which is secure from the corrosive, decomposing impact of consumption, which is *not meant for consumption*, which has *no* use value, which cannot serve any conceivable purpose, cannot be devoured and annihilated in order to satisfy any greed. The 'durable' is something that is not diminished by being enjoyed; if it is 'consumed', that consumption, in sharp opposition to all 'ordinary' consumption, adds instead of detracting from its total volume. The desire that makes it valuable is precisely the desire to preserve it and keep it intact. And the activities that follow that desire are not a zero-sum game; the value of durable goods actually grows in their course. It is as if, through contagious magic, sociating with the sublime that has been in this fashion *eternalized* by non-use, 'rubs off' on those who practise it and allows them to share in the splendours of immortality.

Definitions do not do what they pretend to be doing; they do not establish an opposition as a symmetry between two entities equal in value – instead, they cut out subsets from total sets on the strength of their assumed uniqueness and a superior value that the rest of the set does not possess. In Roland Barthes' words, the opposition ('the knife of value') 'is *always and throughout* between the *exception and the rule*'.[13] If mortality

---

[12] Pierre Bourdieu, *Distinction: A Social Critique of the Judgment of Taste*, trans. Richard Nice (London: Routledge, 1979), pp. 7, 6.

[13] Roland Barthes, *The Pleasure of the Text*, trans. Richard Miller (New York: Hill & Wang, 1975), p. 41. Barthes illustrates the proposition by the way in which the opposition between 'new' and 'old' organizes the contemporary world: 'The New is not a fashion, it is a value, the basis of all criticism: our evaluation of the world no longer depends, at least not directly, as in Nietzsche, on the opposition between *noble* and *base*, but on that between Old and New . . . There is only one way left to escape the alienation of present-day society: to *retreat ahead of it.*' (p. 40) Definition is a way of escaping the ordinary, disliked or rejected. Let us observe that it may serve this purpose precisely because it is a *self*-definition, because it sets the definer apart from the multitude and the ordinary – as the exception, the unique, the *different*.

and transience are the *norm* among humans, durability may be attained only as an *exception*. Its practical achievement is an heroic feat. It will not be assured simply by individuation, though its hope cannot be seriously entertained without it. Most conspicuously, personal immortality is not the lot of any individual. Princes and sages alike cannot work on their future immortality otherwise than by making their individual existences protrude out of the grey, anonymous mass of the present, and then digging, widening and deepening the moats separating them from 'ordinary mortals', by juxtaposing their own individuation with the collectivization of the others into a faceless mass. As Edgar Morin pointed out,

> the sublime individuality of a King is founded on the denial of individuality of others. Universality of royal consciousness exists solely through the negation of its presence in the consciousness of others. Culture of the Master does not grow but on the non-culture of the slave. History of individuality has been perpetrated, in fact, through the brutal de-individualization of the Other . . .
>
> At its limit, the absolute affirmation of one's individuality calls for the absolute destruction of others.[14]

This is, one may say, the one permanent and immutable *social* aspect of the immortality-bound self-estrangement. This outward aspect has its mirror reflection in the inner struggle of the self against everything that – too blatantly for comfort – betrays its own mortality through exposing its association with the parts of the social which has been already cast as transient: ordinary, base, loathsome, lowly, faceless and common. As Simmel observed, the self of 'the profound natures' tends to strive to disengage itself from all earthly contents, from everything 'ephemeral and accidental in the concrete contents of life'.[15]

The bid for immortality means the declaration of war on everything firmly anchored in the 'mere present', in the material being of the world. This is not, however, an easy task to achieve. However radical, distance from the mundane cannot be made absolute. Even the loftiest spirituality cannot fully escape engagement with the this-worldly – if only through

---

[14] Edgar Morin, *L'Homme et la mort* (Paris: Seuil, 1979), pp. 50, 65. The contrast between the few marked for immortality and the many doomed to transience has to be rehearsed (most probably, it is that rehearsal which constitutes its sole reality) through daily display of the gap separating the individuals from the faceless mass. 'The Masters', Morin points out, 'are always surrounded by under-individualities: slaves, buffoons, toadies, moneylenders, courtesans . . . the grotesque living mortals whose satellite presence bears witness to the Sun.' (p. 65)

[15] Georg Simmel, *Mélanges de philosophie relativiste*, p. 172.

leaving real – tangible, visible – imprints on the world with every success in its struggle for transcendence.

As we saw before, the candidates for immortality must present as their credentials the lasting traces of their labours: deeds weighty enough to sediment in the shared tradition, objects alluring enough to be classified as art and thereby durable, thoughts original enough to found an orthodoxy ready to adopt them. 'But although these forms arise out of the life process', Simmel would say, 'they acquire fixed identities, a logic and lawfulness of their own; this new rigidity inevitably places them at a distance from the spiritual dynamic which created them and which makes them independent.'[16] These 'forms' would not be capable of supporting the claim to immortality, were they not to acquire that demonstrable rigidity.

The moment, however, when they have been fixed, they become also, by definition, *objective*. Objectified (reified), they face the immortality-punter as another part of that transient, fixed and rigid reality that has to be transcended so that immortality can be accorded to the one who has accomplished the feat. The bid for immortality, therefore, seems to be incurably afflicted by schizoidal tendency. Otto Rank wrote convincingly of the 'neurotic nature' of all creative power, of the 'impulse to eternalization' being constantly checked by too close a contact with things mortal without which it cannot fulfil itself; of the 'double attitude' of the artist 'to the prevailing art-ideology, which, on the one hand, he uses for the justification of his individual creativity, but, on the other, opposes with all the vigour of his personality'. If 'the individual will to art' must be understood 'as a personal urge to immortality' in view of the fact that creative individuals are 'always animated by the same immortalization tendency',[17] then we should expect, as a norm, the artists' hopelessly conflict-ridden conduct, veering between engagement and escape, between the search for leadership over life processes and the shelter of an ivory tower.

---

[16] Georg Simmel, *The Conflict in Modern Culture and Other Essays*, trans. K. Peter Etzkorn (New York: Teachers College Press, 1968), p. 11. And yet: 'the creative act represents the struggle of life for self-identity. Whenever life expresses itself, it desires to express only itself; thus it breaks through any form which would be superimposed on it by some other reality.' (pp. 16–7) As it usually happens in the case of alienation, the leftovers of the successful drive to individual immortality turn into the most serious obstacle to all further successes.

[17] Otto Rank, *Art and Artist: Creative Urge and Personality Development*, trans. Charles Francis Atkinson (New York: Agathon Press, 1968), pp. 372, 386, 365–6, xxvi (the last quotation comes from Ludwig Lewinsohn's Preface).

This is an additional, perhaps the primary, cause of the notoriously stormy, well-nigh schizophrenic, record of the engagements and disengagements of thinkers and writers with political practice and social reality. The aspiring beneficiaries of the eternality of reason cannot very well secure the social confirmation (the only foundation, as it were) of that eternality without the collaboration of the powers expert in protecting privileges with the might and splendour of law and order; without bidding for such powers for themselves or for the benevolence of such powers held by others. Yet the order they must secure in one of these ways is a thoroughly earthly affair. The guardians of order cannot preserve anything without first 'objectifying' it and thus detracting from its value as the prime vehicle of individual self-assertion and transcendence.

Adorno more than anyone else brought this dilemma into sharp relief (though in an already processed form, somewhat removed from the paradox that underlies it, and certainly not free from ideological self-deception): 'culture suffers damage when it is planned and administered; when it is left to itself, however, everything cultural threatens not only to lose its possibility of effect, but its very existence as well.' This latter dependence is tragic, since 'culture would like to be higher and more pure, something untouchable ... manifestation of pure humanity without regard for its functional relationship within society'; 'the simple fact must be recognized that that which is specifically cultural is that which is removed from the naked dependency of life'. Culture is 'that which goes beyond the system of self-preservation of the species' – that is, beyond all these things the rulers concern themselves; the only things they are fit to be concerned with. Rulers are for that reason exquisitely practical, and hence natural enemies of art, with its 'impractical nature' imprinted in 'its mere existence'.[18] Labourers of culture have no other choice but to entrust the protection of the 'sacrosanct irrationality of culture' to the powers bent of exterminating all irrationality; to cede to the powers dedicated to the self-preservation of the species the task of guarding the this-worldly foundations of the other-worldly, the transient guarantees of the durable – of that which 'goes beyond self-preservation'. Labourers of culture cannot but collaborate with forces that are gnawing at the selfsame immortality they are asked to preserve.

This is not, however, the whole of the dilemma; neither is it the most tragic of its aspects, as seen by Adorno and Horkheimer, his fellow-

---

[18] Theodor W. Adorno, 'Culture and Administration', trans. Wes Blomster, *Telos*, vol. 37 (1978), pp. 93–111.

writer.[19] 'The history of old religions and schools like that of the modern
parties and revolutions teaches us that the price for survival is practical
involvement, the transformation of ideas into domination.' Is this price,
however, worth paying? Whether one follows the development of
struggling-for-survival ideas from Isa-Upanishad to Veda, or from uncouth
and universally ridiculed Cynics to dignified and universally respected
Stoics, or from the arrogantly lonely St John the Baptist to St Paul, the
hugely successful manager with a mass following – one always finds the
same process: the survival success 'shows traces of the betrayal of youthful
radicalism and revolutionary opposition to the dominant reality'. Having
acquired an organized backing, capable of making an effective bid for
domination, ideas cannot but have lost on the way much of their pristine
powers. They had to compromise. They must shed everything that would
make them unpalatable, indigestible, off-putting to their mundane,
common-sense followers – never ready, as Plato's allegorical cave-
dwellers, to look the sun in the face. One may say that what all this
amounts to is that ideas must resign 'the immortal' in them in order to
gain the earthly, temporal survival which they struggle for in the name of
immortality . . . To be immortal in this latter sense – to survive the earthly
struggles – ideas may have to surrender, one by one, every bit of
radicalism, all those elements of transcendence, which made immortality
worthwhile and desirable in the first place.

A vicious circle, indeed. One, as Adorno and Horkheimer sadly admit,
from which there is no easy exit; perhaps no exit at all. No one can escape
it while seriously hoping for transcendence. Even 'the uncompromising
people' could not be all that uncompromising. In as far as they are
'recorded in history', they surely 'did not lack all forms of organized

---

[19] Cf. Theodor W. Adorno and Max Horkheimer, *Dialectic of Enlightenment*,
trans. John Cumming (London: Verso, 1979), pp. 212–15. Adorno would repeat
these ideas, in a still sharpened form, commenting on his failed attempt to re-
enter political practice after return from his American exile. He would say then:
'No transparent relation prevails between the interests of the ego and the collective
to which it assigns itself. The ego must abrogate itself, if it is to share in the
predestination of the collective . . . The feeling of a new security is purchased with
the sacrifice of autonomous thinking. The consolation that thought within the
context of collective action is an improvement proves deceptive: thinking,
employed only as the instrument of action, is blunted in the same manner as all
instrumental reason . . . In contrast, the uncompromisingly critical thinker, who
neither superscribes his conscience nor permits himself to be terrorized into
action, is in truth the one who does not give up . . . Open thinking points beyond
itself.' ('Resignation', trans. Wes Blomster, *Telos*, vol. 35 (1978).

society, otherwise not even their names would have been handed down to us'. True, 'they set greater store by the idea and the individual than by administration and the collective', and thus their theoretical systems were 'not very rigid and centralized' (rigid theories are but corollaries of centralized organizations). They could not, or did not want to 'build strong hierarchies'. But they did not push their rejection of the mundane and transient to the radical extreme; if they did, we would not know of it anyway; their ideas would die with them.

Transcendence is slippery. The seeds of its defeat are firmly planted in its very drive to self-assertion. Its strategy – the only conceivable strategy – is ridden with contradictions. And so is the life of its carriers, the thinkers who transcend the 'it is' and mentally re-forge the succession of mortal lives into immortality of human history. Dangers lie in wait at every corner. Even a 'chance conversation' may be 'already a betrayal'. 'No thought is immune against communication, and to utter it in the wrong place and in wrong agreement is enough to undermine its truth'. Both practical attitudes towards the mundane – the only conceivable ones – are wrong: 'condescension, and thinking oneself no better, are the same.' Hence the tragic paradox: 'For the intellectual, inviolable isolation is now the only way of showing some measure of solidarity.' To attain and preserve such isolation, one should try 'a search for fresh concepts not yet encompassed by the general pattern' as 'the last hope for thought' – and for true autonomy: 'He who offers for sale something unique that no-one wants to buy, represents, even against his will, freedom from exchange.' Thus,

> nothing less is asked of the thinker today than that he should be at every moment both within things and outside them – Münchhausen pulling himself out of the bog by his pig-tail becomes the pattern ... And then the salaried philosophers come along and reproach us with having no definite point of view.[20]

---

[20] Theodor Adorno, *Minima moralia: Reflections from Damaged Life*, trans. E.F.N. Jephcott (London: Verso, 1978), pp. 25–6, 68, 74. These thoughts come, as the subtitle of the book explains, from the experience of a *damaged* life; a life during which mortality of all efforts have been profusely demonstrated, leaving little to imagination; in which the received wisdom of the ostensibly foolproof recipes for transcendence has been again and again discredited, and the practices they recommended have been frustrated. A life, in other words, that forced its bearer to reflect on motions which others 'like him' tend to go through, seldom asking why do they trust them to be effective. This was not a life of an ordinary intellectual, but, as Adorno self-consciously repeats, of an intellectual *in emigration*. Such intellectuals are 'mutilated'. They live 'in an environment that must remain incomprehensible' to them. They experience isolation, which 'is made

If Plato's *Republic* may be seen as the prototype of the constitutive myth of the intellectuals as the collective spokesman of the transcendent and the eternal, Adorno's tormented self-scrutiny may well serve as the archetype of the dilemmas the intellectuals face whenever trying to follow the bid with practical action.

Immortality as shelter

The dilemma is simple, though no less haunting and harrowing for that. Cast in a society which, at the time free of its throat-cutting pursuit of self-preservation, is preoccupied with the daily chase of mundane, eminently mortal pleasures and thus has little time left for the transcendent and the eternal – intellectuals, these latter-day Calvinists, yet more than their erstwhile prototypes crucified by uncertainty, have no way of testing by their earthly success whether they 'have been chosen'. There is a yawning gap between the terrestrial and the heavenly. The first is unlikely to be guided by, or to be a reflection, of the second; one cannot decipher the contours of the second in the fleeing images of the first. On the other hand, the heavenly has now no master one could trust to overrule the earthly verdicts. The eternal, like the transient, are both admittedly man-made and man-administered. Disregarding the sentences of the earthly courts of fame in the name of the timeless tribunal of immortality is a gamble which demands quite a reckless courage – yet still brings no peace of mind. Given that, as Adorno explained, earthly courts cannot be easily forced to abide by the rules set by the tribunal of eternity, the sole strategy left is to set such terms of reference for the second as would be deliberately and blatantly unacceptable for the first and thus, perversely, hoped

---

worse by the formation of closed and politically controlled groups' – an instinctive defensive reaction of individuals cast in a hostile environment which rejects them and blames them for the rejection. The victims learn soon that 'one should beware of seeking out the mighty, and "expecting something" of them', but also of the 'mirror-images of the mighty, lackeys, flatterers and cadgers' who deceive with the hopes they weave of an anchorage that would not hold any anchor and a destination that leads nowhere. Even the 'past life of emigrés is, as we know, annulled . . . even the past is no longer safe from the present, whose remembrance of it consigns it a second time to oblivion.' Such painful, yet sobering experiences 'can flourish' only in the 'extraterritorial circumstances of emigration'. What they reveal, or suggest, is that 'the concept of austerity, though hardly ship-shape or watertight, still seems, in emigration, the most acceptable lifeboat. Only a few, admittedly, have a seaworthy example at their disposal. To most boarders, it threatens starvation or madness.' (pp. 33–4, 46–7)

to remain well beyond its strangling embrace. Perhaps the eternal thought will keep its kingdom after all, providing it reconciles itself to the fact that this kingdom is not of this world?

This was the strategy followed, with abandon but in the end without success, by the artistic avant-garde – and, more generally, by the numerous currents of the *l'art pour l'art* movement. Half-programmatically, half-subconsciously, the movement represented the dilemma at its most incongruous extreme. On the one hand, it wished to force the presence of the culture creator upon public attention and make that presence tangible, audible and heavy – and recognized as such. On the other hand, that presence could not be allowed to hang on public recognition and be left to the vagaries of public approval. To prevent frustration, one would need to disavow and delegitimize public taste as a source of authority; one would need to make an artistic offer the public cannot but refuse (only a totally unpalatable and utterly unacceptable offer could, conceivably, create *facts* which could then be brandished as a proof of *quod erat demonstrandum*); to be most evidently *in*, but most emphatically *not of*, this world, to declare that defeat is the ultimate sign of victory; to derive the ultimate confirmation of 'being chosen' for immortality from the rejection by the mortal world; to use the exile as a shelter, to rename the social margin an *avant-garde*, the foothold of the future and of eternity.

This was not, to be sure, a programme to opt out from the engagement with the world. The avant-garde strategy needed the world and needed it badly – as that which taunts and is taunted, as the constant, reliable source of strength-giving self-immolation. One needed the bourgeois to have someone to shock. 'Ça t'épate, hein?' was, after all, the only point of contact left between eternal values and their earthly manifestations. The values were eternal, indeed: was not the horror of the bourgeois a most convincing evidence of that? The avant-garde artists were no hermits; they needed an audience to startle, deride and humiliate. Some would rationalize the need: humiliation of the public was not an end in itself, but a means to salvage the hapless victims from their abject boorishness, if the rescue was still possible. Humiliation for the victim's own good: to see the light one must first admit that one lives in darkness.

If this was the theory, the practice seemed to veer from the declared aim. The avant-garde feared nothing more than the prospect that the bourgeois (a synonym for the *vulgar* and the philistine) would stop feeling shocked and terrified; that they might even find a sort of vicarious pleasure in the offerings meant to make them suffer; that they might *agree* with the artist on the value of his creation. Such an agreement, if it happened, could not but brand the value hoped to be eternal with a demeaning mark of mundanity. The avant-garde tried hard to postpone indefinitely the moment of conversion; it wanted to be accepted on its own terms, but every instance of acceptance testified – by definition – that the terms were *not* its own. They could not be, could they? If they were, there would be no acceptance . . .

The practice of the avant-garde reversed all the ground rules of military art. Any territory, the moment is had been conquered, was vacated by the conquering troops. Each victory was a signal for retreat. The trouble was, however, that for one reason or another the bourgeois proved to be less 'shockable' than the avant-gardist propaganda painted them to be. Worse still, the shocking power of the most audacious outrage tended to wear off rather soon. The ultimate wonder-weapon of the bourgeois – the market, with its uncanny capacity to absorb, assimilate and digest, however unsavoury and inedible the substance, and to transform any potential liability into an actual asset – proved to be a force much in excess of the nuisance powers of the avant-gardist *provocateurs*. New assaults had to be devised, ever more refined and with an ever accelerating speed. The offerings must have been ever more function*less*, meaning*less*, purpose-*less*, use*less* (as the functionality, purpose and usefulness was admittedly the focus of ordinary mortals' interests). The market had to be challenged to accept, as timeless values associated with works of art, objects and acts never before considered to have anything in common with artistic crea-tion; but the market did accept them with surprisingly little prodding, so that new acts had to be ever more whimsical and new objects ever more outlandish and incongruous. However fast the avant-garde ran, the market scouts ran faster. They had the last and clinching argument: they have beaten the challengers in their own game, having re-forged the very attack against the power of the market into a best-selling market commodity. 'Bizarre', 'devious', 'controversial', 'shocking', 'outrageous' – have all become the favourite terms of advertising scripts and most effective selling points. It soon transpired that the avant-garde stood no chance. As Peter Bürger put it, a few years after Marcel Duchamp's iconoclastic (and in its intention ultimate) gesture of freedom,

> if an artist today signs a stove pipe and exhibits it, that artist certainly does not denounce the art market but adapts to it . . .
>
> Since now the protest of historical avant-garde against art as institution is accepted as *art*, the gesture of protest of the neo-avant-garde becomes inauthentic.[21]

---

[21] Peter Bürger, *Theory of the Avant-Garde*, trans. Michael Shaw (Manchester: Manchester University Press, 1984), pp. 52, 53. This observation is strikingly apt,

The sinister inclination of victories to turn into defeats had two profound consequences, which cast doubt on the very viability of the avant-gardist strategy. The first consequence, to quote Bürger again, was that though 'the historical avant-garde movements were unable to destroy art as an institution', 'they did destroy the possibility that a given school can present itself with the claim of universal validity'[22] – and this it did not just unintentionally, but contrary to both its virtual and genuine intentions. Sapping the credentials of ever new objects of art the moment they had been accepted as such, the avant-garde in the end undermined the very criteria of acceptance, the authority of common consent to pronounce on the value of anything. Provocation was to be a method of asserting above-the-earthness, universality, durability, the timelessness of cultural creation; it proved to be a weapon of destruction instead. Now no one could seriously claim any of the values which were the original stakes and the motives of struggle. *Collectively*, the avant-garde artists rendered null and void the feasibility of their *individual* ambitions. The durable has become transient – at least for the duration . . .

Another consequence was slow yet relentless self-annihilation of the art itself: an effect of the gripping fear of pollution, growing ever more obsessive as the gestures hoped to be purifying proved one by one to be the criminal acts of co-operation with the polluting powers. How far one can go in the desperate search for safe shelter before finding himself forced to surrender to the alluring security of non-existence? Only what has not been made cannot be stolen; only what does not exist cannot be defiled and corrupted. Thus the artists send to galleries erased drawings of their artist friends; or fill the gallery with a truckful of rubbish; or invite

---

though it is questionable whether the desire to 'reintegrate art into the praxis of life' (as Bürger suggests, p. 22), rather than the overwhelming, though often unconscious drive to use the denigration of that practice as a stepping stone, or a catapult, for own elevation, was responsible for the result it portrays.

In the postscript to *The Name of the Rose* (trans. William Weaver (New York: Harcourt Brace Jovanovitch, 1981), pp. 66–7), Umberto Eco thus writes of the self-destructive tendency of the avant-gardist project: the avant-garde 'destroys the figure, cancels it, arrives at the abstract, the informal, the white canvas, the slashed canvas, the charred canvas. In architecture and the visual arts, it will be the curtain wall, the building as shell, pure parallelepiped, minimal art; in literature, the destruction of the flow of discourse, the Burroughs-like collage, silence, the white page; in music, the passage from atonality to noise to absolute silence (in this sense, the early Cage is modern). But the moment comes when the avant-garde (the modern) can go no further . . .' The project to break links with the transient has destroyed the durable.

[22] Bürger, *Theory of the Avant-Garde*, p. 87.

the critics to the private view of an empty gallery; or bore a hole in the ground and cover it with a lid so that no one can see it; or wrap a bridge in plastic sheets ('Now it is wrapped; now it is not!'). Even these, as it turned out, proved to be but half-measures. There has been thus far pretty little which the market failed to turn into commercial profit. If Tertullianus once proclaimed 'Credo, quia absurdum est', the principle of the market, as the avant-garde has learned through own tribulations, seems to be: 'I am selling, because it does not make any sense.' Disinterestedness can be disinterested no more. The last limit for a painter is blank canvas (better still, the absence of one); for a writer, a blank page of the book; for a composer, silence. The struggle for eternal existence ends up as a rehearsal of non-being. Immortality, if ever it is to be achieved, shows all the abhorring features which made the transience and temporality repulsive and inspired the flight into the eternal. The dream of transcendence appears to be self-defeating. That is, if it is pursued through this strategy.

Philosophy, that original stock-exchange of immortality, seemed to have followed, in its own way, the avant-garde strategy – and with a similar result. With the passage of time, it distanced itself far enough from the bustle of mundane interests to be left with itself as its own subject-matter. It located the absolute in what it was left with: what it can do is to decompose what it has composed, and to recompose it again so that the process of decomposition, the only recognizable form of durability, may go on. The deconstructionist programme is the philosophical equivalent of the neo-avant-garde's sullen assertion that the flatness of canvas is the only proper subject-matter of painting. Examples are plentiful, growing steadily in number, and can be found everywhere. Perhaps the following quotation from Roland Barthes may serve as a sample as good as any:

> *Text* means *Tissue*; but whereas hitherto we have always taken this tissue as a product, a ready-made veil, behind which lies, more or less hidden, meaning (truth), we are now emphasizing, in the tissue, the generative idea that the text is made, is worked out in a perpetual interweaving; lost in this tissue – this texture – the subject unmakes himself, like a spider dissolving in the constructive secretions of its web. Were we fond of neologisms, we might define the theory of the text as an *hyphology* (*hyphos* is the tissue and the spider's web).[23]

---

[23] *The Pleasure of the Text*, p. 64. Elias Canetti's diaries have been filled over the years with scorn for philosophy, which considers it its mission to improve the world by purifying it from everything worldly. Here is the characteristic example: 'The thing that repels me most about philosophers is the *emptying* process of their thinking. The more often and more skilfully they use their basic words, the less

The desire to transcend the mortality of the subject led, when pushed to its philosophical limit, to the destruction ('dissolution') of the subject itself. Immortality has not been assured. But it does not count for much now, as life itself has been proved to be but an illusion or pretence. After centuries of modern torments, after bankruptcy of modern hopes, we are invited to relax in the postmodern nirvana.

The precarious survival of immortality

In 1925 Paul Valéry proclaimed, with a mixture of sham humility and unmistakable pride:

> Anyone who cannot be replaced by another – for the reason that he is unlike any *other* – is one who fulfils no undeniable need. So we find in the intellectual population these two remarkable categories: *intellectuals who serve some purpose* and *intellectuals who serve none*.[24]

This was said with the tongue firmly pressed against the cheek. Valéry seemed to entertain little doubt that the 'no purpose' was the nobliest purpose of all, so that its very description as 'no purpose' testified solely to the baseness of the describers. The second category of 'intellectual population' embraced free and self-determining humans living by and for

---

remains of the world around them. They are like barbarians in a high, spacious mansion of wonderful works. They stand there in their shirt sleeves and throw everything out of the window, methodically and steadfastly, chairs, pictures, plates, animals, children, until there's nothing left but whole empty rooms. Sometimes the doors and windows come flying fast. The naked house remains. They imagine that these devastations make it *better* . . . These Oxford philosophers scrape and scrape until nothing is left. I have learned from them: I now know it's better not to start scraping at all.' (*The Human Province*, trans. Joachim Neugroschel (London: André Deutsch, 1985), pp. 126, 177.)

[24]Paul Valéry, 'Remarks on intelligentsia', in *History and Politics*, trans. Denise Folliot and Jackson Matthews (New York: Pantheon Books, 1962), p. 84. The perception of 'uselessness' is, of course, the derivative of what current form of life defines as useful, that is relevant to itself. And the current form of life has little use for things durable, let alone immortal. 'Farewell to all labours endlessly slow: three hundred years for a cathedral . . . Farewell to painting as the final product of a long accumulation of transparent labours . . . Farewell to the perfecting of language . . . We are now *committed to the moment*, to the effects of shock and contrast, and almost compelled to seize upon whatever flashes into the mind from any chance stimulus, suggesting precisely that. We look for and appreciate the *sketch*, the *study*, the *rough draft*. The very notion of *completion* has almost vanished.' (pp. 76–7)

thought, truly unlike anyone else, irreplaceable individuals *sensu stricto* –
as close as one can be to the ideal of Adorno's 'inviolable isolation'. What
they did seemed like 'no purpose' to anyone drowned in the ephemera
of quotidianity, because what they did served no evident need of self-
preservation. They transcended the parochiality of transient and diffuse
daily concerns and reached, above their head, for the totality that was
eternal and centred. They did not 'serve' anything – since, on the contrary,
everything was to be convinced or forced to serve that eternal totality
which they represented.

This was, after all, the time when reaching the absolute seemed but a
matter of time and determination; the transcendence was believed to
depend on the thinker's readiness for ascesis and self-abandonment. In
Ignazio Silone's words, 'one that does not live according to circumstances,
according to his *milieu*, according to his commodities, according to matter
. . . one that lives for justice and truth, in no regard of consequences – is
not an atheist, as he inhabits the eternal and the eternal inhabits him.'[25]
And this was also the time when Jules Benda's *La Trahison des clercs* could
state, as a fact only too obvious, that the intellectuals, *les clercs*, are people
engaged in 'an activity which in its essence does not pursue practical
purposes', people who instead 'derive their joy from the exercise of art,
of science, of metaphysical speculation, in short from the possession of
non-temporal goods, so that they say in a way "my kingdom is not of this
world'".[26]

In 1943 Paul Valéry noted, with sullen humility and little trace of pride:
'The universe was a totality, and had a centre. There is no more a totality
or a centre. But one goes on speaking of the universe.'[27] One hears a
stubborn defiance in the voice that once sounded with quiet and dignified
confidence. Defiance is heard, though, and so there is hope as well. The
task of intellectuals has become so much more complex and risky, but the
job has not been finished yet and must not be allowed to stop. The world,
after all, was never too hospitable a place for the 'useless' seekers of
transcendence.

Half a century later Bernard-Henri Lévy, the one Frenchman still sporting the intellectual cloak with gusto (if only to proclaim, in the attire
proper for the occasion, the end of the intellectual era), calls the intellectual 'an extinct species'; he announces his death 'as a kind of prophet of

[25] Ignazio Silone, *Le Pain et le vin* (Paris: Grasset, 1939), p. 26.
[26] Quoted after R.M. Alberes, *L'Aventure intellectuelle du XXe siècle, 1900–1950* (Paris: La Nouvelle Édition, 1950), p. 287.
[27] Valéry, *Mauvaises pensées et autres*, p. 16.

the universal', a death one could only expect at a time 'when no one believes any more in the meaning of history'.[28] Lévy is not the only writer of obituaries. In fact, epitaph-writing has become of late a highly popular genre among the intellectuals-turned-journalists. Thus, Luc Ferry: 'The function of the intellectual at present is to understand the society in which he lives, not to construct the grand machine for the production of meaning.' And Edgar Morin: 'First of all, we must descend from the throne of the Supreme Judge of the Universe.'[29] Why must we? Because there is no demand for the insights and auguries that may be pronounced from such a throne. Indeed, that society which we have 'the function to understand' has no use or time for history or universe.

To start with, this society has brought to a radical extreme the tendency of our civilization, as Valéry suggested,

> [to take on] the structure and the properties of a machine ... Its precision, which is its essence, cannot endure vagueness or soul caprice; irregular situations are incompatible with good running order. *It cannot put up with anyone whose duties and circumstances are not precisely specified* ... The machine neither will nor can recognize any but professionals.[30]

or, as Adorno would prefer to put it, to 'the departmentalization of mind', which is 'a means of abolishing mind where it is not exercised *ex officio*, under contract'. What has been so described is not just the lot of the long and inconclusive philosophical exploration of the absolute: 'the entire private domain is being engulfed by a mysterious activity that bears all the features of commercial life without there being actually any business to transact' – so that 'not to be "after" something is almost suspicious'. The universal triumph of instrumentality and business principles, leaving no enclave free from its obtrusive interference, empties of content the acts of

---

[28] Quoted after Pierre Billard, 'Inventaire avant liquidation', in *Le Point*, 18 March 1991, p. 38; and Philippe Petit, 'Expliquez-vous, Bernard-Henri Lévy!', in *L'Evenement du jeudi*, 28 February 1991, p. 74.

[29] Edgar Morin, 'Intellectuels: l'adieu aux rêves', in *L'Express*, 8 March 1991, p. 50. To be sure, not all participants of the discussion from which the above statements are taken were fully prepared to accept the practical conclusions from the diagnosis which suggested defeat. Most notably, Edgar Morin himself, the veteran of many intellectual campaigns: 'Our societies are ever more dominated by experts and econocrats. But a specialist can offer but a compartmentalized competence. While it is necessary to integrate the analyses in a total view of the global situation and in the planetary context, and go beyond the immediate when thinking of the current crisis.' But then, self-consciously and apologetically, Morin admits: 'Mission impossible? Well, it is necessary.'

[30] Valéry, *History and Politics*, p. 81.

solitary rebellion; what may be intended as a heroic act of resistance looks more like a clownish farce. In life, there are no more concerns left that could serve as an interface with the intellectual search for the transcendent and the absolute. In consequence, the intellectual preoccupation with the eternal seems both idle and ridiculous; most certainly, illegitimate. Thus the task to maintain the 'inviolable isolation' grows more difficult by the hour, and those who persist against the odds found themselves ridden with doubts:

> So great is the power of the advancing organization of thought, that those who want to keep outside it are driven to resentful vanity, babbling self-advertisement and finally, in their defeat, to imposture ... Between delight in emptiness and the lie of fullness, the prevailing intellectual situation allows no third way.[31]

In an interview with Alessandro Fontana and Paquale Pasquino first published in 1977[32] Michel Foucault composed what amounts to an obituary to the 'universal' intellectual, so called to set him apart from the 'specific' intellectual, one who 'got used to working not in the modality of the "universal", the "exemplary", the "just-and-true-for-all", but within specific sectors', 'at the precise points' where his own conditions of life or work situate him. The now defunct 'universal intellectual', Foucault suggest, was first and foremost a *writer*, whatever his professional assignment; but 'the activity of the writer' is 'no longer at the focus of things'. The stage is taken over by the 'specific intellectuals', who are first and foremost *professionals* – magistrates or psychiatrists, doctors or social workers, laboratory technicians or sociologists – whether or not they write and whatever they may write. The universal intellectual was also an offspring 'of the jurist, or at any rate of the man who invoked the universality of a just law'. The specific intellectual, on the contrary, is 'quite another figure' – an *expert*. If he intervenes in public, he does it 'in the name of a "local" scientific truth'. *Universal* intellectuals, proclaims Foucault, are for all intents and purposes extinct; the day belongs to the *specific* intellectuals.

This being or not being the case, the question is, how does the specific intellectual score on immortality? Can the intellectual work still be con-

---

[31] Adorno, *Minima moralia*, pp. 21–24, 67.

[32] 'Intervista a Michel Foucault', in Michel Foucault, *Microfisica del Potere* (Turin, 1977). Here quoted from English translation by Colin Gordon, published under the title 'Truth and Power' in Michel Foucault, *Power/Knowledge: Selected Interviews and Other Writings, 1972–1977* (Brighton: Harvester Press, 1980), pp. 126ff.

sidered as, among other things, also a personal bid for transcendence and immortality? Most of the work of 'specific intellectuals' has been thoroughly bureaucratized. And whatever else bureaucracies do, they are notorious for their flair for depersonalization and effacement.[33] Individuality is the enemy number one of all organization. No wonder, as it breaks down the confident routine on which the continuous existence of the organization rests. The element of unpredictability it inevitably injects into programmed and co-ordinated activity is not easy to square with the unity of command on which that routine rests in turn. An organization therefore likes to think of itself, and act, as an assembly of roles, not persons. It is the roles that last – persons are interchangeable and disposable: a contradiction in terms, as far as personality goes. An organization follows the pattern of the species: it perpetuates itself through a succession of temporal agents, it assures its own durability by making every one of its members transient. Mortality of its members is the condition of its own survival. Each organization therefore guards jealously its right to decide when and why the organizational life of its members can and should be terminated. 'Specific intellectuals' depend on organizations for their ability to do research, teach or publish. More often than not, their intellectual lives end together with their organizational lives. Their individual prominence, however grand and terrifying it may seem at the moment, has no roots in their own inalienable achievement, being just a pale reflection of their organizational standing. It will wash out, sometimes without trace, once the organizational role has been abandoned. The best that the 'intellectual functionaries' can count on is that their memory will be preserved in the filing cabinets (if they are lucky, also in oral lore) of the organization. This is, however, a kind of durability akin to the family albums and eminently perishable reminiscences of one's offspring. Like its family equivalent, it cannot score better on the scale of universality than its own locality permits.

---

[33] Of science, by common agreement the true paragon of creativity, Abraham Maslow had the following to say once it had been organized as bureaucracy: 'Science, then, can be a defense. It can be primarily a safety philosophy, a security system, a complicated way of avoiding anxiety and upsetting problems. In the extreme instance it can be a way of avoiding life, a kind of self-cloistering. It can become – in the hands of some people, at least – a social institution with primarily defensive, conserving functions, ordering and stabilizing rather than discovering and renewing ... The bureaucrats may actually become covert enemies of geniuses, as critics so often have been to poets, as ecclesiastics so often have been to mystics and seers upon whom their churches were founded' (*The Psychology of Science* (New York: Harper & Row, 1966), p. 33.)

One would therefore expect the 'specific intellectuals' to be tempted, time and again, to break out from their specifity. To do so, they may try to transform the handicap into an asset: to further their personal bid for immortality they can deploy the same depersonalizing role-determination which they experienced as such a confining and suffocating factor in their organizational lives. The stature conferred by the combined impact of the publicly acknowledged importance of the organization that employs them, and the inside role conferred by that organization, can be re-forged into an entitlement to a personal share of public attention: of the impersonal ore, coins of personal uniqueness and significance can be minted. As Michel de Certeau observed,

> in the Expert, competence is transmuted into social authority . . . The Expert pronounces on the basis of the *place* that his speciality has won for him . . [His authority] is no longer a function of knowledge, but rather a function of the socio-economic order.[34]

Once outside the stultifying yet secure shelter of the native organization, out in the windy, noisy and crowded expanses of the agora, the specific intellectuals (if they step beyond the strictly circumscribed expert role, acting as themselves, not as the spokesmen delegated by the organization) find themselves on their own. After what we heard of the collapse of the universal and the fast-fading interest in transcendence, we would not expect the agora to be a hospitable place for immortality bids of the kind developed in past intellectual history (that is, at a time when intellectuals were still 'universal'). More importantly, the agora is no more a town square bubbling with freely milling crowds. Like the rest of the world, it is a domain of organizations and specialists.

In *Extraterritorial*, George Steiner discussed the passing of classic, literature-based model of culture, that swam on three whales – of privacy, silence and time. The stuffed hides of all three whales now gather dust in the nostalgic 'visit your past' museums. The classic model of culture has nothing to rest on. No wonder that knowledge splintered, that broad erudition has been replaced with semi-literacy, that the ability to read extends to simple texts only, and that, in general, 'the literal compass of educated discourse has shrunk'. 'A society with few private libraries and a sharply diminishing readership . . . can be a society of numerous screens, arenas, and playhouses.' All these profound transformations, Steiner

---

[34] Michel de Certeau, *The Practice of Everyday Life*, trans. Steven F. Rendall (Berkeley: University of California Press, 1984,) pp. 7, 8.

observed, led to the

> transformation in the status, in the conceptual focus and attendant mythol-
> ogy, of personal identity and of death ... The trope of 'immortality' together
> with the vital echo of recreative reading constitutes a classic culture. We no
> longer invoke 'immortality' in that sense, or, if we do, it is with a tinge of
> archaicism and ironic solemnity. The notion, almost axiomatic in classic art
> and thought, of sacrificing the present existence or content to the marginal
> chance of future literary or intellectual renown seems to grate on modern
> nerves. To most younger people, it would seem hypocritical bathos and a
> subtle perpetuation of élitist idols.

Notoriety has replaced immortality as viewing replaced reading and
screens replaced books. 'The audio-visual means of the mass media are
calculated toward maximal impact and instant obsolescence.'[35]

One should not facilely assume that instant obsolence cancels the
allurements of maximal impact. 'Being in view' is the way of being an
individual; perhaps the only way of being one. On grand historical
canvases, as a rule, the leaders and commanders are standing or sitting in
the front, painted in sharp focus. They *have faces* – very individual and
recognizable faces, each one with its unique and inimitable lines of lips,
nose, eyes, its own very private grin, frown, wrinkles, warts and all. In
sharp contrast, the others (followers, admirers, onlookers, soldiers –
'people') are faceless: devoid of identifiable features, the vague shapes in
the background are indistinguishable and blatantly exchangeable. They
are not a collection of individuals; they are the *masses*. Their being masses
serves a function: it allows the individuality of those at the front to shine.
Facelessness of the many gives meaning to the faces of the few.

In our era of *mediocracy* (the term has been coined as a deliberate
double entendre, one would guess), which replaced the rule of universi-
ties and grand publishing houses, mass media, Debray suggests, have
made an offer the intellectuals found hard to refuse. Hard, because the
advent of mass media rendered traditional 'classic' vehicles of transcendence obsolete and pitiably inefficient; but hard also because the offer was
not devoid of considerable attractiveness: 'it is as a rule less harrowing for
a professional to seduce amateurs than his colleagues ... No more need
of a school, of a problematics, of conceptual pregnancy.' True, mass media
threaten, as Steiner has warned, an instant obsolence. But they also
guarantee instant notoriety (dubbed, self-flatteringly and above all assur-

---

[35] George Steiner, *Extraterritorial: Papers on Literature and the Language
Revolution* (Harmondsworth: Penguin Books, 1975), pp. 168, 168, 174.

ingly, fame) – a short-cut to prominence that in a surrogate way may assuage, for a time at least (for Warhol's 'fifteen minutes'), the anguish of mortality. 'Everybody', says Debray, 'secretly fears that he does not exist – since he indeed does not, as long as others do not recognize his entitlement to exist. One exists only in as far as others speak of him – praise him, quote, criticize, slander, deride, etc.' And it is the media who make the others speak. Instead of the musings of a couple of thousands of sophisticated 'serious journals' readers, the mass media offer the chance of being talked about by a two-million-strong army of televiewers. Media create fashions – fashionable topics, fashionable scripts – and they fit actors to the lines. What matters in the casting, is not 'truth-value', but 'spectacle-value'.[36] Not (just) what is being said, but by whom. After all, it is the audience ratings that have the final say. And the managers of the media are above all (they had better be!) experts in rating-boosting.

Ten years is a long time in the continuous *Jetztzeit* of postmodernity; it seems now that Debray, writing from the perspective of an early stage of the *mediocratic age*, sorely underestimated the devastating consequences of the change; not just its impact on the stock-exchange of intellectualist vanities, but on the substance of intellectual strategies. 'If public statements of the intellectuals seem today so often futile', writes Pierre Enckell, 'it is probably because they follow the rule of a-thought-a-minute.' 'A formula, ping! A retort, pong! These are matches, not debates. Time for reflection has been reduced to zero, it is the reflexes that one needs. The presence is what count, at the expense of the profundity of thought.' It could be hardly different, if 'lucky he who will be allowed a flash to shout "*J'accuse!*" ' – as 'all the argumentation of Emile Zola would have gone down the drain'.[37] Pierre Billard would concur: 'Today, the university is in ruin and education in a headlong flight. *La grande presse* left the place for mass media, who substituted the values of communication for those of knowledge and pedagogy.' Hence 'the second death of Jean-Paul Sartre': 'the intellectual is judged no more by the justice of his ideas, but by the repercussions of his interventions'.[38] And George Steiner, on his revisit to the society of screens, would concur as well. 'We are in a cosmic casino.

---

[36] Régis Debray, *Le Pouvoir intellectual en France* (Paris: Ramsay, 1979), pp. 97, 168, 98.

[37] Pierre Enckell, 'De la longue controverse à la polémique-minute', in *L'Évenement de jeudi*, 28 February 1991.

[38] Billard, 'Inventaire avant liquidation'. Ibid.

Nothing but rhetorical games, more or less amusing, more or less profound.'[39]

Immortality into notoriety

Like all aspects of life, bidding for immortality is now in the hands of *experts*. The new experts are, however, individuals just as the bidders are. They lack the massive and unchallengeable support of the powerful body of the Church, who could easily, and effectively, re-forge its monopoly of power into finality of their judgements. Like the bidders, experts compete for the social hold of their promotions. They have their victories and their defeats; their impact on social attention is precarious – temporary, revocable and until-further-notice. Their services to immortality are themselves mortal; the durability they promise is itself but transient, and as all things transient, used up quickly in the process of consumption.

Fashion is the name of *transient durability*. Fashion is powerful and overwhelming because it sports the trappings of durability – a well-nigh apodeictic 'naturality', universality, acknowledged authority to exclude – *while it lasts*. Yet unlike truly *durable* durability, it lacks supra-generational mechanisms of self-reproduction, and so it makes up for the absence of social foundations with the intensification of tribal-like allegiances. Fashion is always listless and in haste: it has no time to lose. Thus it cannot afford the reflection of a 'long view'; its efforts must be hectic and uninhibited, all-stops-pulled; its appeals must be deafening, shrill and hysteric. Its hold is, after all, solely the accomplishment of the public attention it succeeds in drawing upon itself. But once it becomes the focus of market competition, attention – fickle at the best of times – is buffeted by cross-waves of seductions and never allowed to have a close look on anything, let alone stay still. Once it is taken hold of, it must be held fast. It is this transient intensity of hold that deputizes, with equally transient success, for genuine durability which alone can afford serenity and delicacy of manners.

---

[39] Interview by Jean-François Duval in *Le Monde*, 11 January 1991. Steiner insists that the response offered by the 'virtuosos of the void' is not the only one possible in the 'cosmic casino': one can still speak of 'real presence', one that lasts longer than even the most amusing and profound game. 'I call the real presence that which exists behind *l'oeuvre*; there is, lodged in the word, something that no dictionary or grammar can fathom.' Thanks to this 'active mystery' we are nothing if not 'shadows of the substance'.

As the bid for immortality goes, fashion appears as *fame* (better still, as *notoriety*). In a market tightly filled with competing commercial agents, fame, as Adorno pointed out, is no longer fortuitous; less still unsought, emerging unexpected from 'objective' tests to which competing creations are subject. 'It has become wholly a function of paid propagandists and is measured in terms of the investment risked.' The contemporary descendant of immortality bidders 'no longer pins his hopes on posterity', but on 'the hired applauder'. This is the function of literary or show business agents, of art galleries and the professional advertisers they hire. Writers and artist need agents who

> assume personal responsibility for becoming famous, and thus in a sense for their after-life – for what ... can hope to be remembered if it is not already known? – and purchase from the lackeys of the trusts, as in former times from the Church, an expectation of immortality. But no blessing goes with it. Just as voluntary memory and utter oblivion always belonged together, organized fame and remembrance lead ineluctably to nothingness, the foretaste of which is perceptible in the hectic doings of all celebrities. The famous are not happy in their lot. They became brand-name commodities, alien and incomprehensible to themselves, and, as their own living images, they are as if dead. In their pretentious concern for their aureoles they squander the disinterested energy that is alone capable of permanence. The inhuman indifference and contempt instantaneously visited on the fallen idols of the culture industry reveals the truth about their fame, though without granting those disdainful of it any better hopes of posterity.[40]

As a matter of fact, the 'falling from grace' of today's cultural idols is as a rule much less dramatic than Adorno suggests. Fame producers have long ago mastered the art of transforming even the fall into the title for fame: indeed, falling may grip public attention even tighter than sudden rise, as the subject of fall, unlike the newly born celebrity, has already had his right to public awareness confirmed. The expedient of disgrace, as carefully stage-managed as the original promotion into fame had been, is quite commonly deployed as a shot in the arm of a fading or ageing star; or, rather, as a means to reinvigorate the wilting attention of the audience. The fall has, potentially, a tremendous spectacle-value, and whatever has such value is utterly unlikely to escape attention of fame-makers.

More often than not, the famous do not 'fall'; they just fade, peter out, evaporate and otherwise *gradually* disappear from view. It is precisely the fact that their disappearance is too slow to draw attention and be noticed, which makes their durability, yesterday still seemingly overwhelming,

---

[40] Adorno, *Minima moralia*, pp. 100–1.

transient from the start. Great celebrities are not transformed into *past* celebrities; neither do they become *lesser* celebrities. Using Michael Thompson's tripartite scheme, we may say that false durables are transferred into the realm of *rubbish*, that 'third' and culturally illegitimate category, which social pretence, having been trained to avert its eyes and studiously 'unnotice', treats as *non-existing*. It is this transfer, whose exact moment, given the socio-cultural casting of rubbish, also passes unnoticed, that finally confirms the erstwhile transience of alleged durables: unlike genuine durables, fame diminishes in the process of consumption.

One may conclude that notoriety, like all other market translations of lasting values, and all other expert-administered translations of lasting *issues* into pragmatically manageable *problems*, is not a contemporary rendition of immortality, or of concerns it begets. It signals, rather, the advanced *deconstruction of immortality*. The search for fame derives substance from the age-old dream of immortality; it is given form by the market which knows of the instant consumer potential as the only measure of value; it rests its fate with the publicity-and-marketing experts. As a version of the immortality bid, it is for these reasons as self-destructive as the other bids we have surveyed before, but in a more decisive, definitive (one wants to say 'ultimate') fashion. If you cannot join them, beat them; if hopes for true durability keep being dashed one by one, let us go for transience instead; but let us make it spectacular and enjoyable so that the loss will not be bewailed – for the duration . . .

3

The Selfish Species

No one has been thus far, nor is likely to be in the future, as scathingly contemptful and bitter in his depiction of incurable futility of life, and as wary of all the illusions to the contrary, than Arthur Schopenhauer. Existence, Schopenhauer tells us, is empty and hopelessly devoid of purpose; indeed, what can possibly be its purpose – an intrinsic or ready-made, pre-given purpose – if 'dying is certainly to be regarded as the real aim of life'?[1] Looked upon in instrumental terms, as 'a means to an end', life is validated only by death, as death is its only obvious, 'natural' and unavoidable point of arrival. Otherwise, life is empty of meaning.

> The emptiness finds its expression in the whole form of existence, in the infiniteness of Time and Space as opposed to the finiteness of the individual in both; in the flitting present as the only manner of real existence; in the dependence and relativity of all things; in constantly Becoming without Being; in continually wishing without being satisfied ... Time, and the *transitoriness* of all things, are merely the form under which the will to live ... has revealed to Time the futility of its efforts. Time is that by which at every moment all things become as nothing in our hands, and thereby lose all their true value ...
>
> What *has been* exists no more; and exists just as little as that which has *never* been. But everything that exists *has been* in the next moment.[2]

If these are all primary facts of life, the conclusion is easy to draw: 'Life has *no true and genuine value* in itself, but is kept *in motion* merely through the medium of needs and illusion.' This, one would say, would

---

[1] Arthur Schopenhauer, *The World as Will and Representation*, trans. E.F.J. Payne (New York: Dover, 1966), p. 637. In *Parerga and Paralipomena* (trans. E.F.J. Payne (Oxford: Clarendon Press, 1974), p. 275) we read: 'Our life might be regarded as a loan received from death; sleep would then be the daily interest on that loan.'

[2] Arthur Schopenhauer, 'The Emptiness of Existence', in *Essays of Schopenhauer*, trans. Rudolf Dircks (London: Walter Scott Publications, n.d.), pp. 54–5.

not be such a depressingly bad news by itself, if it were not for the fact that, given the preordained transitoriness of life, in men 'everything is dubious and uncertain, not merely the solution but even the problem'[3] – and so the conception of what the needs are, and the line separating the needs from illusions, are bound to stay despairingly tenuous and unconvincing. The only thing 'forever' about humans is that they are, and are bound to remain, *underdetermined*.

One may look at it from the other side, though. One may say that life is offered to men and women as an empty container, waiting to be filled with content by its carriers, so that life may be 'given a sense'. The task is enormous; it transcends the mental and volitional powers of any individual carrier. As individual life is all-too-obviously and irrevocably bound to end, and as everything which fills it today will become a *has-been* tomorrow – individual carriers crave for something non-individual, stronger than individual, more lasting than the individual; something that may escape the transience of the merely individual, and make of individual life its servant, thereby imbuing it with meaning. Only a master-idea, it seems, lends meaning to those who serve it. Only as servants may human individuals bask in the radiance of eternity.

What got us in that trouble in the first place, Schopenhauer repeats on every occasion, is nature itself: the species-centred selfishness manifested in the expedient of keeping the group alive through making its survival independent from the survival of any of its members in particular: in making every one of its members *disposable*. The only task nature sets for members of the human species which they must perform individually (or, rather, – in pairs – so that they do not stray from their species-imposed togetherness) is to propagate: to inseminate, to get pregnant and to give birth. Nature has neglected to give them, however, any but purely technical means to fulfil that task. But humans must first stay alive to become able to propagate – and being *human* beings, *thinking* beings, the *aware-of-mortality* beings, they must therefore *wish* to remain alive, they must *have a purpose* to make them wish. Yet that wishing and having a purpose the selfish species has neglected to guarantee.

Schopenhauer admits that nature supplied humans with a remedy against despair: their in-built drive toward happiness. But this remedy, he hastens to add, proves to be a delusion the moment it has been put into action. More often than not, action ends up in a disaster: 'There is only one inborn error, and that is the notion that we exist in order to be happy.'

---

[3] Schopenhauer, 'The Emptiness of Existence', p. 62; *Parerga and Paralipomena*, p. 201.

It is *inborn*, because nature made us so that we cannot stop but strive for happiness; and yet it is an *error*, because dreams of happiness are in each concrete case no more than a wish to get rid of the present suffering, and so happiness

> always lies in the future, or else in the past, and the present may be compared to a small dark cloud driven by the wind over the sunny plain; in front of and behind the cloud everything is bright only it itself always casts a shadow. Consequently, the present is always inadequate, but the future is uncertain, and the past irrecoverable.

Grass is *always* greener on the other side of fence; satisfaction is always there where we are not. The chase of happiness is inherently disappointing; it must generate anguish that – if not contained and held in check – threatens to boil over and turn into aggression. More disastrously yet, the futility of the chase may only speed up the discovery of the ultimate absurdity of life and thus put the very continuation of life in jeopardy. To prevent this, inventiveness of society must fill the void and do the job nature failed to provide for. And it does. All religious and philosophical systems, says Schopenhauer, are 'primarily an antidote to the certainty of death which reflecting reason produces from its own resources'.[4]

Thus the intentions of the selfish *species* (*nature*'s product) cannot be fulfilled without the mediation of selfish *societies* (*human* products). Propagation of the species is a fact of nature, not of culture. By itself, it has no meaning. It cannot inflame imagination (unless the latter is a sexual fantasy), it cannot mobilize emotions (except for sexual desire), it cannot spur into action (except for acts of seduction). To do all these indispensable things which nature cannot do by itself, and so to sustain the process of life without which nature's own ostensible intentions stand no chance of fulfilment, devotion to immortality of the species must be changed into smaller coins of the loyalty to groups and group causes. Thoughtful culture, Schopenhauer implies (without necessarily saying it in so many words), co-operates with nature in making secure the latter's mindless tyranny.

Schopenhauer speaks of religion and philosophy. At the time he wrote, those might indeed have seemed the only 'antidotes to the certainty of death' invented and experimented with by the hapless victims of species' selfishness. Schopenhauer wrote well before the time of mass politics and mass ideologies; at any rate, before the time of 'ideology for itself' – before the time when recognition of ideologies as modern functional substitutes

---

[4] Schopenhauer, *The World as Will and Representation*, pp. 634, 573, 463.

for religion dawned upon those in charge of the spiritual union of society. As a matter of fact, it was the spectacular failure of religion to offer an effective antidote, and the ever more obvious bankruptcy of the philosophers' high hopes to supplant religious grounds of life-meaning with their own reason-assisted sophisticated rationalizations, that prompted Schopenhauer's bitter reflections. But the resourcefulness and ingenuity of the selfish species were soon to dwarf, mock and surprise even an imagination as powerful as Schopenhauer's.

The cultural take-over

The effectiveness of a religious antidote to death (that is, the cogency of religiously founded meanings of life) is not a simple function of the determination, ingenuity and acumen of its prophets, codifiers, preachers and vigilantes. It depends closely on the type of society which it addresses, and the human experience prevalent in that type. For most of human history, up to the rise of the type of society and the kind of human experience which came to be known as 'modern', the timelessness of the religious message chimed well with the stagnant, self-repetitive life routine.

Continuity was the primary experience in a world that knew of abrupt change only in the form of war or plague; under the circumstances, change was not a passage to things which have not been yet before, not a step into the unknown – but a temporary break, a phase in Nietzschean eternal return, an intermission in the smooth flow of self-sameness; it was the *change* in the routine that was truly transient – a ripple on the eternal sea, temporary disturbance, a momentary departure from the place things have been, should be and will be again. Were the uncertainty called the future visible in the fickleness of the present, that world would have conceived of itself as one of 'order'; but it did not. Only later generations, having eaten of the tree of the unexpected and the unfamiliar, will be able to call it that – looking back at what was no more, and with poorly concealed, wistful nostalgia. Until that happens, without the advantage of hindsight, it must have been obvious to all thinking people that the world they knew was made once and for all, and the form it was given was not open to challenge. (It was precisely the latter consideration that precluded the coinage of the idea of order; order must appear first as a *task*, if the idea is ever to become usable as a *description*.)

The timelessness of the world made the timelessness of the human soul plausible; the earthly sojourn was not a stage in time (time had not yet become linear, and was far from winning independence from space); it was devoid of history in the same way as the world in which it was placed. More to the point, the timeless world did not prompt questions about the meaning of life, since what is obvious (unchallengeable, without alternative) is neither meaningful nor meaningless, but stands outside the realm of meanings. One does not demand that the obvious should justify itself. Neither does one feel the urge to justify it.

It is only we, the moderns, who believe – again with a hindsight and with more than a touch of nostalgia – that once upon a time, when everything stayed as it was and everyone knew the place reserved for him or her and it was unlikely ever to change, 'religion gave meaning to life'. On closer scrutiny it appears, however, that in those remote (imagined?) times religious beliefs only corroborated the kind of experience which *made concern with meaning pointless*. Life was not in the hands of the living. Life was *not a task*. Life just *was* – as the rest of the world, which only when prodded out of its self-sameness would become an object of anxiety-fed scrutiny. Religious authorities could confine themselves to curt admonitions often proffered by impatient parents: 'You do it, because I told you so.' In fact, we know nothing of religion making life 'meaningful'. Religion was, rather, a decision to remove life-meaning from the agenda of *human* concerns. More correctly, religion was possible as long as that agenda (if there was such an agenda) did not include the meaning of life among its items.

The idea of life-meaning (of life *having* a meaning, and *needing* a meaning in the first place) may only appear once that meaning (more recently discussed under the rubric of 'self-identity') has already been construed as a *task*. Meaning is what is *meant*; there is no meaning unless action is *intentional*, preceded by a move addressed to a purpose. And there is no meaning where there is no freedom of choice between motives nor between purposes, and thus no responsibility for the choice eventually made. Having taken life out of the hands of the living, religions endorsed the world which had no room for the vexing questions of meaning. By the same token, they barred for a time the discovery of that absurdity which, once revealed, and above all once endowed with the added credential of a reflection of common experience, would make an antidote imperative.

It was precisely the kind of world which did not make 'the meaning of life' or 'identity' a common and daily concern, that the advancing modernity destroyed; and with that world, off went the ability of religion to get away with its non-answer to the question of life-meaning (the clever ability construed in retrospect, wistfully yet anachronistically, as the apposition of the religiously warranted meaning of life). Religion remained effective as long as the question remained unasked. Once it had been asked, it was not the unsatisfactory character of the religious answer that was revealed – but the *absence of an answer*.

If the only reason religion can offer for following a certain route of life is that it has been preordained by a power stronger than man's – then it would be more than likely to encounter the same difficulties (notorious for their inability to stand up to scrutiny the moment scrutiny begins) as those later to beset so-called 'naturalistic ethics': why should not nature or God (for a religiously grounded ethics) see to it themselves that their will should be implemented? Why should this be not theirs, but human concern? If it is nature or God who bears the responsibility for what the world is like, than clearly they have not done a good job and one could do one's best to float their verdicts rather than follow them obediently. In a dictatorial regime resistance to command is a popular virtue; also, each case of suffering is by common consent a charge against the central administration – all the more so the more high-handed are its practices and more monopolistic its ambitions. If such a resistance is possible (that is, if nature or God have endowed humans with free will, and thus burdened them with the excruciating task of self-constitution) then the preordained character of the world is irrelevant to the issue of human identity, which now becomes, for all practical purposes, a *human*, and human only, responsibility. One way or the other, the avalanche of doubts is triggered off once the original sin of questioning has been perpetrated. And it is this original sin of asking the fatal question that has been prompted – indeed, rendered both unavoidable and imperative – by the profound transformation of human experience known as the advent of the modern condition.

This connection has been commented upon by many writers, yet few expressed it more poignantly than Paul Valéry:

> New powers, new men, the world never knew less where it goes . . .
>
> Men have grown accustomed to view all knowledge as transitional, any stage of their industry and mutual relations as provisional. This is new. The general state of life must pay ever more attention to the unexpected. Reality is no more definite. Space, time, matter allow liberties of which once there was not the slightest premonition . . .
>
> One of the most certain, and most cruel, effects of progress has been to add pain to death – a pain that aggravates as the revolution in customs and ideas accelerates and deepens. Now, it is not enough that men perish; they also turn unintelligible, nay ridiculous.[5]

---

[5] Paul Valéry, *Regards sur le monde actuel et autres essais* (Paris: Galimard, 1945), pp. 168, 169–70, 172.

Death suffered, death defied

One of the most painful prices humanity paid for the comforts of modernity was the discovery of the absurdity of being. There was no room for the perception of absurdity as long as the monotony (experienced as *normality*) of being lasted. Monotony made existence un-problematic, hence non-visible; the customary repetitiveness of life-routine (sustained even by the regularity with which routine was punctuated by hardships and calamities) seldom gave occasion to conceive of being as a matter yet to be defined and determined. The entrance of *the unexpected*, of the unexpected as the ubiquitous, constitutive feature of quotidianity, as a new *normality of sorts*, was a blow from which that existential security (or, rather, absence of existential *insecurity* – not necessarily the same condition) was never to recover. It changed, so to speak, the rules of the life-game. More importantly still, it showed life *to be a game*: that is, to be a process with a course and the outcome not just unknown to the participants, but as yet undecided; a course which the actions of the living have the chance to shape, alter or otherwise influence decisively.

An existence without a script written in advance is a *contingent* existence. It is also an existence without 'external' reason – older, more lasting, and stronger than itself; an existence which must yet find or conjure up its own reasons. In the absence of reasons, life would have but one of the Aristotelian causes – the *final cause*: but this final cause happened to be death. Stopping at this point would make the status of all the world's durables incongruous. Everything in life would be transient, like individual life itself (and the sole meaning of transient things is that they are consumed and vanish once they have been consumed). Thus another power – call it the power of reason – was needed if transient things were ever to be lifted above the mire of transience: if some particular things were to *become* durable, that is to be turned into those curious objects that grow and get stronger, rather than perish, in the process of their consumption. Life filled with such things, even if only in part, would borrow and reflect some of their durable splendour. Death's victory would not be then complete.

Philippe Ariès suggested that in pre-modern era death was 'tamed' in a way which we, the moderns, find difficult to comprehend:

> The ancient attitude in which death is simultaneously close, familiar, and diminished, defused – is sharply opposed to our own in which death becomes a terror so powerful that we no more dare to pronounce its name.

This is why, when we describe that familiarized death as tamed, we do not mean that it was savage before and later became domesticated. What we have in mind is, on the contrary, that death has become savage today while it was not wild before. The most ancient of deaths was a tame one.[6]

'Tame' does not mean benign, 'close' does not mean willingly embraced, 'familiar' does not mean accepted without grudge. Death was frightening at all times, and just before the great modern war against the mortal fate was declared the horror of death had reached previously unknown heights – as Johan Huizinga in his epoch-making study of the late Middle Ages so brilliantly demonstrated.[7] Art and literature of the fifteenth Century had articulated the previously diffuse fears and put them into a form which made death and mortality into an abomination, fit to become one of the first targets of the modern challenge to ruthless and mindless nature. Three themes in particular, all introduced at that time, revealed and laid bare the absurdity of human existence haunted by death which no one controlled – by an obstreperous, illogical, randomly striking death. They were: the vanity of earthly glory, the shallowness and brevity of human beauty, and the *danse macabre* – that haunting visual image meant to convey the blind randomness of death's blows, totally unrelated to anything humans do or may do.

François Villon's melancholy sigh, 'Mais où sont les neiges d'antan?' immortalized the first theme – but he was not alone in musing on the futility of the human chase of glory which, however impressive it may seem at the moment, will be cut off without mercy and without warning. Where are today the High and Mighty of yesterday? Where will be tomorrow the proud and powerful of today? Everybody ends – as the second theme would hammer home – as a rotting carcass.

The second motif equally gathered in popularity: in poetry and in scholarly tracts alike the vanity of human concerns with glory or beauty was ridiculed: beauty and charm will rot away, a splendid body will be soon a worms' dinner. A widely read poem by Olivier de la Marche asked: 'Ces doulx regards, ces yeulx faiz pour plaisance, /pensez y bien, ilz perdront leur clarté,/ nez et sourcilz, la bouche d'eloquence/ se pourriont

---

[6] Philippe Ariès, *L'Homme devant la mort* (Paris: Seuil, 1977), p.36. 'Domestication' of death expressed itself in cool, indifferent attitude to graves and funeral rites. Until the eighteenth Century, cemeteries were located in the midst of populated centres; dead and alive mixed freely, the latter being obviously unperturbed by the *memento mori* impact of the daily neighbourhood of the first.

[7] Johan Huizinga, *Herfsttij der Middeleeuwen* (1918), quoted below according to the Polish translation of 1961, published by PIW.

...' But even before the hour of death, before the rot sets in – as one could read, for a change, in a learned tract:

> the beauty of body is no more than skin deep.
> If only men could see what is there under the skin, if only they could see the interior, as they say about certain sharp-sighted Beotian, the sight of a woman would disgust them. Their charm consists of phlegm and blood, moisture and bile. If one thought of what is there inside the nostrils, in the throat, in the belly, one would come to the conclusion that there is nothing but filth.

'How can we wish to embrace a sackful of shit?' asked, bewildered, the monk who put in words what was fast becoming a most popular wisdom of the time.

The word 'macabre' was coined in the fourteenth century. (The image of the *danse macabre* is alleged to have been first broached in 1376 by the poet Jean le Fèvre.) More than any other concept it captured and conveyed the feeling of total *helplessness* that accompanied the late-medieval horror of death: whatever you do, however hard you try to earn survival or to cheat death, all is and will forever be in vain. Faced with death, all people are equal. Death, that gruesome *maître de dance*, invites the pope, the king, the lord, the tenant, the monk, the child, the clown, all people of all trades and all standings, to join it in the fandango – and no one has the power to refuse. The blindness of exceptionless, merciless fate paralysed the will and froze the emotions – leaving but gnawing fear and resigned sorrow.

Thus, what Ariès' 'tameness' of pre-modern death may be seen as referring to is merely a common assumption, unchallenged until the dawn of the Age of Reason, that there was nothing one could do against cruel human fate. Death, so to speak, was there to stay, and was there from the first moment of life, and one had to live daily in its shadow. One could repine the fate, give voice to one's abhorrence and fury – but that was about all, and that 'all' was dazzlingly, despairingly ineffective. One thing which did not cross one's mind was that the frontiers of mortality could be pushed back, that the conduct of death could be controlled, that fate could be made a little less blind and cruel than it was.

The most common explanation of this resigned equanimity with which death was treated in pre-modern times (and this does require explanation *for us*, as it appears *to us* so outlandishly un-natural and, placed in the midst of our own collective experience, constitutes a hermeneutical puzzle) is that in those times death struck frequently, early, blindly and without warning; death was a daily and highly visible occurrence, neither

a secret nor an extraordinary event. Everyone had therefore ample opportunity to get used to its presence, starting from the most tender age; one
had no reason to be puzzled or unduly excited when death, for the
umpteenth time, struck in one's close vicinity. This explanation makes
sense to us; the frequency and obtrusive visibility of death undoubtedly
goes a long way toward explaining its bafflingly 'tamed' character. What is
not, however, strongly enough emphasized in this interpretation is that
death, dying and survival, like the rest of pre-modern life, could be
perceived in *existential*, but not *practical*, terms. Like life, death 'followed
its course'. Like life, death was not 'a task'. There was little or nothing one
could or should do about it. Death was 'tame' because it was not a
challenge, in the same sense in which all other elements of the life-process
were not challenges in a world in which identities were given, everything
was stuck to its place in the great chain of being and things ran their course
by themselves.

The resigned yet peaceful cohabitation with 'tame' death did not survive
the end of that 'existential settlement'. (In our contract-minded society,
but only in this kind of society, we are inclined to think of such settlements
as being ones of 'great compromise'.) The break-up of the close control
over the totality of life, exercised heretofore by all-encompassing and
almost self-sufficient local and vocational corporations, replaced the
settled population with an array of wanderers ('life pilgrims', in the phrase
favoured by the Protestant saints); a seminal transformation of the human
condition if there ever was one, later to be theorized by philosophers as
the *liberation of the individual*: as a welcome process, started off by
history, but calling for the active and planned intervention of legislators
to be implemented, monitored and completed.)

Once the communal ties started to weaken, once their hold became less
sure, so that some room for exceptions appeared at the margins –
'existential determination' showed ever clearer signs of temporality. An
idea could be born then that whatever had remained of determination
(and let us repeat that only now it was seen as *determination*, thanks to
the availability of an 'undetermined' vantage point) was neither inevitable
nor necessary; that things could be different from what they were, that
they were amenable to manipulation, and that they *could* and *should* be
manipulated. The increasingly conspicuous weakness of communal grip
encouraged rebellion; the disconcerted and frightened orphans of social
control were exhorted to turn into valiant fighters for freedom. By the
eighteenth century, a philosophical *individualism* was fully formed which
postulated, as Simmel was to observe, that all the restrictions that confined
the infinite pliability of human identity 'were artificially produced in-

equalities and that once these had been banished along with their historical fortuitousness, their injustice, and their burdensomeness, perfected
man would emerge'. Imperfections were many and varied; perfection
could be only one and the same for everybody. That early modern
individualism postulated equality, and absence of difference. The perfect
man about to be disclosed through his own effort of emancipation was to
be a man without identity and without qualities.

One by one, all elements of communal determination had been theorized as errors or crimes of history or of its obtuse or malevolent, but in
each case illegitimate, human agents. Crimes ought to be punished, errors
rectified. The rulers must muster resources needed to *free* man 'from all
these historical influences and diversions that ravage the deepest essence',
so that 'what is common to all, man as such, can emerge in him as this
essence'.[8] That liberation meant first and foremost the destruction of
oppressive frames. *Les pouvoirs intermédiairies*, bonds of local communities, parishes, kinships, craftsmen guilds had to be shred. A free man was
to be a person without a fixed master or address. All fixity, all determination harmed and maimed. With fixed qualities out of the way, and the
powers capable of stamping them on the 'man as such' disempowered,
man would be pared to the bare bones of his *eigenschaftenlos* essence,
would turn into the genuine clean slate, on which those who can write
will be able to inscribe the *universal*, 'just human', contents.

Power-assisted universality

In the ultimate account, emancipation from particularity boiled down to
a call for unconditional and uncontested subordination to the power of
the supra-communal state, which had now been juxtaposed, as the epitome of universality, to communally based parochiality. Rulers normally
described their conquests as liberation (in case they themselves did not
care about names, their scribes did). In practical terms, liberation of the
territory meant the *uniformity* of its residents – achieved through erasing
their once indifferent, now abominable diversity.

What was meant, moreover, was not a mere substitution of one, state-
sponsored, set of qualities, for the multitude of locally sustained sets.

---

[8] Georg Simmel, 'Freedom and the Individual', in *On Individuality and Social
Forms*, ed. Donald N. Levine (Chicago: University of Chicago Press, 1971), pp. 219,
220.

Between communities and the pre-modern state there was, so to speak, a division of labour – with the state interested in its subjects as taxpayers, sometimes as soldiers needed to conquer more potential taxpayers, but certainly not as the objects of identity-formation. The latter function was the communal accomplishment, and a tacit one, which the state felt no need to supervise – much less still to initiate. But the communally administered formation of identities differed from the state-administered one than was later to replace it, not so much in the contents it promoted, as in the fashion in which the promotion was made effective, and in the existential consequences of that fashion. In the pre-modern context identities were induced rather than imposed, let alone 'taken', sought, constructed. They 'emerged' – matter-of-factly, *naturally*, having but in exceptional cases a chance of being conceived of as the *task* one needed to pursue, bearing personal responsibility for the pursuit and its success. Clearly, this was not to be the case of the state-administered 'universal' identity, whose formation could not be expected from 'natural' processes. Under state management, identities had to be an outcome of planned, managed, 'rational' action. The imparting of beliefs, attitudes and behavioural patterns had to be problematized and structured as *education* (and, more generally, *culture*), run by the expert agents appointed and empowered by the state.

This situation, however, revealed identities as qualities which would not be there if not taken care of and willingly constructed. The 'man as such' was revealed as a 'raw material' empty of qualities, purpose and meaning. Meaningless, unless *given* meaning; purposeless, unless *given* purpose.

At the threshold of modernity one finds the process of the self-constitution, self-distancing and self-separation of the *elite* (now set apart by its 'civilized' mode, with its two faces of spiritual refinement and bodily drill) which at the same time is a process of *formation* of the *masses* as the potential field of the elite's action and responsibility. *Responsibility* is for nudging the masses into humanity; the *action* may take form of persuasion or enforcement, enlightenment or confinement, depending on what strategy is found, or deemed, more expedient. It was that sense of responsibility and the associated propulsion to act that defined 'the masses' in their two permanently coexisting, even if ostensibly sharply diverse, incarnations: of 'the mob' (coming to the fore in as far as force was the order of the day), and 'the people' (invoked when education was hoped to make enforcement redundant).

What applied to the grand separation, applied as well to the grand reunification which was bound to follow. The reintegration of divided society was to be led by the new civilized elite of the educated, now firmly in the saddle. In a sharp summary of Ernest Gellner,

> at the base of the modern social order stands not the executioner but the
> professor. Not the guillotine, but the (aptly named) *doctorat d'état* is the
> main tool and symbol of state power. The monopoly of legitimate education
> is now more important, more central that is the monopoly of legitimate
> violence'.[9].

The processes of the integration and reproduction of society could be no
more left to spontaneous, unreflexively operating forces of sociability set
and kept in motion by the multitude of compact, localized mini-centres.
More correctly – modern elites have consciously and resolutely broken
with what they now came to view, with the horror of hindsight, as such a
decentred, diffuse, chaotic, *irrational* state of affairs, dangerous because
uncontrolled and thus permanently pregnant with catastrophe.

The processes of the integration and reproduction of social order have
now become the domain of specialization, expertise – and of a legally
defined authority. As the processes of separation which preceded them,
they simultaneously constituted the elite as the group at the helm, and the
rest of society as a natural object of elite's action. To put it another way,
they reproduced the structure of domination in its new, much extended
form, stretching far beyond the past redistribution of the surplus product,
shaping the spirits and the bodies of the subjects and penetrating deeply
their daily conduct and the construction of their life-worlds. The call for
the education of the masses was simultaneously a declaration of the
masses' own social incompetence, and a bid for the dictatorship of the
professoriat (or, to use the educated elite's own vocabulary, for the
'enlightened despotism' of the guardians of reason and good taste).

'The masses' belong to the populous family of categories born together
with modernity. The shuffling together of the multiple regional, legal and
occupational identities of *le petit peuple, le menu peuple*, into a mass –
indiscriminate and apparently uniform – or a *mobile vulgus*, did not start
in earnest until the seventeenth century, and had reached its conceptual
maturity only in the thought of Enlightenment. According to Robert
Muchembled,

> All social groups of the 15th and 16th centuries moved at the same level in
> that universe, enormously distant from ours. Real cleavages caused by birth
> or wealth did not result in profound differences in sensibility and common
> conduct between the dominant and the dominated . . .

---

[9] Ernest Gellner, *Nations and Nationalism* (Oxford: Blackwell, 1983), p. 34.

Beginning with the 18th century, the break between two separate mental planets intensifies. The civilized people cannot any more feel the people, in the proper sense of the word. They reject everything which appears to them savage, dirty, lecherous – in order to better conquer similar temptations in themselves . . . Odour became a criterion of social distinction.

There were many divisions and subdivisions, broad or minute, in that *divine chain of being* that the pre-modern mind of Christian Europe forged to piece together its life-world; too many divisions, in fact, for one, all-embracing, all-defining 'division of divisions', like that *modern* division between the 'refined' and the 'vulgar', to emerge. In a truly revolutionary way, the 'civilizing process' that took off in the seventeenth century was first and foremost a drive to the self-separation of the elites from the rest – now blended, despite all its internal variety, into homogenic masses; a process of a sharp *cultural desynchronization*. On one, active end (that of the elites) it produced a growing preoccupation with the task of self-formation, self-drill and self-improvement. On the other, receiving end it sedimented a tendency to biologize, medicalize, criminalize and increasingly police 'the masses' – 'judged to be brutal, dirty, and totally incapable of holding their passions in check so that they could be poured into a civilized mould".[10]

The overall product of the process was a sharply dichotomized society (at least such was its vision from the top; but it was that vision that counted

---

[10] Robert Muchembled, *L'Invention de l'homme moderne: sociabilité, moeurs et comportements collectives dans l'Ancien Régime* (Paris: Fayard, 1988), pp. 12, 13, 150. The idea of the two-pronged, sharply differentiated effects of the 'civilizing process' (aimed polemically against the 'trickling down' model popularized by Norbert Elias) has been systematically pursued by Muchembled also in his other works (see particularly *La Violence en village: sociabilité et comportements en Artois du XVe au XVIIe siècle (Paris: Bregnols, 1989)).* According to Muchembled, the most profound mutations in sensibility and behavioural standards of quotidianity were limited to a narrow elite; they functioned simultaneously as a vehicle of self-distancing and as a vantage point for a new perspective from which the rest of the population was scanned as uniformly vulgar and, for the initial period at least, *uncivilizable*. Self-polishing as the strategy of the elite was juxtaposed to the confinement, policing and universal surveillance as the strategy to be deployed in dealing with 'the masses'. The civilizing process is best understood as the 'recomposition' of the new structure of control and domination once the premodern institutions of social integration have proven inadequate and were gradually decomposed. (I have argued this point more fully in my *Legislators and Interpreters: On Modernity, Postmodernity and the Intellectuals* (Cambridge: Polity Press, 1987).)

most). The children of light versus the children of darkness, reason at war with superstition, civilizing effort facing sinister passions, law and order keeping violent instincts at bay, the humanizing self-culture of the educated set against the raw animality of the lesser mortals; all oppositions being, in the end, but perspectival dimensions of the greatest and most seminal of separations – that between elite and the masses. Separation did not mean opting out, isolation, or refusal to be interested. This was, on the contrary, an active separation – separation as a condition of engagement, as an initial and seminal step, an overture to the transformation of the 'masses' (now homogenized in their shared absence of qualities) into the permanent ward of the elite.

In this sense, as Adorno insisted, 'Enlightenment is totalitarian'. 'The creative god and the systematic spirit are alike as rulers of nature. Man's likeness to God consists in sovereignty over existence, in the countenance of the lord and master, and in command.' The equality of 'human essence' that the enlightening elite promoted was *repressive*; the 'levelling domination' pressed and condensed 'free individuals' into the Hegelian 'herd'. Contrary to Durkheim, the resulting uniformity of thought was not an expression of social solidarity, 'but evidence of the inscrutable unity of society and domination'. To the individual, domination appeared 'to be the universal: reason in actuality'.[11]

From the perspective of the poor and lowly, the advent of state-administered identities meant little change in the subordinate, determined, other-directed condition. It was the elite who knew they were free, responsible, and in urgent need of self-constitution. (But Elias wrote about the bewilderment with which even the high and mighty of their times met the idea that children must be consciously 'formed' into 'proper' adults, when this had been first suggested by the preachers of *Bildung*.) It was the self-proclaimed 'civilized' elite who set to practise their freedom. As to the poor and lowly – they, as in the past, were *told* what to do and how to carry themselves, without being asked to choose; as before, their identity was hardly ever in question. What did change was that they had been now *informed* that they were free, and thus had been told that they were fully responsible for what would have become of them; that they have a *duty* to themselves, and that what they would eventually turn into could only be seen, rewarded or punished, as being of their own making. The 'unanticipated consequence' of the change was that what they were thus prompted to do, was to be concerned with their 'life meanings' –

---

[11] Cf. Theodor Adorno and Max Horkheimer, *Dialectic of Enlightenment*, trans. John Cumming (London: Verso, 1979), pp. 6–22.

with the purpose of life, with survival and self-preservation; in the end also with the purpose of existence which they could not but feel to be miserable. Neither life with all the sufferings it contained and the sacrifices it required, nor its inevitable ending were now 'obvious' – the 'fate' one suffers without soul-searching and self-immolation. Life and everything in it had now to be *given* its meaning.

If the urge to find the meaning of life could spur the elite of the high and mighty into frantic and realistic efforts to make their presence in the world significant and consequential – such a possibility never arose for the 'masses'. To start with, the masses would never be allowed to resort to the weapon of self-assertion, to make their mark as *individuals*; any attempt in this direction would be automatically recorded as unforgivable arrogance and an act of rebellion – a threat to society which demanded action from the guardians of law and order. More importantly still, they lacked the resources any serious attempt at self-constitution would require. As far as they were concerned, there was a yawning gap between the alleged self-made character of identity and the access to means through which identities may be constructed. The brutal fact of residing, for the duration of earthly life, at the bottom end of the scale of domination – appeared, under the circumstances, as the genuine 'reason in actuality'.

In short – though the question of the meaning of life was eminently 'askable', the ways to the construction of such meaning were, for the 'masses', theoretically off-limits and practically beyond reach. The elite had evidently arrogated all recognized means appropriate to rendering life 'meaningful' – endorsed by the authority of lasting values, referring to something infinite and eternal, and thereby transcending the ephemerality of transient bodily existence. The elite reserved for its own use all the 'officially listed' roads leading to individual immortality. 'The masses', already depersonalized in their earthly life, had been by the same token expropriated from the means of immortality production. This was one among many faces of repressive domination – and like all its other faces, it had to be concealed ('social repression', says Adorno, 'always exhibits the masks of repression by a collective'); it had to represent itself as the product of totality, not as the will of that small part of totality which sat in judgement. The very objectified (reified) status of all but selected individuals (for the overwhelming majority, for 'the masses', the 'yardstick is self-preservation, successful or unsuccessful approximation to the objectivity of his function and the models established for it') had to be translated as durable value in its own right: as the 'immortal' moment in what otherwise is, undeniably, a mortal existence, as a *collective* equivalent of the *privatized* immortality of the elite (a 'mass production' version of customized *haute couture*); as a reliable source, and warranty, of life's meaning fit for popular use; as a sort of durable, supra-individual existence, to which everyone, however lowly, has equal access; a share in the public company called immortality that everyone may purchase and the possession of which would truly make everyone equal – albeit post-humously.

Selfish societies

The sought-for formula could only be a rationalized, narrowed down, group-focused version of 'species selfishness'. The pattern to follow was the species' expedient of prompting individual life concerns to contribute to the preservation and perpetuation of the group. Immortality was to be the lot of the group, not of its members; the lot which could be assured only on condition that the fashion in which the members conducted their mortal lives was such as to enable the life of the group to continue unendangered. In the case of the species as a whole, such an effect is produced through the means of biological reproduction. In the case of societies, more is at stake; more is involved than continuation of bodily existence; bodily continuation of the population does not by itself secures the continuation of the society (culture, civilization etc.) 'as we know it'. Durability is to be secured not for life *in general*, but for a *specific form* of collective life; and this means a specific structure of domination, a certain allocation of privileges, a given distribution of freedom and dependency as well as of the chances of individual immortality – all those arrangements chosen from among other conceivable alternatives, to give the group its distinctive identity and the meaning to its survival.

As it has been suggested before, until the advent of modernity the group continuity (its immortality for the duration) was not a matter of conscious concern and focused efforts. It did not appear as a task, as a purpose that was made present ideally before it would, and could, be reached materially. It was only the collapse of the self-perpetuating order of fixed identities that led to the 'grand separation' between the elite and the masses (to the closely related, yet opposite, processes of the personalization of the elite, the 'individualization' of its members, coupled with the 'collectivization', depersonalization of the remainder into a mass) and posited the reproduction of society in its new structure as a task that had to be planned, managed and monitored. The monotony of the behaviour of the masses could not be uncritically relied upon to accomplish the task.

Not unless the masses were first drilled into such monotony, and then settled in carefully designed conditions which made the perpetuation of monotony highly probable, if not certain.

The methods commonly applied to the task have been described in detail: they split, roughly, into two essential categories. The first has been given by Michel Foucault the name of 'panoptical' (in metaphorical reference to Bentham's architectural solution to the issue of the reproduction of order), and entailed close control of conduct through the asymmetry of surveillance backed by confinement (that is, the explicit and coercion-assisted denial of choice) as the last-resort argument. The second category was in different, but related ways captured by Weber's concept of 'legitimation' and Parsons concept of 'central value-cluster': it entailed efforts, concentrated or diffuse, to conceal the repression by the elite behind a 'collective repression', through representing the specific order of a given society as tantamount to order as such, and the perpetuation of such order as a mission transcending the span of individual lives – a mission to which these lives ought to contribute if they are to acquire meaning.

Both methods were deployed by the elites bent on the preservation of the social order which made their privilege secure. The most important stratagem used to make such deployment effective (a meta-strategy, one could say) was to represent it as a 'functional requisite' of society, a condition of its survival – of collective survival, of survival of all individual members as a collective; to represent it as the condition of *group immortality*. Perhaps the foremost, and most spectacularly successful, expression of that strategy practised in modern times was *nationalism*.

Nationalism was, first and foremost, a conjunction of the spiritual elite's bid for political leadership and the political rulers' bid for spiritual hegemony. It was aimed at recapturing the bodies and minds of the 'masses', that end-product of decomposition and pulverization of ancient (local and self-perpetuating) structures of incorporation. It aimed at the substitution of one 'centre', overlooking and supervising the whole of the 'periphery', for the patchwork of multi-focal sociabilities. In this sense, nationalism was a programme of unification and a postulate of homogeneity. But nationalism was also invariably a bid for the sole and exclusive rights to a territory, a population, a populated territory. Much as it was a struggle *of the elite* to tame and subjugate the obstreperous or indifferent masses, it was also a struggle *between* extant and prospective, established and up-and-coming elites for the right to administer the taming effort, to define its rhetoric and to benefit from its eventual success.

There was always an ambiguity, an interplay of inclusive and exclusive tendencies in every nationalism – and in each nationalist crusade or proselytizing campaign. The preservation of the nation could be hailed as a supreme value, hovering above the short-lived, mortal lives of its members, only as long as it could be shown that it was exposed to a threat, in the face of which members had to huddle together to be sure of their survival. The immortality of the collective held a prescriptive authority – because there were enemies who threatened it. Promotion of homogeneity had to be complemented by the effort to brand, segregate and evict the 'aliens' – already a prey of another national elite, converts of another nationalism, and altogether poor prospects for assimilation into the fought-for uniformity. Drawing the boundary between the *natives* and the *aliens*, between the prospective nation and its enemies, was an inseparable part of the self-assertion of the national elite. There was a codicil, however: to acquire and retain an overwhelming grip over the minds and acts of the present or prospective nationals, this boundary-*drawing* could not be seen for what it in fact was.

'What is *la Patrie*?' asked Maurice Barrès, and answered: 'The Soil and the Dead.' It is easy to see that the two constituents of *la Patrie* have one thing in common: they are not a matter of choice. They cannot be *chosen freely*. Before any choice can be as much as contemplated, one has already been born onto this soil here and now and riveted into this chain of ancestors and their posterity. One can move places, but one cannot take one's soil with one, and one cannot make another soil one's own. One may change company, but not one's dead, the dead ancestors who are one's own and not of the others; nor may one transform other people's dead into one's own ancestors. Commenting on the tragic conflict between Creon and Antigone, Barrès made it clear just what the limits of the choice were:

> Creon is a master who arrived from abroad. He says: 'I know the laws of this country and I apply them'. This is what he judges with his intelligence. Intelligence – what a petty, superficial thing!... Antigone, on the contrary ... engages her deep heredity, she is inspired by the subconscious where respect, love, fear are not yet separated from the magnificent power of veneration.

Antigone has what Creon, armed solely with his wit and *acquired* (namely, detachable, free-floating, abstract and unfeeling) knowledge, will never possess: *l'épine dorsale*, the backbone on which and around which everything else in the human creature rests and is shaped (the backbone, Barrès insists, is not a mere metaphor, 'but a most powerful analogy'). By comparison with the solidity of the backbone, intelligence is no more than 'that trifle thing on the surface'. The backbone is a fixed point from which everything else must depart – a point which from the start (*ursprünglich*, as Heidegger would say) must have been already in place; otherwise, no move would have been feasible. The backbone pre-empts the selection: it determines which moves are feasible and which are not (that is, which threaten to break the backbone). Truth is such a backbone; also a fixed point, and a point fixed *beforehand* – not a point of arrival (not the *end point* of the knowledge process, as Heidegger and his countless followers would insist later), but the *starting* point of all knowledge, a point that cannot be created but only found, unravelled, recovered if missed, or lost; 'a unique point, in this, not any other place, from which all things can be seen in their true proportions'.

> I must place myself at the point demanded by my eyes, as they have been formed in the course of centuries, at the point from which all things make themselves to the Frenchman's measure. The assembly of just and true relations between the objects and the concrete man, the Frenchman, are French truth and justice: to discover these relations is French reason. Pure nationalism is nothing else than being aware of such a point's existence, searching it, and – having reached it – clinging to it in our arts, our politics, and all our activities.[12]

An ambivalence, if ever there was one: that magic point has been fixed before I have been born, I myself had been 'fixed' by it before I began to think of points, magic or otherwise (or of anything else, for that matter) – yet finding this point is still my *task*, something *I and no one else* must *do* while exercising my *reason*. I must seek that point actively, and then *choose* what is *not* a matter of choice anyway: to embrace *voluntarily* the *inevitable*, to submit consciously to that deeper truth which has been present all along in my subconscious. The outcome of my free choice is given in advance: while exercising my will, I am not really free to will.

---

[12] Maurice Barrès, *Scènes et doctrines du nationalisme* (Paris: Émile Paul, 1902), pp. 8–13. Régis Debray stressed the uniqueness of French nationalism, owed above all to the pioneering role of the French Revolution in discovering and propagating the nationalist strategy as a response to the tasks raised by advancing modernity. Due to historical circumstances, French nationalism retained some of its unique features to this very day, yet at no time were they more pronounced, and less amenable to borrowing, than in the immediate aftermath of the revolution, in which France was practically alone in describing its population as a 'nation'. At that time, Debray suggests, 'the Frenchman had the privilege of representing a people that embodied The People' – and thus French nationalism could, for a time undetected, 'confound chauvinistic meanness with messianic generosity'. (*Le Scribe: genèse du politique* (Paris: Grasset, 1980), p. 127).

There is only one thing that in my case may be willed effectively: to be in all I do and think of, determined by *la terre et les morts*, to revel in the comfort and security of having stern and demanding masters – to say to myself, 'I wished to live with those masters, and, by making them consciously objects of my cult, to partake fully of their strength.' Yet there are other things as well that I may (wrongly) happen to will, or think (mistakenly) that I am free to will; for instance, disowning my own masters or appropriating masters that are not mine. In both cases I may really come to believe that I am free and that my reason-dictated choice, like reason itself, knows no bounds. In both cases, the result will be equally destructive, disempowering, horrifying: *déracinement*, rootlessness – body without a backbone, thought with no fixed point on which to stand. Against such a catastrophe I am insured in advance. As a matter of fact, I am lured into it by the hubris of freedom.

Thus the nationalist formula of which Barrès was one of the most cogent spokesmen would have been sorely incomplete if it were not for an important addendum: what unites certain human creatures (and sets them apart from others) is not *solidarity* – a contractual link, an agreement they can enter or disavow at will – but *affinity*: liens by which they are bound without having chosen them, and which they are not at liberty to trade off. 'The fact of belonging to the same race, to the same family, is psychologically determining: it is in this sense that I use the word "affinity" .' The status of affinity is precarious: strong enough to inspire faith in the final victory of the unity drive, yet not strong enough to breed complacency and legitimize quietism.

True nationalism (certainly a nationalism of Barrès's style) would shun the kismet-like, quietism-inducing, overpowering and thus disempowering determinism of *race*, one that absolves the individual from the duty of vigilance: 'it is incorrect to speak of a French race in the strict sense of the word. We are not at all a race, but a nation: it (the nation) goes on making itself day by day, and lest we should be diminished, annihilated, we – the individuals it entails, must protect it'.[13] If group membership depends on race, everything had been said and done before anything was spoken and little depends on what is being spoken; if, however, the togetherness of the group hangs on the *willing* acceptance of fate (if the nation is Renan's 'daily plebiscite'), it also (and most importantly) hangs on what is being spoken and those who speak it. Unlike the race, the nation is incomplete without its 'conscience-arousing' *spokesmen* and spiritual leading lights. Unlike race, the nation includes consciousness

---

[13] Barrès, *Scènes et doctrines du nationalisme*, pp. 16, 20.

among its defining attributes: the nation can be *für sich*, but also 'merely', in an inferior fashion, *an sich*.

Nationalism, one is tempted to say, is a racism of the intellectuals. Obversely, racism is the nationalism of the masses: the masses are, virtually by definition, objects of somebody else's choices, products rather than producers, whether the determining forces are genes or the legally fixed narrative of the powers that be. The state of 'belonging' appears to the masses, therefore, as something given and complete, matter-of-fact, non-negotiable; something that cannot be changed, not by human action they know from the inside of their life experience.

Constructing the nation's immortality

For the theorists and spiritual heralds of the nation's immortality (even if not always and not necessarily for those in whose name they spoke) the nation was, quite unambiguously, a matter of affinity, not race. And yet the need to forge a formula of integration that cast those who spoke and wrote in the pivotal role of the integrators supreme, of the wardens of the nation's immortality, had embroiled the nationalist intellectuals (not unlike their ostensible detractors and sworn enemies, the intellectual preachers of class mission, for that matter) into an ambivalence without a good solution. The truth they preached had to rely on something stronger than the mere power of argument; it must have been guaranteed before the argument has started, and independently of the course the future argument might still take – that is, by the kind of forces which reason can only discover and acknowledge, not conjure up or modify. In relation to the powers of human intelligence, the truth of the nation had to be immune – transcendental and absolute. On the other hand, however, it had to be a vulnerable truth, a truth which might come under attack and even be, at least temporarily, defeated – so that it will always need to be defended, and so that its defenders will always deserve respect, gratitude and reward. *Une vérité française* must be *la vérité* for all Frenchmen; but it must not be just any truth, but la vérité *française* – a made-to-measure truth, so to speak, a truth that selects and appoints its addressees in advance and leaves choice to no one. At this point, rational argument grinds to a halt. Sentiment takes over where reason surrenders.

And so we learn that the reality of the nation is (must be) simultaneously absolute *and* relative; a baffling incongruence, indeed, a source of no small trouble. No wonder the nations of the nationalists are constantly at war – an unwinnable war – against their own inner ambivalence and logical incongruence. Fighting, as always, its inner incongruity in a re-projected form of *The Other*, nations are doomed to focus their self-defence on locating, segregating, disarming and banishing the *strangers* rather than *enemies*: those aliens in their midst who are the crystallizations of their own zealously, but ineffectively, suppressed ambivalence.[14] Nation-building, that quest for a uniform world without difference or contingency, turns out ambivalence as its 'productive waste', and cannot but turn it out continuously and on a never diminishing scale. Lest they should suffocate under the rising mounds of ambiguity, nations are called to be vigilant against the strangers in their midst, those false pretenders who claim the soil and blood that are not their own, the outspoken detractors of the sanctity of national symbols or, worse still, the deceitful flatterers trying slyly to drown their alienness in the torrents of mendacious praise.

As Dominique Schnapper has recently concluded – bluntly and succinctly – 'the ambition to integrate a population around a political project and a common culture remains constitutive of all national collectivity'.[15] It is the political action that makes nations durable, and their existence

---

[14] In the words of Reinhold Niebuhr, any 'altruistic passion is sluiced into the reservoirs of nationalism', so that 'patriotism transmutes individual unselfishness into national egoism'; with that task accomplished (but never accomplished securely and once for all), nations bear ill criticism of their selfish parochialism; 'nations crucify their moral rebels with their criminals upon the same golgotha' (*Moral Man and Immoral Society: A Study in Ethics and Politics* (New York: Charles Scribner & Sons, 1948), pp. 91, 88). Niebuhr goes on to propose that nations are inherently immoral (or, rather, that they manipulate individual morality in such a way as to render it deployable for immoral purposes): 'the sentiment of patriotism achieves a potency in the modern soul, so unqualified, that the nation is given *carte blanche* to use the power, compounded of the devotion of individuals, for any purpose it desires ... So the nation is at one and the same time a check upon, and a final vent for the expression of individual egoism.' (pp. 93, 95) One recalls Canetti's words: 'If you had to face one another naked, you would have a hard time slaughtering. The murderous uniforms.' (*The Human Province*, trans. Joachim Neugroschel (London: André Deutsch, 1985), p. 12).

[15] Dominique Schnapper, 'Diversités et permanences', in *Le Débat*, no. 63 (1991), p. 90. In his splendid study of group-sanctioned aggressiveness (*Cannibalism: Human Aggression and Cultural Form* (New York: Harper, 1974)) Eli Sagan scrutinizes the wide class of forms 'of social aggression that societies have certified as legitimate and moral' (p. xv). He finds out that in most cases such forms rely for their effectiveness on implicit or explicit 'defining out' certain members of human species as non-human. The contracted, group version of species selfishness finds itself as a rule in an ambivalent relation toward the self-preservation of the species as a whole, which it simultaneously serves and qualifies.

transcendent. Political action is triggered by a *project*; and having a project, allowing action to be triggered by a project, to be organized and monitored by a project, measured by a project, given sense by a project – is a most remarkable among modernity's innovations.

Modernity, as Jean-François Lyotard recently suggested,[16] can best be conceived of not so much as a socio-political system or a socio-economic formation, but as a certain *mode* – of thought, of rhetoric, of sensibility. We may say that once in this very special kind of mode, thought casts itself as *history*, that is to say, it transcends the present by decomposing it, simultaneously, as the *over*-determined residue of the past, overflowing with meanings, and an *under*-determined preamble to the future, waiting for a meaning yet to be given. The modern mode denies the past its ultimate meaning-giving authority and hands over the right to assign meanings to the still-unknown-and-uncertain future. Before that future comes to be, the present does not really have identity. The present is incomplete (*im-perfect*), not yet quite what it *could* be if fully developed, not yet quite what it *should* be if it duly cut itself free from the hold of the past that drags it down. Indeed, the most pronounced of the present's characteristics it that it has been caught in the moment of the still unfinished *emancipation*: be it from the consequences of original sin, from ignorance, from parochiality, from exploitation, from alienation, from poverty, or from dependence on nature – from anything that makes the present what it is: non-universal, partial – and thus wan, lame, fragile, transient, mortal. In sharp distinction from virtually all other (traditional ist?) myths, the unique *modern* myth of the yet-unfulfilled-emancipation seeks the guarantees of durability (of freedom from the ravages of time, of escaping, by-passing or cheating the decay which no mortal thing could or would avoid) not in the foundational act of creation, not in an event in the past, but in an idea yet to be realized: an idea which – being itself universal – credits the present with an advance sense of a step leading to the universal condition.

In the modern mode, immortality is defined as a *prospect*; one that is identical with attaining freedom from particularity, from *difference*. From this definition, two seminal consequences follow.

First, the lifting of the present from its flawed, imperfect condition is a *task*: it may come out only in the wake of embracing the Idea consciously, followed by a wilful, purposeful and focused act. Unlike the past, the future has a modality of the *product* and is to be *produced*. Hence the relevance

---

[16] Cf. Jean-François Lyotard, *Le Postmoderne expliqué aux enfants: Correspondance, 1982–1985* (Paris: Galilée, 1988), pp. 36–7, 44–5.

of political action, of the resources it mobilizes, of the power to determine the course of events it secures.

Second, annihilation of the morbid consequences of the past is the substance of such political action. Those consequences which are to be destroyed by political action manifest themselves first and foremost in the non-universality, particularity, parochiality of the manifold forms of the transitory present that in all its shapes falls short of the Idea's timeless perfection. If the *telos* of modern politics is universality, its *practice* is the war declared on difference. Ostensibly, the thrust of modernity is towards realization of universality. Its practical accomplishment, on the other hand, is delegitimation of difference, one that daily breeds Adorno's 'fear of social deviation'.

This is not, however, the end of the story. If the advent of universality is to be assured, and in the end brought about, by power-assisted action, then the boundaries of universality can never reach beyond the carrying capacity of that power which brings it about. The thrust toward universality, therefore, cannot but produce and fortify new divisions, separations and differences – and do this at the very same time that it earnestly uproots and sweeps off the old differences that stand in the way of the new uniform standards promoted by the powers that back it. Modernity is branded with a contradiction it cannot wash off: it divides when dreaming of unification, it promotes particularity while striving towards universality. Hence, as Derrida pointed out, the astonishing paradox: 'nationalism and cosmopolitanism make always a good marriage'. National hegemony – a thoroughly divisive bid for distinction, privilege and discrimination – can seldom entertain a reasonable hope of success without flying high, for everyone to admire, the banner of universality.

> Whether it takes or does not take on a national form, whether it is refined, hospitable, or aggressively xenophobic, self-affirmation of identity always responds to the appeal or the assignation of the universal. This law does not bear an exception. No cultural identity ever presents itself as an opaque body of untranslatable idiom – but always, on the contrary, as an irreplaceable *inscription* of the universal upon the singular, a *unique testimony* of the human essence and human quality. Each time, this is the discourse of *responsibility*: I, the unique 'I' have the responsibility for giving testimony to the universality. Each time the exemplarity of the example is unique.[17]

However selfish and intolerant it may be in its practical manifestation – national hegemony is in the end about transcendence of the contingent

---

[17] Jacques Derrida, *L'Autre Cap* (Paris: Editions de Minuit, 1991), pp. 49, 71–2.

and transient, and as such it cannot but invoke, in its self-legitimizing theory, the timelessness of the universal. The efforts of nation-building must be represented as steps on the road to human universality. In a perverse way, nationalism's universalistic disguise is a tribute which the group's selfishness must pay to the humanity of its members. Yet the inner contradiction which results makes of all nationalisms endemically unfulfilled – and in all probability unfulfillable – projects. Nationalism must be forever unsatisfied with every concrete sedimentation of its past labours. Nothing can quite come up to the standards that make nationalist practices, simultaneously, feasible to perform and doomed to failure. Nationalism must remain loftily confident about its proclaimed purpose and contemptuously critical of everything that has been done, ostensibly, to promote that purpose.

In the result, nations can never stay still; complacency and fading vigilance is their worst sin – a mortal (suicidal) sin, to be sure. The order that sustains them and which they sustain by their 'daily plebiscite' is, after all, artificial (even though proclaimed to be, and conceived of, as 'natural', that is 'merely reflecting' what the soil and blood dictate), and hence precarious from stem to stern. The paradox of all and any order – 'the ludicrous thing about order', in Canetti's expression – is that it wants to be total and all-embracing while it 'depends on so little. A hair, literally a hair, lying where it shouldn't, can separate order from disorder. Every thing that does not belong where it is is hostile. Even the tiniest thing is disturbing: a man of total order would have to scour his realm with a microscope, and even then a remnant of potential nervousness will remain in him.'[18] Nationalism breeds such an endemic nervousness in the nations it spawns. It trains the nations in the art of vigilance that cannot but mean a lot of restlessness while promising no tranquillity; it makes nationhood into a task always to be struggled for and never to be fulfilled in the degree justifying that pleasing and restful complacency which comes with the conviction of victory. It prompts feverish defence of the soil and frantic blood-testing. It creates the state of permanent tension which it claims to relieve; it thrives on that tension, it draws from it its life juices; it is, after all, the selfsame tension which it sustains that makes it indispensable – indeed, welcome, sought after, and once found or offered, eagerly and gratefully embraced. Nationalism is self-defeating, but it needs its 'unfulfillingness' to make an impression, an impact, to be effective – to survive.

A quarter of a century ago Karl Deutsch spelled out the role played by the tension born of anxiety born of uncertain (withdrawn, questioned,

---

[18] Canetti, *The Human Province*, p. 160.

under-determined) identity, in riveting together the 'push' and 'pull' factors in nationalism. The nation-state, he wrote,

> offers most of its members a stronger sense of security, belonging or affiliation, and even personal identity, than does any alternative large group
> . . .
>
> [The] greater the need of the people for such affiliation and identity under the strains and shocks of social mobilization and alienation from earlier familiar environments, the greater becomes the potential power of the nation-state to channel both their longings and resentments and to direct their love and hate.[19]

That the need for affiliation is indeed great and growing, is the seminal, perhaps also unique, accomplishment of modernity. Affiliation has become a *need* in the course of the atomization which followed the tearing up of primordial, 'natural' bonds tied together in spatially confined, and for that reason temporally unbound, 'communities of belonging'. Before that tearing-up, the timelessness of communities was not a matter of intention and intentional practice; it called for no action. Mortality was the lot of the individuals, not communities. Only individual mortality was evident; like the immortality of community, it was given and came ready-made. One may say that having destroyed the spontaneous *sociability* of in-group-living, new powers (now rising high above the level at which that sociability used to operate) had to replace it (or to try to replace it) with *socialization*.[20] Men and women had to be *made* into the members of community, which could reveal itself to them only through the faculty of imagination; a community which they did not know even if they knew *of it*, and of which they had no direct, and certainly no totalizing, experience. The new timeless totality had to be built up, made credible and sustained in its precarious existence through constant prod-

---

[19] Karl Deutsch, *Contemporary Political Science: Toward Empirical Theory* (New York, 1967), p. 217. See discussion in Peter Alter, *Nationalism*, trans. Stuart McKinnon-Evans (London: Edward Arnold, 1989), p. 123ff.

[20] In *L'Ombre de Dionysos: contribution à une sociologie d'orgie* (Paris: Klinck-sieck, 1985), Michel Maffesoli proposes a different terminological distinction: *social* to denote 'mechanical-rational relations' of the kind promoted and protected by the legislating/coercive powers of the organized society, and *sociétal*, to denote that 'togetherness' that 'surpasses simple rational association'. *Socialité* would then stand for the 'ground solidarity', which is the manifestation of the *sociétal* in action (see particularly pp. 15–16).

Myself, I have discussed at length the substitution of societally promoted *norms* for uncontrolled and essentially uncontrollable ('non-rationalizable') moral drives in 'Effacing the Face' and 'Moralizing Actors, Adiaphorizing Action', both published in *Theory, Culture, Society* in 1990.

ding of *imagination*. 'Popular education' came to be the major instrument
of inducing and keeping alive the collective fantasy which now replaced
unreflective practice of daily togetherness. 'Only beginning with the 18th
century the school was conceived here and there in Europe as a crucible
of nationhood able to develop the civic consciousness. One had to wait
till the next century for the State arming itself with that weapon in order
to realize its objective' [of nation-building].[21]

Unlike the unreflectively self-perpetuating 'communities of belonging'
of which it pretends to be one but is not – the nation must defend its
existence: actively, daily, full-time. Natural as the traits by which it defines
itself might be, the nation may survive only through a contrived and
constantly invigorated, ongoing, guided, structured, rule-led discourse,
and at the cost of enormous work of defining, arguing, legitimating,
heresy-banning.[22] Because of that, nationalisms normally demand power
– that is, the right to use coercion – in order to secure the preservation

---

[21] Willem Frijhoff, 'L'Etat et l'éducation (XVIe–XVIIe siècle): une perspective
globale', in *Culture et l'idéologie dans la genèse de l'Etat moderne* (Ecole
Française de Rome, 1985), p. 101.

[22] In a non-modern (or, to use Kant's terms, non-republican) setting, identity,
in Lyotard's interpretation (cf. Lyotard, *Le Postmoderne expliqué aux enfants*, pp.
68–79), is perpetuated in an automatic, indeed tautological, way, which staves off
both the need and the occasion for critical reflexivity: certain stories are reiterated,
deriving their identity-defining authority from the fact that they are told by 'right
persons', that is persons bearing that identity, but those persons bear that identity
for the very fact that they tell these particular stories. In the modern setting, identity
discourse is, on the contrary, *deliberative*. It must posit questions and undertake
to answer them in a rule-abiding way; it must produce justifications and legitima-
tions, needed to make the enunciations identity-effective, in the course of its own
development. The questions are: 'What ought we to be?', 'What ought we to do so
that we are what we ought to?', 'What can we do for this purpose?'. Questions of
this kind immediately open space for specialists, experts, consultants, and their
work – research, surveys, reports, statistics. They also institute the *regime of
argumentation*. Such a regime is characterized by concerns with decision-making
and legitimation of decisions through reference to careful observation of norms,
the right to make binding statements, and the procedure to eliminate statements
that are not legitimate parts of the discourse. 'Deliberative discourse' of identity,
and its products, are endemically fragile – and that fragility is incurable, as it
conditions whatever affectivity that discourse may have and demonstrate. In
principle, a number of discourses may run alongside each other, resulting in
ambivalence about identities. Deliberative discourse 'makes sense', indeed may
take place at all, only because the ends and values it strives to ground are not
given or certain, and identity is not pre-established, even if the pre-establishment
is used as rhetorical device in the conduct of discourse. Each one of them can in
the end of the day claim no other authority but that of a *project*, that is of a 'will
turned towards an end'.

and continuity of the nation: the condition of immortality is the right to manage the earthly discourse. *State* power fits the bill best. State power means monopoly over the instruments of coercion, including that all-important coercion that forces subjects to abide by the rules of the discourse; only state power is capable of *enforcing* uniform rules of conduct and laws which everybody must obey. As much as the state needs nationalism for its legitimation, nationalism needs the state to be effective. The *national state* is the product of this mutual attraction.

Once the state has been identified with the nation (represented as the organ of the 'self-government' of the nation), the prospect of nationalist successes grows considerably. Nationalism need not rely any more solely on the persuasiveness and cogency of its arguments, and still less on the willingness of the members to accept them. It has now other, more efficient means at its disposal. State power means the chance of enforcing the sole use of the national language in public offices, courts and representative bodies. It means the possibility of mobilizing public resources to boost the competitive chances of the preferred national culture in general, and national literature and arts in particular. It also means, above all, control over education, which is made simultaneously free and obligatory, so that no one is excluded and no one is allowed to escape its influence. Universal education permits the training of all inhabitants of the state territory in the values of the national formula promoted by the state: to make them 'born' patriots, and so to accomplish in practice what has been claimed in theory, namely the 'naturalness' of nationality.

The combined effect of education, of ubiquitous though diffuse cultural pressure, and of state-enforced rules of conduct is the attachment to the way of life associated with the 'national membership'. More often than not, this spiritual bond manifests itself in a conscious and explicit *ethnocentrism*: in the conviction that one's own nation, and everything which relates to it, is right, morally praiseworthy, and beautiful – and vastly superior to anything that may be offered as an alternative; and that what is good for one's own nation should be given precedence over interests of anybody else.

The strength of nationalism rests in the end on the 'connecting' role it plays in the promotion and perpetuation of the social order as defined by the authority of the state. Nationalism, so to speak, 'sequestrates' the diffuse *heterophobia* and mobilizes this sentiment in the service of loyalty and support for the state and discipline toward state authority. It therefore makes the state authority more effective. On the other hand, it deploys the resources of state power to shape social reality in such a way that new supplies of heterophobic anxiety, and hence reserves of mobilizing opportunities, may be generated.

As the state jealously guards its monopoly of coercion, it prohibits, as a rule, all 'private settling of accounts', like ethnic and racial violence. In most cases, it would also disallow and even punish private initiative in petty discrimination. Like all the rest of its resources, it would deploy nationalism as a vehicle of the one and only social order (that is, the order defined, sustained and enforced by the state), while at the same time persecuting its diffuse, spontaneous and thus potentially 'disorderly' manifestations. The mobilizing potential of nationalism will then be harnessed to appropriate state policy – beefing up nationalist sentiments and the patriotic identification with the state through preferably inexpensive, yet prestigious military, economic or sporting victories, as well as through restrictive immigration laws, enforced 'repatriation' and other measures often reflecting, but always reinforcing, the popular heterophobia. The immortality of the nation and the survival of state power merge into a single task one is no more allowed to dissemble.

Survival as group privilege

During the recent 'Operation Desert Storm' the phrase most often pronounced by the generals and the politicians, most emphatically broadcast by the media, and most heartily welcomed by the audience on this side of the battlefront was that the major consideration of the allied commanders was 'to save lives'. That rule was implemented, for all to see and everyone to applaud, through the non-stop carpet bombing of enemy targets, burning and exploding shelters, shooting at close range soldiers in retreat, and – more generally – 'the cut them off and then kill them' policy.

Saving lives turned to mean *taking* them; the survival success of one side had no other measure than the number of corpses on the other. In order to save some lives, one needed to kill more of the others. This all-too-evident paradox raised few eyebrows, and – considering the ocean of printing ink and sound waves which the war released – prompted a negligible amount of comments. Perhaps what was undoubtedly a paradox for a logician or a moralist did not look at all paradoxical to those few who took it upon themselves to secure the triumph of superior, universal values of freedom, justice and world order and to all those, much more numerous, who wished them luck. The faculty of all universal values is to particularize. As French folk wisdom concluded long time ago – *Deux poids, deux mesures*. There are no universal rights for the enemies of universality. And this includes the right to survival – let alone the right to immortality.

Survival of Y (the non-X) defies the *universal* principle of survival of which the survival of a *particular* X is the embodiment, supreme example and ultimate end. Seldom has this truth, built into the existence of selfish species split into selfish groups, been expressed so frankly as in the Nazi project of the world made fit for the immortality of the healthiest and most virile of races. There, the particularity of the Aryan race was proclaimed the universal principle of world order; and the road to transform that particularity into a universal principle was depicted as one leading through the extinction of all other, admittedly numerous, particularities. To express this intention, the language of inter-species competition was borrowed. What the natural sciences of the day (by no means insensitive to the competitive practices of the society in which it was set; Darwin, the naturalist, gleaned his idea of the survival of the fittest from Malthus, a social analyst) believed to be the principle of species' survival, was applied to one part of the species, this part having been declared to be the carrier of the species' universal principle. Non-Aryans were marked with death; they were the less-fit or the un-fit, doomed to extinction, and they exuded the stench of putrefaction and decay, contaminating the atmosphere which the healthy stem of humanity needed clean so as to be able to breathe freely. Their survival was an obstacle to the survival of the healthy race, now made identical with the survival of the species as a whole. Because of that, their extinction was now the condition of species' preservation.

And yet the Nazi project of universal extermination was but an extreme and blatantly vicious solution to the problem which transcends the realm of admittedly totalitarian practices and seems to be endemic to a social condition in which the immortality of the group – whether verbalized as the survival of a nation, of an ethnic tradition, of a culture, or of a civilization serving sacrosanct values – is conceived as an accomplishment not automatically assured, and hence as a problem – as a task calling for conscious design, social engineering, carefully monitored action. *Particular* interests in survival are under such condition always fought for under the banner of *universality*: the transient must *become* durable, the particular must rise to the level of the universal. This has not happened yet, not in a secure, confidence-inspiring fashion; neither can it happen if not fought for with all the acumen and energy that the as-yet-particular carriers of postulated universality can muster. With the present identity unsure of itself and uninsured, still struggling to acquire the certainty which only elevation to universality might eventually bring, and with that universality cast by the present uncertainty into the modality of *becoming* – reality seems to be conspiring against realization of the purpose (which in terms of the universalistic historiosophy is *its own*, innate and endemic, purpose).

Reality (manifested in the resistance to the purpose; perceived *as reality* thanks to that resistance; defined as reality in terms of resistance responsible for the unfulfillment of purpose) must be bridled and subdued, and then forced to become something different from what it is now. With its meaning fully negative, defined by the unfulfillment of the project, reality (both 'natural' and 'social') is denied authority to justify its own right to persist. But neither is there a universal way to legitimate universal credentials of the project bound to supplant it.

It is in the end a group, admittedly something less than the whole – a particularity – which wraps itself in the robe of universality to justify its own survival. Its universal legitimation holds, however, only in as far as other particularities are not allowed to claim universality. Theirs must be a 'sham universality'. Any particularity struggling earnestly for survival must posit other particularities as flawed, at odds with universal principles, as ugly blots on the pristine landscape of universality, on no account worthy of preservation, yearning for a clean-up operation. In the absence of a disinterested verdict which all particularities would be ready to accept, it is invariably the politically organized force which in the end settles the contentious issue of the right to universality. To quote Lyotard again, 'the crisis of identity which the Nazis tried to remedy ... is potentially contained in the republican principle of legitimity'.[23] Always and in all places, in each instance.

Generally speaking, the strategy of group immortality consists in exempting one's own group from the condition of transience which extends to all other categories and collectivities of the human species. Other groups are temporalized; their presence in history is made into an episode. Those groups make a brief entry onto the historical stage which is bound to be promptly followed by an exit. History itself is given the unity of an eternal, uninterrupted continuum by the perpetual, indeed non-temporal presence of one's own group or of principles of which that group claims to be the last and final, the most fulsome incarnation. The permanence of one's own group, and the transience of all the rest, condition and legitimate each other. No wonder the advent of historical thinking, the 'historicity' of the world-view, coincided with the advent of modernity, which posited immortality as a project, a *human task*, and

---

[23] Lyotard, *Le Postmoderne expliqué aux enfants*, p. 81. Lyotard speaks of the 'aporia of authorization' – to be found in every instance when a *particular* institution, say the French General Assembly, signs a declaration of *universal* rights. 'How to know in the end whether the wars conducted by a particular body in the name of universal principles are wars of liberation, or of conquest?' (p. 79)

interpreted that task, for all practical intents, as the *group's* struggle for the universality of its uniqueness.

Indeed, a most prominent feature of the West-European-born modern civilization was temporalization of cultural difference. The different was cast as backward, underdeveloped, retarded, arrested – a relic of the past which outlived its usefulness, its right to exist and its welcome to the stage of fast-moving history. The different stood for the transient; the superior civilization, from which it differed, stood by the same token for all that is durable and potentially timeless: for the ultimate state expected to arise after the principles, which civilization saw itself as promoting, will have been universally implemented. That ultimate state was visualized as a time that denies its own temporality: as an existence no more afflicted by ageing, senescence, senility, decay. Once perfection had been attained, history would stop.

The other way of saying this is that perfection is the state of immortality; once civilization reaches its proclaimed objective of perfection, it will become truly immortal. And, as long as it fights for perfection, it is on the way to that immortality which makes any other pretended durability blatantly transient by comparison. If history is to grind to a halt, and the transience of things human is to be finally overcome, history must be the history of civilization striving for perfection.

The West-European-born modern civilization had won the right to narrate the history of the world; the right which until quite recently it enjoyed and practised unchallenged. (It is today challenged all over the place – by the once 'weaker' sex, by ethnic groups denied their language and by aborigines denied their land – but this challenge, as we will see in later chapters, can be easily taken in its stride by a society not any more excessively worried with immortality.) The right to tell history was gained by force, but the superior killing potential of guns was interpreted as the superiority of Western reason and form of life, so that its practical impact could be in good conscience taken for the clinching argument, if one was needed, on behalf of the peak historical position on which the gun-carriers were perched. As V.G. Kiernan commented in his marvellous study of European military, commercial and spiritual domination, 'colonizing countries did their best to cling to a conviction that they were spreading through the world not merely order, but civilization; which implied that other peoples were not civilized yet, but were capable of becoming so'.[24]

---

[24] V.G. Kiernan, *The Lords of Human Kind* (London: The Cresset Library, 1988), p. 311.

Marx wrote, as of a great philosophical discovery which would determine historical thinking from now on, that in the same fashion in which the anatomy of man was a key to the anatomy of the ape, so the new and improved state of the 'most developed' countries is the key to the understanding of the sore state of those not-yet-so-developed: it approves of some aspects of the latter's present state – such as resemble most the traits prominent in the history-tellers' self-portrait – as endowed with surviving potential, while relegating the other, idiosyncratic and bizarre aspects to the category of living fossils and tomorrow's ashes. From Hegel to Dilthey, the nineteenth century took the globalization of European rule for the proof of achieved or imminent universality of human history.

The past was thus retold as the succession of 'historical nations', each laying bare another small part of the human universal and perpetual essence, each carrying the torch of civilizing fire a step or two further, only to hand it over to its successor (this loudly recited story was complemented by deadly silence in which all sorts of dregs and left-overs – nations which never, even for a brief moment, managed to lift themselves to 'historicity' – were sunk). Those who discovered this ruthless cunning of history's reason were the first successors who announced that they needed no more successors of their own and that by the behest of history they would not be succeeded, thus achieving what all predecessors dreamed but none could attain – true immortality. The civilization which has discovered history and its own historicity, was – by the same token – programmatically ahistorical: it had a beginning, but denied having an end. Having situated itself at the telic point of history, it claimed immunity against history's corroding impact.

Immortality dressed as history

This was the general strategy, applied on the most global of scales. But it also set a pattern for a multitude of smaller-scale imitations. In a history-conscious culture, the general plan of history-telling which sustains immortality as the privilege of history-tellers tends to be applied universally, and on all levels. The struggle for national privilege which filled the modern era was as a rule a struggle for the exclusive right to history-telling: a struggle for the right to represent the past of one's own nation (more precisely – the past aspired to and claimed by one's own nation, appropriated by it as the object of exclusive administration, and hotly defended against impostors claiming it as part of their own 'tradition' or 'heritage') as *history*. This could be done only at the expense of the power-assisted forgetting of some other pasts – unfit to be accommodated, too obviously associated with contemporary competitors, and hence bound to be devalued and disowned. That condemned past was glossed over in silence and thus made into non-history. Alternatively, in case such radical treatment was not feasible, it was diminished in significance or degraded in moral value.

This was an expectable strategy. After all, the vehemence with which the right to tell history is fought for derives from the crucial role which the length and weight of the group's past existence plays among the resources deployed to assure the group's future survival, which always means making out of immortality the group's privilege. (Often, symptomatically, that past existence is talked about from the start as 'our *immortal* heritage'; an expression which – cleverly because it is on the sly – pre-empts all discussion of grounds or substance, and all doubts as to the power of the past to secure the durable future.) The pattern is repeated endlessly, but with variable success. Some successes are more lasting than others. Sometimes, because no competitor seems to be eager to steal the 'heritage'; but more often because the odds are overwhelming – as the current might of the history-tellers gives the opposition little chance to reclaim the stolen property or to restore splendour to the objects officially consigned to the 'dustbin of history'.

Attempts of the conquerors to sap the identity of conquered groups, and thus to make their own coercive domination more lasting by re-forging it into cultural hegemony, include as a rule the ban on historical narratives of the vanquished groups as one of the most urgent and doggedly pursued measures. Through enticement or threats, the defeated groups are goaded to forget their history; short of forgetting – to feel ashamed and embarrassed of it and thus unwilling to narrate it in public. Group identity is shown as having no future if it has been effectively denied a past worth preserving. The writers and tellers of the conquered people's history are muzzled, put in jail, or bribed or befuddled to retune their narratives. Educational institutions of the conquered – those principal vehicles of continuous memory dressed as tribal immortality – are disbanded, forbidden to give instruction in history, or supplied with new textbooks and new curricula. Prohibition of the group's own language, that carrier of separate history sedimented in autonomous culture, is the extreme and the most radical of measures to which the conquerors gladly resort whenever they find it practicable.

With each change in the balance of power, history-telling starts anew. Hegemony over historical consciousness is closely correlated with the domination over material conditions of the present – and the mutual dependence shows itself in both directions. Hegemony follows the domination – but often the challenge to the second starts with a guerrilla warfare against the first.

The efforts to retell history in a different fashion, to distribute the highlights and shadows in a novel way, often reflect the internecine, inter-elite struggles for the hegemony over the group. In the same way as it is done in the case of inter-group contests, competing elites defend and prove their entitlements to the sole representation of 'universal values', appropriated collectively by the group, by claiming the particular antiquity of their own respective heirlooms within the ostensibly common tradition; they need to play up the prominence of their own ancestry and belittle or decry that of the competing elites. To achieve this effect, they struggle to immortalize in retrospect their own selection of great names or deeds; they promote their own rosters of saints and villains; they strive to redraw the lines between the 'historic' and the 'non-historic', noble and base, transient and durable.

An almost clinical example of this role of past history as the battle-ground on which the present power conflicts are fought out, could be observed recently in the orgy of history-book shredding, museum closures, street-renaming and dismantling of monuments which over-whelmed the whole of post-communist East-Central Europe; most illumi-natingly, in the territory which for the last forty years was styled as the 'German Democratic Republic', and through all these years struggled to construe its own version of German identity by rewriting the heretofore shared orthodox version of the German past. The jubilant rejection of the rewritten narrative, with all its symbolic corollaries, was the first and perhaps decisive link in the long chain of surrender acts which combined into the *Anschluss* of the 'other Germany'.

Mortality collectivized

Construction of group immortality can be interpreted as an attempt to harness the energy generated by death-anxiety in the service of specific group interests and, of course, the interests of the group's extant or aspiring elites. The ubiquitous drive to transcend biological mortality, whether in a consciously embraced and reflected-upon form, or as an unrecognized, subconscious pressure, saturates the life-pursuits of all 'normal' individuals and actively seeks outlets through which gathering energy could be released. Some of such outlets are as individual as the anxieties they serve. As long, however, as individual autonomy remains a privilege which only relatively few individuals possess (and it does remain such a privilege, a criterion of distinction, a stratifying principle in most societies),[25] individually operated outlets are not a feasible proposition for a great majority of people. In addition, and perhaps more importantly still, they are potentially disruptive from the point of view of the extant and defended societal structure of domination.

The individuals who can release their own drive to transcendence through autonomously operated outlets can do to a large extent without institutionalized, power-assisted facilities. This gives them a measure of independence which bodes ill for social discipline, and worse still for the security of dominant elites. The privileged individuals can in principle win their own share of immortality in open defiance of official immortality-bestowing agencies. Perhaps they can even win a better quality, a 'more securely immortal' kind of immortality than the one which the official distributors are capable of mustering for themselves. (And they know it – well enough to tease the powerful and make them diffident by asking, with malicious glee, who in the French government of the time was in charge of culture when Balzac wrote his novels.) In this respect at least (and this is, politically, a potent respect) they are able to take lightly the blackmail of the rulers and deride the baits of the appointed gatekeepers of immortality – and thus deprive the powers of the day of their most effective weapon. Max Frisch, the great Swiss writer remembered as a symbol of defiance against legislating ambitions of the powers that be, could afford to define identity 'as the alienation from what others demand you to be and what they fix in the name they give you'. Frisch could also afford to oppose to the principle of residence (that is, sovereignty defined as a property of state-territorial domain), the principle of the *oeuvre* as the defining trait of life and immortality.[26]

The self-confidence and obstreperous self-reliance which only the availability of individual outlets of transcendence might offer was and remains one of the main reasons of that endemic mistrust of the intellectuals from which no dominant elite has thus far managed to be entirely free. On no account can the fear of the potential 'individual immortals' be dismissed as a manifestation of the power-holders' paranoia. Quite realistically, political elites expect the challenge to their domination to emerge from among the privileged, and from the privileged only; from those who

---

[25] For the comprehensive argument to this effect, see my *Freedom* (Milton Keynes: Open University Press, 1988).

[26] Quoted after Michel Contat, 'L'homme sans identité', in *Le Monde*, 6 April 1991, p. 11.

have already gained the bridgehead of individual autonomy from which they can launch the conquest of universality. It is such people, and such people only, who can escape the hold of the current rulers. Worse still, they are the only ones who can find enough zeal and courage to poach those rulers' game; to put together a seductive, credible counter-offer to the masses whose needs of transcendence have been thus far channelled through collective outlets administered by the extant elite.

As for the masses – that is, those not yet lifted to the level of individual autonomy, or possessed of but a limited, truncated, or make-believe individuality – they have no access to the individual outlets of the transcendence drive, which makes them likely, and indeed eager, to fall into the 'collective immortality' nets. That collective immortality does not promise them individuality – no more than their life secured it for them in practice. The future of the group they are asked to assure through their labours and sacrifice will not have their names engraved upon it. They will at best enter that future anonymously, in the same fashion they live now – as a mass, a 'people' – numbers graspable solely through statistical tables. As far as they are concerned, the group is selfish not only outwardly, but inwardly as well (perhaps inwardly above all): it demands, loudly and convincingly, that they renounce all private ambitions and invest their cravings for survival solely in the 'welfare of the group'. It requires that they disregard many, perhaps all, deeply felt needs   dismissed in advance as 'mere wants', declared irrelevant for the supreme task of the group continuity which 'is in everybody's interest' (and that they are publicly condemned as 'selfish' in case they persist calling their 'wants' needs). If the group can get away with all this, it is because to the masses, with their earthly lives blatantly and irredeemably collectivized, the chance of surviving in a similarly collectivized form seems the only sensible bet; one that is both accessible and desirable.

This circumstance cements 'the masses' (the underdog, the 'uneducated' 'lower classes', the disprivileged, the non-individuals deprived of the individually operated vehicles of transcendence) – into the staunchest bulwark of nationalisms and xenophobia. It makes them the most enthusiastic fans and most resolute warriors of collective glory – be it, as far as they are concerned, but a derived, reflected one. The might of the selfish group is, after all, their only recompense for the depressing lack of individual power – such power as would make them, on the contrary, into autonomous and self-reliant individuals (like the intellectuals and the rich are) were they in their possession. With their private hopes for transcendence doomed from the start and thus seldom consciously entertained, the perpetuity of the group is the masses' only (even if second best) chance of immortality. They bask in the glow of the group's superiority over its competitors; they will do a lot to assist the group's selective survival – that is, the survival of the group bought at the price of the demise or denigration of its competitors. This is the only defiance of mortality they can reasonably contemplate; the only form in which immortality can (if only obliquely, as an anonymous share) become their lot.

The connection was well understood by Johann Gottlieb Fichte, an early prophet of modern German nationhood. Indeed, it has turned into a guiding idea of his *Addresses to the German Nation*. 'The thirst for posthumous fame is contemptible vanity', Fichte – one of the most ambitious men of his generation, who proclaimed the right of intellect, and intellect alone, to immortality – reassured his less endowed would-be compatriot; as for the latter, he hastened to explain, 'does he not wish to pay for his place on this earth and the short time allotted to him with something that even here below will endure forever, so that he, the individual, although unnamed in history ... may yet in his consciousness and his faith leave behind him unmistakable memories that he, too, was a dweller on the earth?' For him who in his earthly life had little chance to find out that he indeed was an 'individual', unique and unrepeatable as well as undisposable – the only realistic form immortality may take is one 'founded on the hope of eternal continuance of the people without admixture of, or corruption by, any alien element which does not belong to the totality.' This is the immortality he can sensibly bid for as the 'eternal thing to which he entrusts the eternity of himself'. With that collectivization – indeed, depersonalization – of immortality dreams, death itself sheds its individuality, so that it can chime in with the life that had been denied it before: 'he to whom a fatherland has been handed down ... fights to the last drop of his blood to hand on the precious possession unimpaired to his posterity'. To the loyal sons of their nations, who mind not their lives if a glittering prospect of the nation's eternity is brandished beyond the corpses of nation's enemies, Fichte has consolation to offer: 'For it, for an order of things that long after his death should blossom on their graves, they so joyfully shed their blood ... [A] true German could only want to live in order to be, and to remain, just a German and to bring up his children as Germans.'[27]

The mass condition, as long as it persists, is for this reason as well a fertile soil for totalitarian group politics – sternly disciplinarian inwardly, selfish and cruel outwardly. Groups stay selfish – *can* and *must* stay selfish

---

[27] Johann Gottlieb Fichte, *Addresses to the German Nation*, trans. R.F. Jones and G.H. Turnbull (Westport, Conn.: Greenwood Press, 1979), pp. 133–7, 142, 144.

– as long as the bulk of their members are denied individuality. Peaceful coexistence between groups and equal distribution of freedom inside the groups are intimately intertwined.

Group selfishness, group concern with collective competitive survival stems from the denial of resources of individual transcendence to group members, or to the great number of group members, transformed by the act of that denial into masses. Once set in motion, however, the prevalence of actions aimed (realistically or not) at the attainment of group survival tends in its turn to reinforce the conditions which made it indispensable in the first place; it sinks the group members deeper still into their existential predicament of the masses. The group can offer a decent service to its masses (to wit, make the demonstration of the group's chance of immortality ever more spectacular and convincing) only if the surrender of group members to 'collective welfare', to the detriment of their own chances of individualization, is irrevocable and more complete by the day: if the access of individual outlets for transcendence drive is cut off for good. There is no easy exit from the resulting vicious circle.

The group sees to it that the more complete and unthinking the surrender, the more it feels like the passport to immortal glory. In an apt summary of such a formula by Tsvetan Todorov, 'it becomes possible to sacrifice an indeterminate number of human lives in the name of the defense of The Man ... The heroes are thus ready to sacrifice their own lives as well as lives of the others, providing the sacrifice serves the chosen objective'.[28] The chosen objective in question is the idea of the group – and it does not matter how many members of the group die for the sake of the survival of that idea; in a macabre dance of means and ends, the immortality of the group worth dying for – the proud, dignified, glorious group – comes to be measured by the readiness of its members to give up their lives at the group's behest. The group reassures itself of immortality through counting its dead. It is death that turns into a symbol of the group's immortality. The more of it, the better.

This, one must admit, is no mean accomplishment. The basic resource of human survival – the capital of spontaneous sociability, of human fellowship, of togetherness – has been expropriated, hoarded into a treasure entrusted to the sole administration of the group's properly established authorities, and used to finance the demotion of human survival in the hierarchy of values worth defending. The group does not teach its members altruistic concern with the well-being of their fellows; it only creams off the propensities and skills which are already there, and

---

[28] Tsvetan Todorov, *Face à l'extrême* (Paris: Seuil, 1991), pp. 14, 16.

having gathered a sufficient volume, dismisses the remainder as contemptible clannish selfishness. Collectivized selfishness of the group sucks its life juices out of elemental human openness toward fellow humans – until only a desiccated hulk in the flaccid non-shape of the masses is left.

As Paul Tillich suggested, anxiety about emptiness and meaninglessness of life has in our times supplanted the older anxieties about fate, guilt and condemnation. I propose that this change has been intimately related to the expropriation of sociability by the groups bent on self-preservation.

Anxiety about death is a universal human feature, indeed the defining trait of specifically human existence. But what is the anxiety about death an anxiety about? Of what, we fear, our death will deprive us? While seeking an answer to this question, we can do worse than consider one offered by Joseph Haroutunian:

> Since human life is a transaction, a communion, human death is the end of transaction or a failure of communion. The being which is annihilated by death is a *being with*, a coexistence, a fellowmanhood. Death, therefore, is not the cessation of physical life, or the dissolution of organism as such, but the separation of fellowmen from one another, which is the death of the human being. [Anxiety about death] is not anxiety about the loss of being as such, but anxiety about the absence from the company of these fellows . . . The anxiety about death which is proper to a human being is a function of love. We are anxious about death, or rather about annihilation, because, on whole, we love our neighbours as ourselves.[29]

The expropriation of sociability, the far-reaching atomization, displacement of fellowhood by administration – which are all marks of modern mass society – replaced the traditional anxiety about death with the specifically modern anxiety about emptiness and meaninglessness of the life itself. The loneliness resulting from the 'failure of communion' is not any more the terrible fate lurking at the horizon of death. It starts well before death becomes an immediate prospect – it permeates life itself. This makes perhaps the task of group survival easier; the demanded sacrifice does not seem that big anymore. Wars, complete with the mass murder and mass suicide that accompany them, may seem an eminently more meaningful alternative to the emptiness of peaceful life. This circumstance, however, also makes living that much more difficult. One is tempted to say that the true price paid for the immortality of the selfish group is death which is easier than life.

---

[29] Joseph Harontunian, 'Life and Death Among Fellowmen', in: *The Modern Vision of Death*, ed. Nathan A. Scott, Jr (Richmond: John Knox Press, 1967), pp. 84 –5, 87–8.

4

Modernity, or Deconstructing Mortality

Norbert Elias noted 'a peculiar embarrassment felt by the living in the presence of dying people. They often do not know what to say. The range of words available for use in this situation is relatively narrow.' Elias added a comment: 'Feelings of embarrassment hold words back.'[1] *Civilization* – that code-word modernity has chosen in order to set itself apart and put itself in a commanding position regarding its predecessors and neighbours in space – lifted the threshold of shame. Unlike our distant ancestors and 'people unlike us', we do not discuss cruel and gory matters. We hide in closets things which the others did or do in public. We are abhorred by the flashes of realities we have chased down into the no-go cellars of our orderly and elegant existence, having proclaimed them non-existent or at least unspeakable. Death is just one of those things that have been so evicted; hence embarrassment, the trained emotion of shame, that makes us numb when we meet death face to face.

Though Elias's description of our curious verbal and attitudinal ineptitude in the face of dying is unquestionably correct, his explanation of it is not the only one that comes to mind. Indeed, we do not know what to tell the dying, though we gladly and easily conversed with them before. Yes, we feel embarrassed, and to avoid feeling ashamed we prefer not to find ourselves in the presence of the dying, though before they came to be dying we avidly sought their company and enjoyed every moment of togetherness. Is it then the trained incapacity to verbalize deep, harsh, harrowing emotions that condemns us to silence? Is it our civilized aversion to cruelty that condemns the dying to loneliness?

Perhaps it is not just the delicacy of manners that deprives us of speech

---

[1] Norbert Elias, *The Loneliness of the Dying*, trans. Edmond Jephcott (Oxford: Blackwell, 1985), p. 23.

(not that delicacy alone), but also the simple fact that, indeed, we have nothing to say to a person who has no further use for the language of survival; a person who is about to leave the world of busy pretence that that language conjures up and sustains. For a few centuries now, death stopped being the *entry* into another phase of being which it once was; death has been reduced to an *exit* pure and simple, a moment of cessation, an end to all purpose and planning. Death is now the thoroughly private ending of that thoroughly private affair called life. Death, therefore, has no meaning that can be expressed in the only vocabulary we are trained and allowed to use; the vocabulary geared, above all, to the collective and public denial or concealment of that limit to our potency. We may offer the dying only the language of survival; but this is precisely the one language which cannot grasp the condition from which they (unlike us, who may still desert them and look the other way) can hide no more.

The language of survival is an *instrumental* language, meant to serve and guide instrumental *action*. It is a language of *means* and ends; of actions that derive their meaning from the ends they serve, and their reason from serving the ends well. This language can accommodate the phenomenon of death only the way it accommodates all other elements of instrumentalized life: as an object of practice, of an informed, targeted and focused effort. As a specific event, with a specific and avoidable cause: an event which enters the vision, the realm of the meaningful, only through the *task of prompting or preventing it*, of making it happen or not allowing it to happen. To be expressed in such instrumental language, death must first be translated into the vocabulary of *potentially* terminal, yet also potentially curable, diseases. The most exceptionless of *norms* of human existence must be thus re-presented as *abnormality*; the most certain (the only truly certain) of all life events must be dissolved in a collection of contingent conditions, each with an uncertain consequence: not-unavoidable conditions, conditions-which-may-be-changed, *manipulable* conditions. Certainty of death incapacitates; uncertainty of outcome boosts energy and spurs into action. In the language of survival, practical concerns with specific dangers to life elbow out the metaphysical concern with death as the inescapable ending to existence. Keeping fit, taking exercise, 'balancing the diet', eating fibres and not eating fat, avoiding smokers or fighting the pollution of drinking water are all feasible tasks, tasks that can be performed and that redefine the unmanageable problem (or, rather, non-problem) of death (which one can do nothing about) as a series of utterly manageable problems (which one can do something about; indeed, which one can do a lot about).

This serves well the needs of all *except* the dying; that is, those who can do nothing, as they face no task requiring action and making action meaningful. What advice can we offer them? Whatever we say will sound false and meaningless, because whatever they do will serve no purpose. This is why we prefer to keep them at a distance, at which communication is no more possible. The dying die not so much in *loneliness*, as *in silence*. There is nothing we can communicate about in the only language we both command and share – the language of survival. It is the impossibility to communicate, the silence between us, the cowardly silence that hides the impotence, that is the deepest cause of embarrassment. Our usual resourcefulness and industry have failed us, and this is something to be ashamed of in the world that measures human quality by the amount of know-how demonstrated in the efficiency and effectiveness of action.

The failure to communicate with the dying is the price which we, the denizens of the modern world, pay for the luxury of life from which the spectre of death has been exorcised for the duration; the price for the peculiarly modern way of (to recall Franz Rosenzweig's poignant words) taking 'from death its sting and from Hades his pestilential breath'. Modern instrumentality has *deconstructed mortality*. Deconstruction does not abolish death. It has only left it unadorned, naked, stripped of significance. Death is nothing but waste in the production of life; a useless leftover, the total stranger in the semiotically rich, busy, confident world of adroit and ingenious actors. Death is *the Other* of modern life. True, death was always 'the Other' of life. Being the Other of *modern* life is, however, a peculiar condition as modernity has its own and uniquely modern way of coping with the Other of itself.

Claude Levi-Strauss suggested that one of the crucial differences between our, modern, type of society and other, simpler, societies is that they are 'anthropophagic', while we are 'anthropoemic': they *eat* their enemies, while we *vomit* ours. Our way of dealing with the Other (and thus, obliquely, of producing and re-producing our own identity) is to segregate, separate, dump onto the rubbish tip, flush down into the sewer of oblivion. How differently do the 'cannibals', literal or metaphoric, genuine or imagined,[2] behave. As Eric Cheyfitz suggested in his recent

---

[2] There is really no way of knowing to what extent the horror stories with which the narratives of the European 'encounter with the savages' abound were reports of the true practices of alien tribes, and to what extent projections of the narrators' own tribe's forcefully promoted identity. The very word 'cannibal' was introduced into European languages by Columbus, who allegedly heard it from his Indian informers, with whom, however, on his own admission he could not converse. 'Cannibalism' quickly turned into a definition and proof of the savagery of the

study of the Western 'writing of savagery', 'cannibalism expresses, or figures forth, a radical idea of kinship that cuts across the frontiers of hostile groups'; 'cannibalism, like kinship, expresses forthrightly the essentially equivocal relationship that obtains between self and other'.[3] Cannibalism, one is tempted to say, is an oblique – both perverse and surreptitious – tribute to the non-finality, non-absoluteness of the division between the self and the other; to the same continuous and irresolvable dialectics of unity and difference, separation and reunion, which in a different, less dramatic and more routine mode is encapsulated in the 'pre-modern' tendency to articulate intra- and inter-societal *divisions* in terms of *kinship* and *affinity*, or in the interplay of marriage union and incest prohibition. In the modern anthropoemic posture, none of the kinship dialectics is left. The rift between self and other tends to be constituted as absolute and irrevocable. Separation would not betray its relativity in the prospect of reunion. Its finality needs to be sustained through material or symbolic annihilation of the other.

The modern treatment of death and the dying – the behavioural code through which the modern 'deconstruction of mortality' is attained – is but one case in the generally 'anthropoemic' way of constituting the Other and coping with its constituted presence.

The Other of emancipation

Modernity is drive to mastery; a mode of being shot through with hope, ambition and confidence – a behavioural-attitudinal complex correlated

---

savages. Eating one's enemies, after all, was a habit diametrically opposite to our own, *anthropoemic*, style – and one that for this reason and in accordance with the selfsame anthropoemic style could not but be revolting and arouse a most intense desire of self-distancing.

[3] Eric Cheyfitz, *The Poetics of Imperialism: Translation and Colonisation from 'The Tempest' to 'Tarzan'* (London: Oxford University Press, 1991), p. 149. In *Time and the Other: How Anthropology Makes its Object* (New York: Columbia University Press, 1983), Johannes Fabian elaborates on the concept of *chronopolitics*: following the European drive to global domination, 'anthropology emerged and established itself as an allochronic discourse; it is a science of other men in another time'. To 'rationalize and ideologically justify' Western superiority 'always needed schemes of allochronic distancing' (pp. 143, 149). Fabian comes too close to implying a rather crude, interested functionality of the form in which the 'savage other' had been constituted in European mind and its scholarly expressions. It would be more prudent to put aside the imputation of calculated propaganda exercise, and confine oneself to the intimate link between the practice of domination and the world-view intellectually reflecting the universe shaped by the power relations such practice could not but sediment.

with what François Lyotard described as the Cartesian determination 'to graft finality upon a time-series ordered by subordination and appropriation of "nature"'. This mode came to dominate European life by the eighteenth century, and found its most manifest theoretical expression in the philosophy of Enlightenment.

Mastery over nature could mean nothing else but emancipation from necessity. The meaning of *emancipation* derived from the fashion in which *necessity* was theorized (it could be the emancipation from ignorance, from parochiality, from exploitation, from poverty); so did the vehicles trusted to bring emancipation about (it could be cultural crusade, uniformity of law, revolution, scientific-technological progress). The discord and differences notwithstanding, all the models of emancipation, and all the tools of their fulfilment, converged ultimately on the vision of history as a time-series leading eventually to 'universal liberty, the acquittal of entire humanity'.[4]

The drive to mastery (to emancipation from necessity, from dependence, from un-freedom) which we call 'modernity' would suffer resistance badly. Voltaire's *écraser l'infamie* paired with Helvetius' *l'éducation peut tout* stood for that mixture of breath-taking ambition and boundless self-confidence that rebounded in the sense of mission which recognized no obstacles and tolerated no excuses. We can do it, we want to do it, we will do it. The ignorant will be enlightened, the savages civilized, the disorderly made to serve the order of things. The world will be the playground of reason – human reason. No more the unexpected, the unpredicted and unpredictable. No more contingency. Everything permitted to be will have first to pass the reason's test of utility. The fête of universal liberty will be by invitation only.

Should one wonder, therefore, that in the eighteenth century 'death was for the first time conceived as the major scandal of the whole of human adventure'?[5] Until then, in Ariès's famous expression, death was 'tame'; but so was the world in general, with all its daily calamities, plagues, wars and

---

[4] Jean-François Lyotard, *Le Postmoderne expliqué aux enfants: Correspondence, 1982–1985* (Paris: Galilée, 1988), pp. 44–5.

[5] Michel Vovelle, *La Mort et l'Occident, de 1300 à nos jours* (Paris: Gallimard, 1983), p. 382. Expectedly, the first reaction to the realization that the scandal would not go away and would not be easily talked down was a conspiracy of silence: 'Philosophers or simply men of good taste ... agreed on one point: one should stop to agonize about death, and to make it into the main worry of one's life. Commenting on Pascal's thought that "it is easier to bear death without thinking, than to think of death without dying", Voltaire remarked derisively that "it cannot be said that the man bears with death well or ill, if he does not think of it at all. He who feels nothing suffers not."' (p. 384)

floods. Not that violent and cruel breaks in the life routine were easy to put up with, let alone could be enjoyed: but the sudden and ruthless violations of the routine seemed equally 'normal', immutable, inescapable – indeed, God-send – as the routine itself. They all belonged to the human fate, and it was not the task of the humans to change the fate. What cannot be changed may be regretted or bewailed, but in the end it has to be lived with. Most importantly, it does not spur into action, does not threaten with the sense of failure, and thus does not humiliate. But what if the fate can be changed, the world can be made into a safer and more agreeable place, and if it is human practice, guided by human reason, which can secure that change? The 'tame' turns then into 'wild'. Its persistence is now a reproof and a challenge, as it has no right to be what it is and as it has been only by the dint of human sloth, wrongdoing or ineptitude that it is allowed to remain in its present disagreeable state. Its persistence is a scandal. Of all adversities of earthly existence, death soon emerged as the most persistent and indifferent to human effort. It was, indeed, the *major* scandal. The hard, irreducible core of human impotence in a world increasingly subject to human will and acumen. The last, yet seemingly irremovable, relic of fate in a world increasingly designed and controlled by reason.

Death was an emphatic denial of everything that the brave new world of modernity stood for, and above all of its arrogant promise of the indivisible sovereignty of reason. The moment it ceased to be 'tame', death has become a guilty secret; literally, a skeleton in the cupboard left in the neat, orderly, functional and pleasing home modernity promised to build. The most arduous precautions were to be taken to prevent the skeleton from being discovered; short of that, aired; short of that, advertised as one of the property's features. The sad fact that it has not been, and is unlikely ever to be, removed was to be hidden beneath a thick protective cover of silence. Death, in Geoffrey Gorer's memorable rendering, turned into that 'aspect of human experience' which 'is treated as inherently shameful and abhorrent, so that it can never be discussed or referred to openly, and experience of it tends to be clandestine and accompanied by feelings of guilt and unworthiness'.[6] Death has become unmentionable. One did not

---

[6] Geoffrey Gorer, 'The Pornography of Death', first published in *Encounter* (1955). Here quoted after Geoffrey Gorer, *Death, Grief, and Mourning in Contemporary Britain* (London: Cresset Press, 1965), p. 171. The topic of death has been, so to speak, *tabooed*: it can be vented only in fantasy 'charged with pleasurable guilt or guilty pleasure' – the distinctive mark of *pornography*. 'If we make death unmentionable in polite society – "not before the children" – we almost ensure

speak of death – not willingly, at any rate, and never without embarrassment. (Indeed, bringing a secret into the open is always embarrassing, as
it calls for a publicly acceptable reaction for which no publicly accepted
rules or guidelines may, or should be established.) Prolonged silence had
resulted in a collective inability to discuss death meaningfully and behave
sensibly towards those whom death affected in a fashion impossible to
hide – towards the terminally ill, the bereaved, the mourners.

Robert Fulton summed the effects up succinctly: 'We are beginning to
react to death as we would to a communicable disease . . . Death is coming
to be seen as the consequence of personal neglect or untoward accident.
As in the manner of many contagious diseases, those who are caught in
the throes of death are isolated from their fellow human beings.' Gorer
remembers reactions of friends to the grief caused by bereavement:

> The people whose invitations I had refused, educated and sophisticated
> though they were, mumbled and hurried away. They clearly no longer had
> any guidance from ritual as to the way to treat a self-confessed mourner;
> and, I suspect, they were frightened lest I give way to my grief, and involve
> them in a distasteful upsurge of emotion.

Furtive glances, incoherent mumblings that masked the absence of
words, the all-too-obvious relief at taking one's leave – are unmistakable
signs of *the trained incapacity* sedimented by the protracted conspiracy
of silence. There are no taught and learned ways of reacting to other
peoples' grief; nor are there socially taught and approved outlets for the
grief of one's own. Hence the 'maladaptive behaviour' 'from the triviality
of meaningless "busy-ness" through the private rituals of what I have
called mummification to the apathy of despair'.[7] (One may note that the
manifestly irrational behaviour Gorer observed was strikingly reminiscent
of the incongruous tussle of a stickleback, the nest-building fish, recorded
by the experimenters who put it in an aquarium too small to separate the
'defended territory' from the avoided 'out there'; with the instinctual

---

the continuation of the "horror comics".' (p. 175) And pornographic fantasy comes
into its own when and where realistic conduct is not a viable proposition: 'in
England, at any rate, belief in the future life as taught in Christian doctrine is very
uncommon today even in the minority who make churchgoing or prayer a
consistent part of their lives.' Expectably, 'Without some such belief natural death
and physical decomposition have become too horrible to contemplate or to
discuss' (p. 173) – that is, to discuss rationally, rather than fantasize about with that
'pleasurable guilt' proper to pornography.
    [7] 'Introduction' to *Death and Identity*, ed. Robert Fulton (New York: John Wiley
& Sons, 1965), p. 4; Gorer, *Death, Grief, and Mourning*, pp. 14, 110.

guidance useless in that extraordinary situation, the hapless victim of the experiment took neither offensive nor defensive posture, instead burying its head in sand as if preparing for the nest building.)

The overall result of collective de-skilling had been the characteristically modern mixture of public callousness and private squeamishness, which marked most common reactions to the emotional pain gone through by the bereaved and people in mourning. Equally modern was the emphatic refusal either to display or to watch the spectacle of death. Off went the elaborate conspicuousness and ostentatious splendour of public funerals; the executions of criminals, once the favourite occasion for public festivities, came to be performed surreptitiously, at unsocial hours, behind thick walls, with as few witnesses as absolutely necessary; finally, the dead themselves, once accommodated in the churchyards as if to remind the churchgoers every Sunday of the vanity of their earthly pursuits, had been removed to a secure distance from the living quarters, and confined to the graveyard ghettos meant to separate and banish not just the corpses but also the bereaved who visited them. In Michel Vovelle's words,

> The ultimate formulation of that refusal of the spectacle of death, after the decline of baroque pomp [of public funeral processions] and the repugnance of public executions, is found in the process of removing the dead themselves away from the world of the living ... All authorities – civilian, scientific, ecclesiastic – conspired to establish in big cities, towards the end of the 18th century, cemeteries located at a longest possible distance from the heart of the city. The Royal Edict of 1776, which forbade burying the dead in churchyards, merely sanctioned the spontaneous evolution.[8]

The itinerary of the funeral cortege had been cut to the bare minimum, and in most cases ensconced within the walls of the graveyard, so that it would not offend the eyes and the feelings of the 'innocent by-passers'. As a matter of fact, through the new habit of the hospitalization of the dying, isolation from public view starts long before the last rites – indeed, at the first sign of the approaching death. As Philippe Ariès suggested, death (alongside all other acts betraying the 'biological underside' of Homo *Sapiens*) became *indecent* – dirty and polluting. People blighted with such a shameful and repelling affliction were to be kept out of sight. A new image of death was formed: 'death ugly and hidden, hidden because ugly and dirty'.[9]

---

[8] Michel Vovelle, *Mourir autrefois: attitudes collectives devant la mort aux XVIIe et XVIIIe siècles* (Paris: Gallimard, 1974), p. 200.

[9] Philippe Ariès, *L'Homme devant la mort* (Paris: Seuil, 1977), p. 563. Ariès suggests that it was the abhorrence of death that spilled over onto all perceptible

And yet better still than by thick walls of remote cemeteries, the semi-secrecy of funerals, the isolation of the mourners and the eviction of the dying from family homes (and, indeed, from the space where life was to be conducted in a manner oblivious of mortality) to hospitals, hospices or nursing homes, the conspiracy of silence had been protected by the expedient of the *analytical* deconstruction of mortality. In modern times, writes Ruth Menahem in *La Mort apprivoisée*, 'death is resented as something coming "from the outside"; one does not die, one *is killed* by something ("what was it that killed him?" – we tend to ask)'.[10] From the existential and *unavoidable* predicament of humanity, mortality had been deconstructed into diverse events of private death, each with its own *avoidable* cause; death as the fact of *nature* has been deconstructed into a set of outcomes of many and varied, yet unmistakably and invariably *human*, actions. Death came perilously close to be declared a personal guilt; in the wake of the modern deconstruction of mortality, it is barely conceivable that there should be no one guilty of the cessation of life; no nameable, identifiable culprit behind the criminal act of 'killing'. 'One does not address death anymore', says Ariès, 'as phenomenon that is natural and necessary. Death is a defeat, a *business lost* ... When death arrives, it is considered as an accident, a sign of impotence or misdemeanour ...'[11]

The truth that death cannot be escaped 'in the end' is not denied, of course. It cannot be denied; but it could be held off the agenda, elbowed out by another truth: that each *particular* case of death (most importantly,

---

signs of its imminence – sights or scents of approaching death. Hence, indeed, the loneliness of dying. The living were to be spared, if possible, visual or olfactory reminders of irremediable transitoriness of life. 'Death has been pushed into the underground.' (p. 555) Around 1870 cremating the dead – the ultimate method to dispose of the corpse completely and definitely – was introduced and fast gathered popularity.

Modern men and women, notes Vovelle, 'decided not to speak of death anymore' (*La Mort et l'Occident*, p. 670). In the last third of the nineteenth century death, according to Ariès, 'would be effaced, would disappear. It would become shameful and forbidden ... One must avoid – no longer for the sake of the dying person, but for society's sake, for the sake of those close to the dying person – the disturbance and the overly strong and unbearable emotion caused by the ugliness of dying and by the very presence of death in the midst of a happy life.' (*Modern Attitudes toward Death: From the Middle Ages to the Present*, trans. Patricia M. Ranum (Baltimore: John Hopkins University Press, 1974), pp. 85, 87.)

[10] Quoted after Odette Thibault, *Maîtrise de la mort* (Paris: Editions Universitaires, 1975), p. 34.

[11] Ariès, *L'Homme devant la mort*, p. 580.

death which threatens the particular person – me; at the particular moment – *now*) can be resisted, postponed, or avoided altogether. Death as such is inevitable; but each concrete instance of death is contingent. Death is omnipotent and invincible; but none of the specific cases of death is.

All deaths have causes, each death has a cause, each particular death has its particular cause. Corpses are cut open, explored, scanned, tested, until *the cause* is found: a blood clot, kidney failure, haemorrhage, heart arrest, lung collapse. We do not hear of people dying of mortality. They die only of individual *causes*, they die *because* there *was an individual cause*. No post-mortem examination is considered complete until the individual cause has been revealed. There are so many causes of death; given enough time, one can name them all. If I defeat, escape or cheat twenty among them, twenty less will be left to defeat me. One does not just die; one dies of a *disease* or of *murder*. I can do nothing to defy mortality. But I can do quite a lot to avoid a blood clot or a lung cancer. I can stop eating eggs, refrain from smoking, do physical exercises, keep my weight down; I can do so many other things as well. And while doing all these right things and forcing myself to abstain from the wrong ones, I have no time left to ruminate over the *ultimate* futility of each thing I am doing; over the sombre and potentially incapacitating truth that however foolproof each measure I take could be made, this does not in the least detract from the uselessness of them all taken together. Thus the cause of instrumental rationality celebrates ever new triumphant battles – and in the din of festivities the news of the lost war are inaudible.

This is how we are trained to think (or not to think). According to some American research, an average child who reached the age of fourteen by 1971 would have watched about 18,000 cases of death on TV.[12] Most of those people who died on the screen were killed. Some others (though not at all that many) failed in their fight against a disease, or did not fight it promptly or keenly enough. Each case of death ('as seen on TV') had a cause, and for the same reason was *avoidable* – contingent. That contingency, that avoidability, that encouraging and reassuring gratuity of death is, as a rule, the main topic of the TV drama in which people lose their lives – individual people, individual lives and in individual circumstances.

In his fascinating study of medical practices in Belfast, Lindsay Prior documented contemporary deconstructing practices and the impact they exert on the imagery of death and, obliquely, also on life strategies:

---

[12] Cf. John Hick, *Death and Eternal Life* (San Francisco: Harper & Row, 1976), p. 86.

In Belfast, as in most other parts of Western Europe, one dies from one's diseases rather than, say, of old age, malfeasance or misfortune ... Death and dying are hospitalized precisely because they are understood, first and foremost, as physical events. And the fact that it is the doctor rather than the priest who is first summoned on the occasion says much about the ways in which human mortality is comprehended ... Death is primarily regarded as an illness and an aberration rather than something that is natural [and] the physician is supposed both to certify death and state its cause ... These certificates also illustrate the belief that although human beings die from many causes at once, it is always possible to isolate a single and precipitate cause of death ... Death is conceptualized as ailment that is amenable to intervention.[13]

The doctors who stand between me and my death do not fight mortality; but they do fight, gallantly and skilfully, each and any of its particular cases. They fight *mortal diseases*. Quite often they win. Each victory is an occasion for rejoicing: once more, advancing death has been stopped in its tracks and pushed back. Sometimes the doctors lose the battle. And then, in Helmut Thielicke's words, the death of a patient – *this* patient, *here* and *now* – is 'felt to be a personal defeat. Doctors are like attorneys who lose cases and are thus forced to face up to the limit of their own powers. No wonder that they conceal their faces and turn aside.'[14] A lost court case does not put in question the importance and the competence of lawyers; at the very worst, it may cast shadow on the skills of a particular barrister. Similarly, a death that has not been prevented does not undermine the authority of the medical profession. At worst it may stain the reputation of an individual doctor. But the condemnation of the individual practitioner only reinforces the authority of the art: the doctor's fault was not to use the tools and the procedures he *could* use. He is guilty precisely because the profession as a whole is *capable* of doing what he, a member of that profession who should have known better, did not do, though could have done. Or, if the learned council resolves that the suspicion of neglect has been ill founded, as the proper tools and procedures were not available *at the moment* – the cause of hiding the lost war against mortality behind loudly hailed victorious frays and skirmishes with cholesterols, infections and tumours receives another powerful boost: we hear that the means have not been invented *as yet*. The equipment has not been developed, the vaccine has not been discovered, the technique has not been tested. But they will, given time and money. And so they should.

---

[13] Lindsay Prior, *The Social Organization of Death: Medical Discourse and Social Practices in Belfast* (London: Macmillan, 1989), pp. 26, 25, 32, 33.
[14] Herbert Thielicke, *Living with Death* (Grand Rapids: Eydermans, 1983), p. 44.

Conquest of no disease is *in principle* impossible. Did you say that another disease will threaten life once this one, here and now, has been conquered? Well, we will cross that bridge when we come to it. Let us concentrate on the task at hand, on this trouble here and now. This we *can* do; and this we will go on doing.

In the effect, death has been turned from a hangman into a prison guard. The big carcass of mortality has been sliced from head to tail into thin rashers of fearful, yet curable (or potentially curable) afflictions; they can be now fit neatly into every nook and cranny of life. Death does not come now at the end of life: it is there from the start, calling for constant surveillance and forbidding even a momentary relaxation of vigil. Death is watching (and is to be watched) when we work, eat, love, rest. Through its many deputies, death presides over life. Fighting death may stay meaningless, but fighting the *causes* of dying turns into the meaning of life.

This is a most radical reversal of the ancient stoical reasoning calculated to avert the terror of death: so long as we exist, Epicurus said, death is not present, and when death is present, we do not exist: therefore, death affects neither the dead nor the living ... In our modern times, death *is* present among the living and *does* affect them – through those countless little daily prescriptions and prohibitions that not for a moment allow one to forget. Doubtful gain, one is prompted to say. Commenting on Pascal's suggestion that death which comes unexpected is less terrifying than thinking of death when one is not in danger, Thielicke observes that the most terrible thing about death is 'death as *thought*: in the thought that lies like a shadow over the whole of life and impresses upon it the stamp of a being for death'.[15]

In the wake of the deconstruction of mortality and the ensuing 'privatization' of dying, precisely because it has been cast as a 'curable disease', death is transformed from the ultimate, yet distant horizon of life into its daily nightmare. The life-giving promise rebounds in a life-poisoning threat. Now the whole of life serves the purpose of war against 'causes of death'. The permanent horror can only be dispelled in the bustle of 'doing something about it', in near-hysterical busyness and incessant sniffing for cloak-and-dagger conspirators. The outcome, as Gorer suggested, is an 'excessive preoccupation with the risk of death' – as if what was at stake was more than replacing *one* 'cause' of death by *another*. For instance, 'implicit in quite a lot of agitation to stop the sale or advertisement of

---

[15] Cf. Thielicke, *Living with Death*, pp. 5, 18.

cigarettes is the suggestion that, without this indulgence, people would be immortal'.[16]

Eschatology has been successfully dissolved in technology. It is 'how to do it', not 'what to do', on which the survival concerns now focus; not what is to be done, but 'how well' it has been done, is the measure of each episode in which the struggle for survival now splits. Transcendence of mortality has been replaced with the mind-and-energy-consuming task of transcending the technical capacity of living. This is a triumph of mundane life-size instrumentality over metaphysical purpose inscribed in eternity. A triumph of event over time, livable present over future death. The future has been abolished, evicted from the field of vision. It has been replaced by Benjamin's *Jetztzeit*, non-flowing time, time without continuation or consequence, a continuous present.

The existential worry can be now all but forgotten in the daily bustle about *health*. Mortality generates *Angst* for which there is no cure, disease is pregnant only with *anxiety* which can be dealt with *therapeutically*. Illness can be conquered, and so anxiety (unlike *Angst*) does not paralyse, but spurs into action. If cancellation of death cannot be made into a realistic goal of life, health can. There are so many things and deeds one should avoid to protect health. And avoiding them is a time-consuming labour. It fills the time that would otherwise be shot through with metaphysical dread – and this is indeed the most gratifying and attractive aspect of the anxiety over health. One does not need to stand idle; one can do something about death: not about death in general, true – but about this and that cause of death one has been warned against. We are mindful of doctors' remonstrations: let us concentrate on this trouble here and now; we will cross that other bridge when we come to it. We hear and read that even 'the longest-living' men or women whose exceptional longevity of life was a title to world fame (not to mention the 'ordinary' very old) die finally of kidney disease or liver trouble or pneumonia; no one seems to die because of human mortality.

A paradoxical reflection of such thinking is a belief, promoted by the medical profession and ossified into *objective fact* through widely publicized statistics of *medical practices*, that 'death from natural causes alone is diminishing. There is an even more telling trend because many deaths from disease often have human intentionality – conscious and unconscious – as part of the cause'.[17] It is obvious that the compilers of statistics

---

[16] Gorer, *Death, Grief and Mourning*, p. 114.

[17] Cf. Kenneth L. Vaux, *Will to Live – Will to Die* (Minneapolis: Augsburg Publishing House, 1978), p. 62–3.

are reluctant to concede that death was 'natural' (that is, that no blameable reasons can be found). Medical practice declared 'natural death' illegal and made its residue suspicious; 'unexplained death' is a challenge to a world-view that splits mortality into a multitude of individual occurrences, each with its own cause, each with a principally *preventable* cause.

However thorough and prolonged the succour this policy of survival may bring, it has its own drawbacks. One may forget that the most a successive victory may offer is a temporary lull in enemy action, not final victory. But one is not allowed to enjoy the respite for long. Death is a momentary event, but defence of health and vigilance against its enemies is a lifelong labour. If death comes at the end of life, the defence of health fills the whole of it. The price for exchanging *immortality* for *health* is life lived in the shadow of death; to postpone death, one needs to surrender life to fighting it. The self-care policy of survival construes death as an individual event. Each death is different; each death is individual; each death is a private experience; each death is lonely.[18] And so is life, once colonized by this kind of death: individual, self-enclosed, separated, unshared, lonely. If my death is caused by something I have done, or by something I could prevent from happening (and thus by my inaction or neglect), survival is reconfirmed as my private matter and private responsibility. The more consistently I deploy the collectively suggested or enforced strategy of survival, the more alone I am left.

---

[18] Norbert Elias's 'loneliness of the dying' seems to be an expectable outcome of the 'episodization' of death brought about by the self-care strategy. Rather than being a manifestation of the delicacy of civilized emotions, the sight of the dying is repulsive to our contemporaries in as far as it demonstrates the ultimate futility of the effort to substitute the 'problem of health' for the 'problem of life'. The loneliness of dying – keeping them out of sight (and preferably, through entrusting them to the professionals, also out of mind) – is a fitting corollary of the loneliness of irreparably individual concerns with health and fitness of the body. Similarly, one doubts whether Elias does not mistake the self-pretence of our age for the truth of history, when suggesting that in 'less developed societies' 'the magic practices' meant to deal with death are more widespread than in our own (p. 46), or when he implies that our scientific knowledge representing death as regular natural process is 'capable of giving a sense of security' (p. 77) – in contrast to 'fantasy-explanations' of the pre-modern age. One may think of the numberless survival, death-exorcising practices that fill the whole life of modern men and women; they may be sanctioned by contemporary experts as sound, but so were their predecessors by the experts of their times; and the way our own death-defying practices are performed does not differ greatly from the compulsion of magical rites. One may as well observe that the 'security' offered by modern science scores poor second to that promised by the beliefs modern sciences discredited and tried to root out.

The stratifying magic

With all the breath-taking miracles modern medicine offers, and more still which it (given sufficient funds) promises, death – as Charles Wahl soberly observed – 'does not yield to science and rationality'. Having cast death as a concern and responsibility of reason and reason-fed technology, modernity could not but expose reason's inadequacy to the task. And so, in the end of the day, 'we are perforce impelled to employ the heavy artillery of defence, namely, a recourse to magic and immortality'.[19] Odette Thibault asks, rhetorically: 'Are not the techniques which give the illusion of power over death our new exorcistic rites, a new form of magic?'[20] Lying (or not telling the whole truth) about its ultimate limits, surreptitiously substituting effective concerns with partial ailments for the (hopeless) struggle against the incurable malady of existence, medical science and the technology it spawns turns itself into a variety of magic. It promises (though by default rather than explicitly) what it cannot deliver, while diverting the attention from the idleness of promise through an ever more dazzling display of staggering surgeries, wonder drugs and awe-inspiring high-tech installations.

The very costliness and sophistication of the 'most advanced' modern medicine seems to be a powerful psychological – reassuring – factor. A thing so costly, so complex, so mysterious to a layman must indeed possess some magical potential. And whoever takes the trouble of using it, must have a most serious of intentions to combat the disease and a good chance of winning the battle. 'We will stop at nothing to defeat the enemy', *whatever the cost*. The exorbitant price of the gadgets adds to the prestige and, indeed, to the perceived trustworthiness of those who operate it; it also gives a new lease of life to the hopes of those on whom the gadgets are to be tried, and protects those hopes from being disavowed by the lack of practical success. (There is always an exonerating interpretation which would keep both the hopes and the production of the gadgets alive: 'if only we had more money available; if only the needed equipment had been purchased in time; if only researchers speeded up their experiments . . .')

But the rising costs of advanced medical techniques mean, inevitably, further limiting of their availability. A sharp stratification of medical

---

[19] Charles Wahl, 'The Fear of Death', in *Death and Identity*, ed. Fulton, p. 57.
[20] Thibault, *Maîtrise de la mort*, p. 124.

services follows. Only relatively few patients can conceivably benefit from the techniques that require huge investment of resources. The very existence of highly refined, highly expensive and not-yet-discredited, and so intensely coveted, combat weapons splits the potential users into those 'deserving' and those 'less deserving' of the treatment, and this not necessarily according to the 'purely medical' (whatever that may mean) merits of their cases. Whether the medical practice and medical facilities are completely commercialized, or fully socialized (that is, distributed according to some non-market rules), the outcome is very much the same; some choices must still be made, and only the factors of discrimination change. In the USA, with its private medical service, the almost sole criterion of choice is the financial standing of the patients and their willingness to commit their resources to purchase exquisite medical care.

In his famous 1960s study of two hospitals, code-named 'the County' (publicly subsidized and caring mostly for impecunious patients) and 'Cohen' (fully private, with a predominantly affluent clientele), David Sudnow found profound differences between what in each of the hospitals was considered to be the standard of medical care and routine medical practice. To start with, in the County doctors and nurses paid much less attention to sparing the feelings of the patients and their relatives, or to disguise the ultimate constraints of their craft. 'The sheer likelihood of hearing the word "autopsy" is greater at County, despite the fact that the number of autopsies conducted is roughly the same in both settings.' At County the doctors routinely tend to locate the 'cause' of death *outside* 'their own limited involvement in the health affairs' of their patients. They resist what they see as unwarranted demands of the relatives to deploy more means or make greater efforts to save their loved ones. They hasten to distance themselves from the possible outcome of the treatment and insist on staying aloof from the 'real causes' in case the outcome turns to be adverse. 'In their daily interaction with families (which are seldom "daily"), they seek to avoid making reassurances, conveying instead the general disaffiliation from "this kind of medicine". Doctor-relative encounters have the character of so many bureaucratic-like interactions which lowerclass persons confront in the various welfare agencies, e.g. "Well, we'll do what we can" character.' All this, point by point, is in sharp contrast with the practice considered routine and proper in Cohen. At County no instances were recorded in which 'external heart massage was given a patient whose heart was stethoscopically inaudible, if that patient was over 40 years of age. At Cohen Hospital . . . heart massage is a normal routine at that point, and more drastic routines, such as the injection of adrenalin directly into the heart, are not uncommon.' (Let us note that in the time since Sudnow completed his study massages or adrenalin injections have lost much of their initial spectacularity and have ceased to impress, so that their discriminating power has all but dissipated; 'the frontiers of medicine' have been pushed back much further, with organ transplants and the electronic, computerized gadgetry in the role of the avant-garde, distinction-conferring techniques. This – given the costs of the new equipment and the skills necessary for their use – only exacerbated the discriminatory processes which Sudnow captured at their relatively more primitive stage.) All in all – Sudnow sums up his findings somewhat allegorically – 'one can observe a direct relationship between the loudness and length of the siren alarm [of the patient-carrying ambulance] and the considered "social value" of the person being transported'.[21]

With death redefined as an outcome of an essentially curable disease, the prolongation of individual life, redefined in terms of expert medical services, becomes a value unevenly distributed. Disease-fighting medicine joins the long list of stratifying mechanisms. For all practical purposes, individual lives are valued differentially. Though those occupying the upper strata of society may not necessarily live longer, their *right* to live longer is (if only obliquely or on the sly) either bureaucratically decreed, or offered to be insured through the mechanism of the market.

Modern promises, modern fears

The promise to conquer if not mortality, then each and any specific *cause* of death, fit well the self-confidence, nay hubris, that marked the modern spirit from the beginning and through most of its history. Drawbacks seemed but a temporary nuisance, all evil but a relic of past human folly which triumphant civilization will eventually extirpate, all affliction but a

---

[21] David Sudnow, *Passing On: The Social Organization of Dying* (Englewood Cliffs: Prentice Hall, 1967), pp. 51, 98, 103, 104. The stratifying impact of medical craft has been pushed (as a prospect or promise, rather than a material fact) to new and unprecedented extremes when 'cryonics societies' began to be formed among the wealthy after R.C.W. Ettinger suggested in 1966 that 'corpses might be frozen and defrosted later when medicine had discovered a cure for what the person had "died" from.' (Jack B. Kamerman, *Death in the Midst of Life: Social and Cultural Influences on Death, Grief, and Mourning* (Englewood Cliffs: Prentice-Hall, 1988), p. 34.) Cryonics was the ultimate version of stratification: it was, from the start, an undisguised offer of selective survival (immortality?) to those able and willing to pay.

side-product of ignorance soon to be replaced with foolproof knowledge. Libraries were written on the not-yet-realized, but certain to materialize, human omnipotence; the following self-assured statement of belief, already penned down in 1775, may serve as a sample as good as any: 'Is it not evident that by management the human species may be moulded into any conceivable shape?'[22]

The greater the hope, the ruder the awakening. As reason-dictated reforms succeeded one another, each triggered by the bitter aftertaste of dashed hopes left by its predecessor, the evidence of the stauncher that expected resistance of reality to human manipulation was ever more difficult to ignore. As the nineteenth century went by, the original optimism was gradually smothered by the rising tide of dark forebodings. As J.R. Searle found out in his study of the new feeling of desperation which fed the acute concern with 'human breeding',

> middle-class commentators on the 'social question' from the 1870s onwards viewed with fear the casual labourers and the inhabitants of the slum areas of the big cities; they noted with both disappointment and apprehension that these people had not 'responded' to attempts by legislators and charitable organizations to raise them to a higher material and social plane, and some were tempted to explain this by the hypothesis of urban degeneration . . .[23]

'Degeneration' was the *mot clé*: it conveyed a new anxiety, and it did it in a form that struck right at the heart of the earlier, comforting image of progress as a straight line with one direction only – up and up. Phenomena of *degeneration* differed radically from those which used to be explained away as the 'unfinished business' of the unstoppable civilizing process. They were not relics or residues yet to be burned out (soon) and disposed of (immediately afterwards). They proved to be much more sinister still than used to be implied by the more benign, less disquieting version of cultural pessimism; one that viewed the resilience of the 'negative' phe-

---

[22] James Burgh, *Political Disquisitions* (London: Filly, 1775), vol. 3, p. 176. Quoted after Andrew Scull, 'Moral Treatment Reconsidered', in *Madhouses, Mad-Doctors and Madmen: The Social History of Psychiatry in the Victorian Era*, ed. Andrew Scull (London: Athlone Press, 1981), p. 114. Scull comments that 'this faith in the capacity for human improvement through social and environmental manipulation was translated in a variety of settings – factories, schools, prisons, asylums – into the development of a whole array of temporally coincident and structurally similar techniques of social discipline.'

[23] J.R. Searle, *Eugenics and Politics in Britain, 1900–1914* (Leyden: Noordhoff, 1976), p. 20.

nomena only as a signal that – contrary to euphoric expectations – reason and the action it inspired and guided were not (not quite) omnipotent or invincible, and that one would need to admit the presence of some stubborn and unencroachable limits to progress. The idea of 'degeneration' went further that that. It implied that the undesirable phenomena, which caused concern of the law-and-order-loving urban dweller and the legislator alike, were of a *post*-civilizational, rather than *pre*-civilizational origin; that they were unanticipated, yet in all probability inescapable, *products* of the civilizing effort and the seminal change in human condition that followed. In 1909 Karl Pearson summed up the new anxiety, proclaiming that the 'survival of the unfit' is a 'marked characteristic' of modern town life. Civilization has its own diseases; it would not be wide of the mark to conclude that civilization itself is a disease. If the progress so far failed abominably to deliver on its promise, if mankind came nowhere near the hoped-for victory over death, it is because the old causes of mortality on which the ameliorating efforts focused have been replaced by new causes, most of them of civilization's own making.

The idea of degeneration assumed that, however great the improvements in daily comforts (Freud, as we remember, lauded civilization for victory over pain and dirt, if not for much else), the civilizing process has an overall *degrading* impact. According to one version, civilizational pressures – that constant violence against the innermost human needs and drives – cause widespread neurosis, saturating daily life with pathological conduct. According to another, the artificially peaceful, cushioned life permits survival and reproduction of an inferior, 'unworthy' stock, which in less distorted, naturally severe conditions would wither and perish without issue. According to another still, the cosy and sheltered life of plenty and comfort leads, paradoxically, back to the pre-civilizational state from which the affluence promised to emancipate – this time, however, not in the form of untamed savagery, but of *decadence*: the fall from the state of refinement and sophistication into the abyss of uncontrolled passion or the prospectless void of *ennui*.

Whatever the imagery woven into the complex vision of degeneration, one feature was present in all versions: that, of a radical *medicalization* of most private or collective worries, everything felt vexing, undesirable, frightening in individual life or in socially shaped conditions of life. Vice had been redefined as illness, immorality as pathology.[24] Toward the end

---

[24] Cf. Ruth Harris, *Murders and Madness: Medicine, Law, and Society in the Fin de siècle* (Oxford: Clarendon Press, 1989), p. 255. For instance, the term 'alcohol-

of the nineteenth century, sin and crime were blended – in public debate dominated by medical experts – into one, all-embracing category of the *disease*. Scratch any 'social problem', any 'personal misfortune', and a *pathology* will be revealed which calls for some medical action – surgery, regime, drug prescription, hospital-style supervised confinement. Behind the bane of the inner cities – vagrancy and begging – there was the neurasthenic condition; behind striking workers there was mob psychosis making its victims susceptible to the incendiary exhortations of the demagogues; there were specific, ubiquitous pathology in the 'normal' life conditions of the hyper-active and hyper-tense bourgeois buffeted by the cross-waves of competitive pressures, of the dissipated and idle offspring of privileged, affluent families, of middle-class women debilitated by the lack of function to the point of sexually rooted hysteria. In Ruth Harris's summary, 'everywhere medical men saw danger ... They increasingly insisted on curative procedures.'[25]

This is not to say that the dramatic change in public discourse is to be blamed on the conspiracy the of medical profession. Even if the acquisition by the medical discourse of a pivotal point in social and political thought could be, to an extent, ascribed to the zestful efforts of medical men to advance the standing of their profession – doctors would certainly labour in vain were not the social conditions ripe for the apprehensive interest in, and hence wide acceptance of, the vision structured by the dichotomy of normal/pathological (or, more to the point, of health/disease).

Students of the history of fiction and political thought alike have long noted that popular and/or dominant narratives convey as a rule more information about the mentality and concerns of the socio-cultural setting in which they had been conceived and circulated, than about their declared objects. This semantic link has been widely explored, for instance, in the studies of the imagery of the 'wild man', the 'savage', the 'native' in European literature. Thus we read in some of the most authoritative of the recent explorations of the topic that 'The kinds of values being tested by the symbolic Native figures in any particular work often

---

ism', coined in 1852 by the Swedish physician Magnus Huss, differed from the traditional names for excessive attachment to alcohol, like *ivrognerie*, in that it defined profuse drinking as a 'disease condition' (*ibid.*, p. 245). It is interesting to note that the disease was primarily related to blatantly *modern*, 'artificial' and hence particularly potent brews, like absinthe, sharply opposed in the medical literature of the time to relatively innocuous, because 'natural', *boissons hygiéniques* – like wine and cider.

[25] Harris, *Murders and Madness.*, p. 13.

reveal which aspects of the laws of civilization and nature are of especial concern to a society' (with sexual licence and legally unregulated violence looming particularly large in the nineteenth century literature); or that 'The indigene is a semantic pawn on a chessboard under the control of the white signmaker' (thus reflecting the mixture of fear and temptation felt by the 'signmakers' toward their own barely suppressed longings); or that

> The notion of 'wildness' . . . belongs to a set of culturally self-authenticating devices which includes, among many others, the ideas of 'madness' and 'heresy' as well. These terms are used not merely to denigrate a specific condition or state of being but also to confirm the value of their dialectical antitheses: 'civilization', 'sanity', and 'orthodoxy' respectively . . . [M]odern cultural anthropology has conceptualized the idea of wildness as the repressed content of *both* civilized *and* primitive humanity.[26]

I propose that the conceptual 'pathologization' of daily life (with 'medicalization' or 'psychiatrization' as its inalienable companions), this most protruding accomplishment of the discourse of 'degeneration', was an unavoidable outcome of the fear of death which the deconstruction of mortality, as the prime strategy of modern times, could only suppress – yet never dispel. Barely veiled by daily preoccupations with health and with fighting the innumerable diseases, lay the finite truth of mortality. It was that truth (too awesome and incapacitating a sight when naked), which was exteriorized, conceptually processed, and then readmitted into the

---

[26] Gordon Johnston, 'An Intolerable Burden of Meaning: Native Peoples in White Fiction', in *The Native in Literature*, ed. Thomas King, Cheryl Calver and Helen Hass (Oakville, Ontario: ECV Press, 1987), p. 53; Terry Golde, 'Fear and Temptation: Images of Indigenous People in Australia, Canada and New Zealand literature', in *ibid.*, p. 70; Hayden White, 'The Forms of Wildness: Archaeology of an Idea', in *The Wild Man Within: An Image in Western Thought from the Renaissance to Romanticism* (University of Pittsburgh Press, 1972), pp. 5, 7.
Hayden White proposed the term of 'ostensive self-definition by negation' for a wider class of similar discursive practices: 'It appears as a kind of reflex action in conflicts between nations, classes, and political parties, and is not unknown among scholars and intellectuals seeking to establish their claims to elite status against the *vulgus mobile*. It is a technique that is especially useful for groups whose dissatisfactions are easier to recognize than their programmes to justify . . . Like the "wild man" of the New World, the "dangerous classes" of the Old World define the limitations of the general notion of "humanity" which informed and justified the Europeans' spoliation of any human group standing in the way of their expansion, and their need to destroy that which they could not consume' (*Tropics of Discourse: Essays in Cultural Criticism* (Baltimore: Johns Hopkins University Press, 1978), pp. 152, 193.)

realm of rational discourse tightly wrapped in the protective costume of organic or mental ailments, or of the uncouth, unbridled, passion-ridden savagery of the 'wild man' out there or inside here, or of the 'dangerous classes' round the corner of the civilized street, or of the feeble and weak-willed femininity oozing out of the appointed female quarters and contaminating the manly, resourceful world meant to be inhabited by the fittest only.

In tune with the spirit of modernity, 'degeneration' was intended as a precise, scientific concept – and pretended to be one. It owed its impact and its world-view-shaping authority to this pretention. And yet it would fail virtually every single test that truly scientific concepts are meant to pass – were it ever subjected to such a test. As Daniel Pick has found out, '*dégénérescence*'

> was never successfully reduced to a fixed axiom or theory in the 19th century despite the expressed desire to resolve the conceptual questions once and for all in definitive texts. Rather it was shifting term produced, inflated, refined, and re-constituted in the movement between human sciences, fictional narratives and socio-political commentaries . . .
>
> Degeneration constituted an impossible endeavour to 'scienticize', objectify and cast off whole underworlds of political and social anxiety . . .
>
> Social commentary was transformed into 'scientific truth' . . .
>
> Crucially, there was no one stable referent to which degeneration applied; instead a fantastic kaleidoscope of concerns and objects . . .[27]

I suggest that – contrary to contemporary retrospective lamentations – the notorious diffuseness (should not one rather speak of omnivorousness?) of the concept was not a product of neglect or lack of scholarly care; and that it hardly diminished the concept's intellectual and practical potency. That concept would hardly be half as effective as it was, were the repeated efforts to 'pin it down', to reduce and specify its meaning, more successful. Only in its actual state of imprecision and confusion could the idea of degeneration perform the role which truly assured its heady career: that of a safety valve for the unsuccessfully repressed truth of incurable mortality of the species which had been repeatedly assured of its ability to defeat and conquer every obstacle on its way to ideal life; the role of a refuse bin for all and sundry substitute worries, all tied by the same unspeakable, secret link to one great worry which members of that species were not allowed to worry about, and which for that reason was

---

[27] Daniel Pick, *Faces of Degeneration: A European Disorder, c. 1848–c. 1918* (Cambridge University Press, 1989), pp. 7, 9, 10, 15.

in constant need of other, surrogate worries and made those other worries worrisome.

What would disable and disqualify any scientific concept, was the main source of intellectual attractiveness and public influence of the idea of degeneration. The fact that it could be freely stretched to serve virtually any social panic, whatever its fashionable focus or current name – be it alcoholism, the spread of venereal diseases, the lack of able-bodied recruits for the Boer War, anarchist bombs, crowds on the march, feminist agitation, the influx of 'racially alien' immigrants, too big or too small a birthrate; the fact that it referred to tendencies or states which were invisible, impossible to detect by direct empirical observation, known only in their manifestations, and thus immune to unambiguously falsifying experiments; the fact that the idea remained blatantly unspecific, suggestive of a virtual ubiquitousness of the degenerating tendency, of its capacity to afflict everything, everywhere, at any time – all contributed to the persistent popularity of the vision, which (thanks to these, scientifically disqualifying, attributes) permitted practices as ambivalent and contradictory as the predicament which triggered them off was irrational:

> Degeneration, with its potentially vitiating and fragmenting effect on the will of the sufferer, was at once universalized as the potential fate of all and, paradoxically, particularized as the condition of the other . . .
> On the one hand, the 'experts' desired to isolate a social threat – to reveal, transport, castrate and segregate 'noxious elements'. On the other hand, it seemed that degeneration lay everywhere, demanding massive campaigns of public hygiene, the closer investigation of whole populations.[28]

Again, the logical contradictoriness apparently endemic in the idea of degeneration did not detract from its practical usefulness; on the contrary, the contradiction might have well been indispensable to make the idea of degeneration resonant with the fears and neuroses it was called to explain away, placate and pacify, if not cure – and was thus adequate to the excruciatingly difficult task it was faced with. Thanks to the diffuse and contradictory image of degeneration, the danger which used to be, intellectually and emotionally, so incapacitating because of its merciless, cruel universality (it was notorious for offering no remissions nor exemptions, and honouring neither merits nor privileges) – has been pinned down, comfortably, to a specific category of 'others'. Now the danger – once ubiquitous, elusive, dispersed and all-pervasive – had an address, and an exact one. It had its spot in space, its carriers, its earthly, identifiable

---

[28] Pick, *Faces of Degeneration*, pp. 42–3, 106.

culprits. Through them as an effigy, it could be charted, isolated, sur-rounded by barbed wire and warning signs, confined and fought against – perhaps even, in the end, tamed or disposed of. The danger now had a name. It became an *object* – and objects can be handled, worked upon, given a better shape or thrown away. Objects have nothing supernatural about them; they stay, reassuringly, within human reach and human capacity to act. One can submit them to purposeful, planned, consistent, effective, *rational* treatment.

One does not despair if one can act, and if one can hope that the action will be rational. One can keep despair in abeyance as long as one *acts*: as long as one knows that not all has been lost, that 'something can be done yet' – and as long as that 'something' which 'can be done' has not been done and hence one can trust it and believe in with all one's heart. Rational efforts go on draining the abysmal depths of irrationality; They will never reach the bottom, but at least one need never again think of the bottom unless the effort stops.

Killing death

Contrary to its seldom reported, yet daily dreamed dreams, modernity did not conquer mortality. Having failed to achieve the ultimate, it zeroed in its effort instead on second best solutions and surrogate targets. As we have seen before, it banished death and the dying out of sight and thus, hopefully, out of mind. It reinterpreted the chimera of final victory over death as the long chain of temporary triumphs over its currently most publicized causes. It replaced the big worry about survival with many small – manageable – worries about the assorted causes of dying. All in all, it 'de-metaphysicized' mortality. Death under modern conditions was no more 'tamed'; but it has been *rationalized* instead. It has been given its own location in social space, a segregated location; it has been put in custody of selected specialists boasting scientific credentials; it has been mapped into a mental space populated with named and knowable objects and events; it has been linked to a network of techniques and practices of measurable efficiency and effectiveness.[29]

---

[29] Thanks to those expedients perceived as progressive achievements of mod-ernity, measures offered as 'defence against death' became subject to the empiri-cally testable criteria of 'usefulness'. Of that, writes Elias Canetti: 'With usefulness, men have called themselves gods, although they must die. The power over usefulness deceives them about this ludicrous foible of theirs. Thus, in their self-

The frequent outbursts of panic – be it about degeneration, decadence, loss of vigour or spread of 'defective genetic stock' – were unavoidable and expectable supplements of this process to rationalization. Were it to spur into action, instead of merely stultifying the mind and paralysing the will, the panic would need to find its outlet, through appointing a 'sensible object' of compensatory efforts in the form of the carriers of impending doom. Naming the agents of degeneration, segregating them, confining, neutralizing, eliminating, was therefore also an integral part of the modern rationalization of death – and an essential part, not a fortuitous, freak, regrettable and preventable chance event.

Once the diffuse and inhuman prospect of mortality had been localized and 'humanized', one need no more stand idle waiting for impending doom. One can *do something*, something 'reasonable' and 'useful'. One can be active, and act in an instrumentally rational fashion. Conforming to modern mentality, one can cast death and survival as 'problems'. And then one can think seriously about the solution to these problems, and apply to the solution all the tested faculties and skills with which modernity armed its residents. One can carefully set the means against the end, search for the resources necessary for the means to be implemented, calculate the cost of the resources and draw the cost-and-effects balance sheet of the whole operation. One can, in other words, be a *rational* agent in the face of (in spite of) the predicament that bars rationality.

Focusing the fear of death on the appointed carriers of degeneration and disease is not, therefore, an irrational act; not the mysterious, primeval, 'Dionysian' hiccup in an essentially transparent, constructed, 'Apollonian' world; not an outcome of the resurfacing of emotions which the rule of reason failed to extirpate; not a transient, however worrisome, irritant, to be eventually left behind for good. Zeroing in the mortality-fed anxiety on the alleged agents of decline and putrefaction is a thoroughly rational proclivity. Or, rather, it is the necessary condition of keeping alive the

---

conceit, they grow weaker and weaker. Usefulness multiplies, but men die like flies. If only usefulness were more seldom useful; if there was no possibility of precisely calculating when it would definitely be useful and when definitely not; if it had jumps, moods, whims – then no one would have become its slave. People would have thought more, prepared themselves for more, expected more. The lines from death to death would not be erased, we would not be its *blind* prey. It could not mock us in the midst of our security . . .' As we stand now, Canetti suggests, 'my hatred of death implies an incessant awareness of it . . . The slavery of death is the core of all slavery.' (*The Human Province*, trans. Joachim Neugroschel (London: André Deutsch, 1985), pp. 60, 82.)

fictitious assumptions which make rational action possible, and hence a *sine qua non* accompaniment of modernity.

The price of the specifically modern way of coping with death anxiety – putting mortality in an institutional and mental confinement and keeping it there – is a constant demand for the 'dangerous other' as a carrier of contagious and terminal disease. Where there is a demand, an offer will soon follow. The only 'buffer' science could provide against anxiety, writes Sander L. Gilman, 'was to create categories that where absolutely self-contained. Thus disease-entities were invented which defined a clearly limited subset of human beings as the group solely at risk.' Well, not really 'absolutely self-contained', though. The diseased subsets must have not only been at risk, but themselves be a risk for the 'healthy' part of society. They must have been potentially contagious (that is, if precautions were not taken to disempower, isolate or destroy them) – otherwise their 'discovery' will do little to alleviate the anxiety which made the creation of diseased subsets needed in the first place.

Among the diseased subsets of the sort scrutinized by Gilman the groups defined in racial terms were particularly popular (no wonder; after all, race invokes 'suprahuman' factors resilient to cultural manipulation – akin to, and resonant with, the equally uncontrollable elements of the human condition originally responsible for the paranoiac fever): 'tied to the prestige of the nineteenth-century science the idea of racial difference in the twentieth century became the means of manipulating and eventually destroying entire groups ... Racial stereotypes have been linked with images of pathology ... [The Other is] both ill and infectious, both damaged and damaging.'[30] With racial discourse tightly interwoven with that of disease and pathology, separation and insulation techniques were driven into the focus of practical concerns. It had become imperative – literally, a life-and-death matter – to keep races apart (that is, to keep

---

[30] Sander L. Gilman, *Difference and Pathology: Stereotypes of Sexuality, Race and Madness* (Ithaca: Cornell University Press, 1985), pp. 215, 129–30. Definition of 'dangerous groups' in *racial* terms implies, if only obliquely, the *incurability* of the disease they carry; hence its particularly sinister consequences. About one of the racially defined subsets, the Jews, Joseph Goebbels noted in his diary: 'There is no hope of leading the Jews back into the fold of civilized humanity by exceptional punishments. They will forever remain Jews, just as we are forever members of the Aryan race.' (Cf. *Survivors, Victims, and Perpetrators: Essays on the Nazi Holocaust*, ed. Joel E. Dinsdale (Washington: Hemisphere, 1980), p. 311.) Things and people one could do nothing to improve had no room in a world that entailed only such objects one 'could do something about' to repair, make useful, pleasing and perfect.

inferior, death-carrying races apart from the superior, healthy one); indeed, it had turned into the crucial commandment of *hygiene*.

Hygiene, as the modern technology of keeping disease (the only, yet scary disguise in which death is allowed to haunt daily life) at bay, boils down in most cases to an activity of separating and maintaining distance. One should steer clear of 'filthy places' and 'unsavoury substances'. Avoiding bodily contact with whatever is cast as dangerous to the prolongation of life is the major concern of everyone who is hygiene-conscious. Hygiene is served by devices meant to facilitate the separation: brooms and brushes, soaps, cleaning sprays, washing powders. The substances set apart by separating operations are *dirt*, and ought to be dumped into ghetto-like or cemetery-like, isolated, closely guarded spaces, or preferably destroyed altogether (in sewage- or waste-processing plants).

Hygiene is, let us repeat, the product of the deconstruction of mortality into an infinite series of individual causes of death, and of the struggle against death into an infinitely extendable series of battles against specific diseases. This deconstruction being an attempt to exhaust the inexhaustible, an attempt doomed from the start and thus bound to suppress the knowledge of its own impossibility merely to be able to continue, it can only suspend anxiety temporarily and drown it for a time in the noise of the hue-and-cry accompanying the flurry of hunting and chasing of passing and elusive targets. No hunting escapade is a conclusive one, no trophy final and ultimately gratifying. Hence the obsession, the tension, the hysteria that surround hygienic concerns and activities. The dirt ('the dirt that you see and the dirt that you don't' – as the advertisers, always eager to graze on human fears, hasten to remind their punters), bacteria, viruses, putrefying and thus surely toxic substances, all arouse intense fear and *disgust* (that emotional corollary of desire to create and maintain distance between oneself and offending object), themselves surrogate outlets for the great metaphysical horror of mortality. Such irrational emotions, and the irrational practices they trigger are, again, the other side of the modern rationalization of death.

One can understand racial discourse and racist politics of the modern era (conspicuous manifestations of mainly *anthropoemic* – as distinct from *anthropophagic* – strategy of modern order-maintenance) as a case of the more general modern preoccupation with hygiene, that realistic surrogate for the irrealistic dream of death-avoidance. Hygienic terms and rhetoric figures which saturate racial discourse are neither accidental nor gratuitous. They are also more than mere metaphors: racial discourse, as all other numerous differentiating/separating discourses, is indeed an integral part of hygienic thinking and hygiene-informed practices of modernity.

Thus the measures taken to defuse and neutralize the dangers inherent in 'foreign races' and other 'disease carriers' are drawn from the arsenal of hygienic prescriptions. Identification of the offending substance; limitation of its freedom to move; bringing it 'under control'; confining it to specially designed and well marked places; transportation to places far enough away to preclude contact; finally, physical destruction, genocide, holocaust – that symbolic death of the death, killing the death in effigy.

Killing the disease-and-degeneration carriers, as killing the bacteria or viruses, is a life-serving and life-enhancing exercise. One does not think of it as of murder, but as of life-saving. The lives destroyed are 'lives devoid of value'; they are also lives inimical to life, lives which have to be killed so that they shall not kill. The destruction of unworthy lives is a cleaning-up action to be judged solely in the light of the precepts of hygiene, validated by the supreme task of the preservation of life – a task not merely morally unquestionable, but a foundation ground of all moral precepts.

Killing of the appointed disease-carriers is a symbolic surrogate of death-killing. But much of daily life in a modern society appears to be in its turn a symbolic surrogate of a second degree: the killing of disease-carriers in effigy. The holocaust has not been a daily event of modernity. But it did serve as a archetype and arch-metaphor for many a daily concern and activity. It surfaces in infinite number of symbolic disguises – countless modern phobias, those garrisons of death in the midst of life. Sometimes, it surfaces as a 'moral panic' focused on the most recent incarnation of the 'folk devil' (two felicitous terms coined by Stanley Cohen) – be it a new widely publicized form of youth fashion of dress, public conduct and sexual mores, or some other offence against average taste and routine behavioural code, like a new musical or visual-art style outrageously irreverent to entrenched habits, or a public display of aspects of human conduct previously forbidden or kept secret, or the sudden effacing of categorial (generational, gender, class) boundaries once kept watertight. Some other times, it surfaces as the horror of a once uncommon, now rising form of criminality or a similar threat to the current model of 'law and order', followed by a new wave of public outcry and demands for stiffer, harsher, more 'radical' punishment – the more corporal and (literally or allegorically) closer to death penalty, the better. At still other times – as scary rumours of sinister conspiracy or criminal neglect perpetrated by the high-and-mighty ('big corporations', foreign firms or 'internationals', occasionally the government agencies), guilty of contaminating, adulterating or poisoning food, air, water, if not the totality of the life-giving 'environment' (that grass-root, and slightly more benign, version of the *Lebensraum* of the genocide managers). Sometimes – as

the scare of new and yet unexperienced biological dangers: new viruses, bacteria contagions, toxic substances, frightening mainly for their novelty effect and apparent absence of 'guaranteed cure', rather than actual spread and documented morbidity.

At all times and at all places the symbolic 'death killing' urge manifests itself in tribal-defence manoeuvres: in the appointing of a categorial enemy of tribal safety and designing measures to stave off the assumed enemy's tendency to infiltrate and subvert from inside the security of one's own tribe. These are tribal practices, not to be confused with the 'territorial behaviour' of nation-states. They are tribal, rather than state-national, as they are only secondarily concerned with the defence (still less with the conquest) of a territory. Tribes are non-territorial, they exist not in space but in historical-cultural discourse. To survive (or, rather, to feel secure) they do not need a territorial, but a cultural sovereignty (though legislative mastery over territory, and coercive means standing at the disposal of territorial masters, may help to insure cultural dominance – and hence tribal postures often extend to the demands of quasi-state-national autonomy). The prime target and the defining (by negation) factor of inner-tribal solidarity is not the enemy on the *other side* of the territory, but 'the enemy inside' – a fitful, iconic symbol of death which – though *foreign* – does not come from 'out there', but leads a kind of parasitic existence *inside* the living organism from the moment of birth. The invidious horror of a tribal enemy rests precisely in its death-like attributes of intangibility, elusiveness, ambiguity of 'outsidedness' and 'insidedness', ambivalence of its partly foreign (which one would wish to assign it), yet partly native (which it claims) status.[31]

---

[31] For a fuller discussion of this point, see my *Modernity and Ambivalence* (Cambridge: Polity Press, 1991), chapters 2 and 3.

Fear of the degenerate body and its polluting effluvia merged throughout with social fears of boundary transgressions; each served, so to speak, as a vivid metaphor of the other. In Catherine Gallagher's words, 'unavailable as a metaphor of order and harmony, equally untranscendable and unperfectible, the body came to occupy the centre of social discourse obsessed with sanitation, with minimizing bodily contact and preventing the now alarmingly traversable boundaries of individual bodies from being penetrated by a host of foreign elements, above all the products of other bodies. Medical doctors became the most prestigious experts on social problems. Society was imagined to be a chronically, incurably ill organism that could only be kept alive by the constant flushing, graining, and excising of various deleterious elements.' ('The Body versus the Social Body in the works of Thomas Malthus and Henry Mayhew', in *The Making of Modern Body: Sexuality and Society in the Nineteenth Century*, ed. Catherine Gallagher and Thomas Laquer (Berkeley, University of California Press, 1987), p. 90.) In his highly

The most favourite candidates for the role of enemies sedimented by tribal practices while simultaneously keeping them alive, are immigrants – that epitome of volatile others (nomads, people 'without fixed address', people 'out of place', mobile people, unstable people, under- and over-defined people) who *come in* and suddenly, uncharacteristically, stop moving; come with the intention of *staying*. Gypsies, who galvanize wherever they go the previously dormant tribal instincts, who are chased with the otherwise unnoticeable tribal solidarity from whatever site they wish to settle, supply a permanent, timeless prototype for the plight meted out to all tribe-infiltrators. (As if to let the cat out of the bag, Gypsies are widely perceived as carriers of infectious diseases, and the campaigns for their eviction are as a rule conducted in 'hygienic' terms.) The presence of migrants exposes the fragility of the social and cultural security of the natives; it shakes, by proxy, all security, since it is the social and cultural security that is outspokenly at stake in all that matters. The socially and culturally shaped life-strategies weave the security one is busy building, so that one can forget the fundamental insecurity one can seek to escape but in vain since one can do about it nothing that truly matters. Migrants, therefore, attract charges invoking metaphorically the deep-seated fear of death and death-bearing disease. They divulge the closely kept secret; they symbolically expose and unravel the essential precariousness of human defences, and the futility of all pretention to durability of human arrangements. They are, indeed, much like disease, frightful because of its uncanny penchant for making visible what one tried hard, with mixed success, to remove from sight and evict from memory. And so they are fought as the diseases are, with the help of all the tried techniques of medical praxis.

Most widely, spontaneously demanded are the above mentioned techniques of segregation, isolation and removal (deportation). They all express the same intention to set a 'secure' distance (that is, a distance which the feared infection is not potent enough to travel) between the population to be defended and the 'foreign tribe' which renders the defence vulnerable. The measures to be taken are hoped to restore the broken balance in the status of two sympathetic links recognized, as Frazer

---

influential study of London labour and London poor, Mayhew expressed no doubt that pickpockets, beggars, prostitutes, street sellers, street performers, cabmen, coachmen, watermen, sailors – all those bearing too close a resemblance to nomadic, homeless, rootless tribes – show 'a greater development of the animal than of the intellectual or moral nature', and that this morbid inclination was closely correlated with the changes in the body induced by living without fixed address and being 'on the move' – i.e. 'high check-bones and protruding jaws'.

discovered long ago, by all magic thinking: that of similarity and contiguity. The *dis*-similarity of the 'foreign tribe', discursively established and objectified by the differential treatment it has been accorded in daily practices, jars with the stubborn physical closeness of the 'foreigners' and the resented frequency of contacts. Segregation is hoped to ,remove that off-putting and vexing ambiguity: it would supplement the lack of similarity with the prohibition and prevention of contiguity.

This is the strategy long established by modern medicine and, more generally, by modern 'therapeutic' society deeply influenced in its world-image and in its pragmatic principles by medical discourse. The strategy consists, by and large, in identifying the 'causes' of death (or of the danger of death), locating the causes in social space (tantamount to pinpointing their most likely carriers), subjecting the 'dangerous sites' (or 'dangerous categories') to a special regime of surveillance and treatment and preferably isolating (hospitalizing) them to ward off the harm they can do to the 'healthy core' when milling around and mixing in. Destruction of the causes of death looms constantly on the horizon as the ultimate, radical, final solution. It also provides a ready-made, tempting model for the 'final solution' to the deadly horrors of tribal infiltration.[32]

We may repeat once more that medical practices are surrogate solutions to the existential predicament that allows no solution. They merely avert attention from big things which cannot be done to other, smaller things

---

[32] As Stephen L. Chorover observed, the 'destruction on unworthy life' (a code name for the genocide planned or performed by the Nazis upon all categories considered dangerous to the healthy survival of the Aryan race) 'followed in time, technique, and justification the precedent set by what purported to be a scientifically objective and morally and ethically neutral exercise' (*From Genesis to Genocide: The Meaning of Human Nature and the Power of Behaviour Control* (Boston: MIT Press, 1979), p. 7.) The link was revealed, but by no means created or even invented, by the Nazis. Contrary to the widespread 'drive to confine and forget' – to what we try, for the sake of our own comfort, to believe – Germany was not 'aberrant or degenerate, a kind of cancer in the healthy body' of Western civilization. (Pick, *Faces of Degeneration*, p. 240.) 'The period 1939–45 may . . . appear as the realization, the crystallized evidence, of all that had been sinister in the Victorian and Edwardian literature on progress and decay, crime and social pathology.' (p. 239) As Robert Proctor found in his eye-opening study of essential harmony between the science we respect and the Nazi practices we condemn, 'racial hygienists drew upon the examples of American immigration, sterilization, and miscegenation laws to formulate their own policies in these areas'. 'Racial science was "normal science", in the sense that Kuhn has given this expression.' (Robert Proctor, *Racial Hygiene: Medicine under the Nazis* (Boston: Harvard University Press, 1988), pp. 286, 285.)

that can. The impotence in the face of the 'biggest of problems' is to be compensated (stifled? masked? shouted down?) by the zealotry and ardour of the agitation about the smaller ones. Hence the hysteria – whether the sniffed dangers come from salmonella-infected chicken, smokers, mad cows, homosexuals, Turks in Germany, Algerians in France, Blacks in England, or Gypsies everywhere. The genuine fear of premature death is beefed up and inflated to neurotic levels by the repressed knowledge of non-finality, the hopelessly temporary nature of any salvation and the precariousness, as well as endemic inconclusiveness, of all survival.

All too often, and certainly much too often for moral comfort and political placidity, the audacious dream of killing death turns into the practice of killing people. It is the specifically modern project of deconstructing mortality which (not entirely paradoxically) infuses modern society with its unyielding and probably incorrigible genocidal drive that lurks just beneath the surface of modern forms of tribalism. It would surface more often, were political precautions and countermeasures not to be taken. Such measures, however, treat the symptoms, not the cause of the innate defect.

5

Postmodernity, or
Deconstructing Immortality

Here, you see, it takes all the running
you can do, to keep in the same place

Lewis Carroll, *Through the Looking-Glass*

'If I wished to characterize the present state of affairs', writes Jean
Baudrillard, 'I would say this is the state after the orgy. The orgy – that is
all the explosive moment of modernity, the liberation in all domains.' 'All
finalities of liberation are already behind us' – whatever could be liberated, has been. The practical effect of a liberation that in the end ran short
of targets, having declared and won the war on all constraints, is that 'we
are now accelerating in the void'.[1]

Modernity declared all constraints illegitimate and hence offensive;
more to the point, it declared illegitimate all such constraints that *could
be* (considering the current or expected state of technological arts), and
had to be (considering the militant self-confidence of the modern posture)
declared unwarranted. All, or virtually all, non-man-made constraints fell
into this category. Mortality, that ultimate offence against human omnipotence, that final challenge to human reason, was the foremost among
them: indeed, the prototype and the archetype of all constraints. All other
constraints seemed minor by comparison, no more than imperfect
metaphors, pale reflections of the ultimate boundary – weak, transient, just
waiting to be swept out of the way, easy to be replaced with sensible,
reasonable, by-humans-made and for-humans-made rules. They were
merely temporary irritants, as-yet-unresolved *problems* – to be resolved
tomorrow or the day after.

In that world-picture, 'nature' stood for everything not yet appropriated,
mastered and redesigned by reason. Empowering of reason meant no

---

[1] Jean Baudrillard, *La Transparence du Mal: essai sur les phénomènes extrêmes*
(Paris: Galilée, 1990), p. 4.

161

more (yet no less either) than legal incapacitation of nature. Nature was denied moral authority; reason was to be in the end left alone in the field, free as God once was, the sole legislator and the only executor of its laws. Until that fateful moment will have arrived, no existent has a sufficient right to exist. What is, derives its significance and value from paving the way for something else. The present has no value of its own: whatever value one can assign to it can be only drawn from the future (the Blochian *Noch-nicht-geworden*),[2] from the great vision of the indivisible sovereignty of reason to which the present is but a step.

Modern time was an arrow with a pointer. What made it into such arrow, was the *projects* (Lyotard's *métarécits*) – themselves already revolutionary narratives, narratives totally unlike the traditional 'legitimizing', sense-making tales, unlike those etiological myths which had always pointed back to the origins, to the zero point of the world, of the land, of the tribe. What the fables of (pre-modern) yore set to do was to 'explain' and 'legitimize' the being by its birth. After birth, there was nothing left to explain. The birth was the unique, the *only* 'moment in time', after which time has stopped, ground to a halt, is no more. Not so the modern projects (a pleonasm, to be sure; a project cannot be anything else but modern): these *meta*-narratives, narratives composed to legitimize (or delegitimize), to make sense (or to expose the absurdity) of all other narratives, to set the legitimate narratives apart from the fraudulent ones. They 'do not seek legitimation in the original founding act, but in a future still to arrive, that is in an Idea still to be realized'. Construed by such metanarratives, time is not being arrested – it gathers speed instead. All competing narratives are invited to test themselves in the yet-unwritten chronicle-of-the-future, to prove themselves in tomorrow achievements. No more point in looking back, brandishing birth certificates and meticulously composed charts of genealogical trees. The vision, the postulate of the finishing line (not a myth; as the line has not been reached yet, its vision is neither true nor false, it still is to be *authenticated*) has replaced the myths of the origins.

The projects were many. But they were all *projects*. And so time stretched from 'now' to 'later'. This was a kind of time that devalued the

---

[2] 'Man is something which still must be found.' (Ernst Bloch, *Spuren* (Frankfurt-am-Main: Suhrkamp, 1969), p. 32.) 'In both man and the world the essential thing is still outstanding, waiting, in fear of coming to naught, in hope of succeeding.' (Bloch, *Das Prinzip Hoffnung* (Frankfurt-am-Main: Suhrkamp, 1959), vol. 1, p. 285.) In his most poetic yet precise summary of the modern posture, Bloch describes both humans and their world as existing in the state of 'explosive possibility'.

'now', measured but by its closeness, its affinity with the 'later'. The link between the 'now' and the 'later' gained in strength as much as the 'now' lost in content. To assure the arrival of the future, the present had to refrain from pre-empting it, from draining the resources the future would need. The present could contribute to the future gratification only by *delaying the current one* – by forbearing its own measure of happiness and joy. Projects presented abstemiousness as self-fulfilment.

At the totalitarian extreme, the present and its residents were offered all the importance of the manure (of history – but history that was about to *begin*) – which, as is the way of all manure, had to decompose so that new life might be born. In modernity's dull and ordinary quotidianity, the present was to be viewed by its residents as no more pleasure-promising than the dull and harrowing time of cramming the lines in the name of the future splendour of the gala première.

Eternity decomposed

Modernity, as we have seen before, deconstructed mortality one cannot overcome into a series of afflictions one can. Modern *projects* deconstructed the ultimate bliss which one is unlikely to savour soon, into a series of little gains one can hope to enjoy tomorrow. Still, tomorrow – not today. Whether it is denigrated by the splendours of the next day, or of a distant and hazy 'sometime', the results for the present are pretty much the same. As long as the project remains the only source of meaning, the present is meaningless unless it abandons itself completely to the service of the future.

Now, as Lyotard says, it is the modern way of living-with-the-project, in-the-shadow-of-a-project, toward-a-project – that today has been not so much abandoned or forgotten or forcefully suppressed, as *liquidized*. It lost, so to speak, its former solidity. 'Liquidization' is, in Lyotard's words, a 'way of destroying the modern project while creating an impression of its fulfilment'.[3] To create the impression could not be easier: it was enough

---

[3] Jean-François Lyotard, *Le Postmoderne expliqué aux enfants: Correspondence, 1982–1985* (Paris: Galilée, 1988), p. 36. Lyotard opposes the manner in which the modern project (or, rather, the modern habit of 'project-making' as such) has been 'liquidized', to the 'destruction', for which Auschwitz provides the paradigm (standing as a symbol of the 'tragic inachievement of modernity'). Liquidizing means that the ends have been slowly dissolved in ostensible means, that the capitalist technoscience brought into being the richly satisfying emotion of attained mastery over reality, without offering visible gains in liberty, public education, equality or common wealth.

to accept that *the future is now*. Or, rather, that the bliss future once promised – liberty, democracy, equality, wealth, security and what not – has (barring minor corrections still to made, soon) arrived. No more history. No more unresolved conflicts of value. No more alternatives to what is. Tomorrow will not be distinct from today; at best (and one means *best*), it will bring more of the same. There is no reason, therefore, why today should be handled as a sacrificial lamb offered to ingratiate the God of tomorrow. Indeed, we may say, 'creating the impression of its fulfilment' *is* the destruction of the modern project – of the modern way of living for the sake of a project.

If modernity deconstructed death into a bagful of unpleasant, but tameable, illnesses, so that in the hubbub of disease-fighting which followed mortality could be forgotten and not worried about – in the society that emerged at the far end of the modern era it is the majestic yet distant immortal bliss that is being deconstructed into a sackful of bigger or smaller, but always within-reach, satisfactions, so that in the ecstasy of enjoyment the likeness of the ultimate perfection may dissolve and vanish from view. Time still runs, but the pointer has been lost in the flow. Now one moment is no different from another. Each moment, or no moment, is immortal. Immortality is here – but not here to stay. Immortality is as transient and evanescent as the rest of things. Immortality is as nomadic as the nomads it serves ... Indeed, being nomads is the existential condition of the orphaned descendants of modernity.

In pre-postmodern time, a project-oriented philosophy of the world was an apt and plausible correlate of the project-oriented life. There was resonance between the two: the social (historical) project of modern philosophers and the individual (biographical) project of the modern person. Both history and individual life ran towards a *goal ahead*; and both in the flow of time came *closer* to their respective goals. History and individual life alike were *cumulative*. They climbed the ladder of time counting the steps made and left beneath – each step having been made 'in a direction', hopefully 'in the right direction' – upwards, towards the peak. Projects gave meaning and direction not only to the present, but also to the past: it was the past presents already 'objectified', frozen into a coherent continuum, sedimented as a past solid and fixed (considered as inalienable gain, legal possession, irreversible achievement, earned interest added to the account), rather than evanescent and risky 'present present' which may yet go up or down on the stock exchanges of history or biography, that truly supplied the 'pointer' to the arrow of time.

'Identity' (of society and of person alike) was something built and to be built level by level, storey by storey, from the ground floor up. Each floor rested on the one beneath. From savagery to barbarity, from barbarity to civilization – this is how history moved, never jumping stages, always reaching for the higher floor with the feet set firmly on the floor below. From childhood, through adolescence, into the mature age – this is how biography moved, never jumping stages either. The history-built identity was plotted along the line of rising knowledge and know-how; the biography-built identity (in both aspects distinguished by Paul Ricoeur: *la mêmeté*, 'identity with itself over time', and *l'ipseté*, 'distinction from other identities at the time') progressed along the line of the occupational career. Both lines were straight lines; like in any straight line, there was but one and one only way connecting any two points – one could move from one point to another only passing through a specific stretch of the line. Both history and biography, one may say, were of the nature of *Markov chains* (and not, as we will see later, of the 'forget the past'-type *Markov processes*, typical of the postmodern condition): in the stochastic time of collective and individual identity building, probabilities at each successive point were, simultaneously, products of the probabilities of the points behind and determinants of the probabilities of the points ahead.

The modern world was a full world ('Nature detests the void' was one of the most popular – scientifically certified – beliefs of the era). No holes in time; no holes in space. André Lervi-Gourhan[4] coined the concept of 'connexity' to describe life-experience in a traditional habitat: one could only pass from one location to another following a continuous, unbroken path – without for a single moment 'getting out' from the world around. We may say that modernity tried its best (though with a mixed success) to make secure the hold of the 'connexity' principle over historical and biographical time. Everything one did was serious and important, since

---

[4] Cf. André Lervi-Gourhan, *Le Geste et la parole* (Paris: Albin-Michel, 1964). Jean-Pierre Dupuy ('Myths of the Informational Society', in *The Myths of Information: Technology and Postindustrial Culture*, ed. Kathleen Woodward (London: Routledge, 1980), pp. 10 ff), recalling Lervi-Gourhan's concept, suggests that already in its modern phase capitalism willy-nilly sapped the rule of connexity by dividing the personal space between separate locations (family home, work place, diverse symbolic foci of the city, shopping centres, as well as 'the mythical elsewhere of leisure and escapism'). The whole impact of that division, we may observe, was to be felt, however, much later, when the late-modern technology and style of life offered a real opportunity to opt out – physically and spiritually – from the spaces in between the selected and significant spots, making those in-between spaces into genuinely meaningless 'wilderness' and casting the traveller into a position of imaginary omnipotence: fragments of the world may be made to appear or vanish at will, just like images on the screen of a remote-control TV set.

everything in the present weighed heavily on everything still to come: the future fate of the project hung on the deeds of today. No void, no momentary lapse, no opting aside from the unstoppable and *continuous* march of time, as *il n'y avait pas de hors-temps*.

In fact, modernity proved to be more ruthless than its predecessors in observing the connexity principle. The remnants of discontinuity tolerated in traditional society found themselves at odds with the cumulativeness of the modern time flow. No wonder Weber insisted that Protestantism, having rejected life sliced by the Roman Church into stretches of sin extending from one confession to another, and replaced it with the 'pilgrimage through life' in which every day trip and every overnight stay counted, bringing the coveted destination nearer – was in tune with modernity in the way in which Catholicism, its declared adversary, never was and could not be. Modernity was about the impossibility of 'starting from scratch', about the prohibition of 'another try'. The question put in the mouth of Judas by the authors of *Jesus Christ, Superstar* – 'Can we start again, please?' – was not a question likely to pass through modern lips.

Now, wonderful now

Postmodern nomads, unlike Protestant 'pilgrims through life', wander between *unconnected* places. It is on this that they differ – not in the concern with *establishing* and *preserving* their identities, a concern which they share with their pilgrim ancestors. Most attributes of the modern conception of identity, listed persuasively by Anthony Giddens,[5] apply to the nomads as much as they did to the pilgrims. For both, identity is a task, and a task which has to be reflexively monitored, and a task the monitoring of which is their own and constant responsibility; for both, the construction and maintenance of identity are tasks that can never be abandoned, an effort that cannot be relaxed. Where the nomads and the pilgrims differ, and differ rather sharply, is the *disconnexity* of the time/ space in which the identity of the nomads is plotted, as against *connexity* of the time/space canvas on which the pilgrims' identities are woven.

---

[5] And particularly the features captured in the following generalizations: 'The self is seen as a reflexive project, for which the individual is responsible.'; 'The self forms a trajectory of development from the past to the anticipated future.'; 'The reflexivity of the self is continuous, as well as all-pervasive.' (Cf. Anthony Giddens, *Modernity and Self-Identity: Self and Society in the Late Modern Age* (Cambridge: Polity Press, 1991), pp. 75ff.

Pilgrims select their destination early and plan their life-itinerary accordingly. We may say that they are guided throughout by a 'life-project', by an overall 'life-plan'. Nomads, on the other hand, hardly ever reach in their imagination beyond the next caravan-site. If pressed to make sense of their itinerary, they would rather look back, than forward, tracing (with the 'wisdom of hindsight') the connections between stations which they failed to note at the time. Only in retrospect, if at all, the series of contingencies appears to them as a stochastically determined chain. Only in this *ex post facto* sense they would speak of their lives as of implementation of a life-project. If there was a life-project, it was not a part of the nomads' own psychological reality. The nomads, like the pilgrims, were all along busy constructing their identities; but theirs were 'momentary' identities, identities 'for today', until-further-notice identities. Nomads do not bind the time/space, they move through it; and so they move *through* identities.

Comprehension can be impaired by too large a distance (not enough shared points of experiential reference for a satisfying translation) or by too intimate closeness (too few opaque 'objects'   references without immediately obvious referents – to trigger off the effort of translation). If the nomadic experience escapes our full comprehension as long as we remain the 'insiders' of that experience – as long as the nomadic condition continues for us – so does, though for the opposite reasons, the Buddhist experience of the world and life-in-the-world. And yet the apparent resonance of the two creates a unique chance for translation. Because of that resonance, the postmodern mind opens more fully to the Buddhist vision that its modern predecessor. In the process, it may learn more about itself. This is an impression one gets rereading in the 1990s Mircea Eliade's account of the Indian symbolism of time and eternity, composed as long ago as the 1940s and first published in 1952. At that early stage of his long and distinguished writing career, Eliade was still at pains to 'make sense', *our* sense, out of the lore his readers had to view as unquestionably bizarre and 'archaic' (that is, destined for a museum place in the land of modernity). Again and again Eliade reminded the readers of the 'specific marks' which 'differentiate the archaic world from that of our modern societies'. As one of those specific marks (perhaps the crucial one) Eliade named the fact that 'in the traditional societies men endeavoured, consciously and voluntarily, to abolish Time – periodically to efface the past and to regenerate Time ...' Such an endeavour had to be, of course, classified among the traits of an odd, opaque otherhood – as it flied in the face of the most sacred modern myths, those of continuous, whole and irreversible time. Today, however, the picture which follows, scrupu-

168   *Mortality, Immortality and Other Life Strategies*

lously and with great effort and flair painted by Eliade, neither offends nor puzzles.

And so we learn from Buddhist scriptures that 'every existence is precarious, evanescent and illusory' to the point where 'Universe itself vanishes into unreality'. The thoughtful among men would 'conceive man's temporal existence not only as an infinite repetition of certain archetypes and exemplary gestures [that the novelty-loving modern mind would expect from the 'traditional mind' – Z.B.] but also as *eternal recommencement*'. 'The nature of any thing is its own momentary stasis and destruction', wrote Santaraksita, a Buddhist sage. Fluidity endemic in things deprives them of reality; in fact, that 'fluidity conceals unreality'. For the Buddha (and thus for his disciples), 'there is neither past nor future', all times 'have become present times'. The Buddhist world is one of the 'total present'.

Two important consequences follow from this vision. First, each moment is important; there is, after all, nothing to expect in the future which will not be another 'moment', fluid, bound to self-destruct. Those who live in the 'eternal present', the Buddha advises 'not to lose the moment', for 'those who miss the moment will lament'. The Buddha congratulates the monks who 'have seized their moment' and pities those 'for whom the moment is past'. Comprehension of reality, as it were – the *true* reality, not the illusion offered instead in the moments of profane time – can be *revealed at any moment*; if it comes, it 'comes *suddenly*, like a *flash of lightning*. Beware, this may happen at any time, and the moment it happens in no way depends on all moments that preceded it ... And the second consequence, already ensconced in the first: '*nothing distinguishes any moment of profane time from the timeless instant attained by the enlightenment*'.[6] There is no way of telling in advance which is which. All moments are *equal* before the only thing which truly matters and lasts beyond death.

In a life composed of equal moments, speaking of directions, projects and fulfilments makes no sense. Every present counts as much, or as little, as any other. Every state is as momentary and passing as any other, and each one is – potentially – the gate opening into eternity. Thus the distinction between the mundane and the eternal, transient and durable, mortal and immortal, is all but effaced. Daily life is a constant rehearsal of both mortality and immortality – and of the futility of setting one against

---

[6] Mircea Eliade, *Images and Symbols: Studies in Religious Symbolism*, trans. Philip Mairet (Princeton: Princeton University Press, 1991), pp. 58, 67, 69–70, 81–2, 84.

the other. If in the pre-modern era *death* was 'tamed' – now, in the wake of the destructive job performed by modernity, it is *immortality* that has been 'tamed' – no more an object of desire, distant and alluring; no more the remote and high-handed God, commanding ascesis, self-immolation and self-sacrifice.

From the Markov *chain* it used to be in the project-oriented world, life turns into the likeness of a Markov *process* – in which probability relations of some future state depends only on the present state and not on the history that led to it. Modernity has had its way, and the past does not bind the present any more. As the war waged by modern spirit and modern practice was coming to its victorious end, Claude Levi-Strauss could in clear conscience declare history to be our own variant of tribal myth, and the synchronic network of relations (and not the diachronic sequence favoured by historically minded etymologists), a network fully enclosed in the present and disdainful to the past, to be the only setting in which meaning of anything could be explored and found. *Simultaneity* replaced history as the location of meaning. What counts – what has the power to define and shape – is what is around here and now. 'Older' and 'younger' objects are all on the same plane, that of the present. The present is a large pool of such objects, which differ in many aspects – the aspect of 'origin' or 'history' not being, however, one of them.

In the postmodern world whose philosophy Levi Strauss' precept antici-pated, the present does not bind its future more than it itself is bound by its past: what will the future be, if not another 'present state' unbound by *our* present that will have turned out to be *its* past? Life is a succession of self-cancelling determinations. Since our present, that *past of our future*, will be sooner or later declared null and void and its hold on the way things are (if there ever was one) will be broken, consideration of the distant, not-immediately-experienced consequences of our present actions is waste of time. Whatever the present may offer, it offers now – 'until the stock lasts'. The offer will be rescinded (or won't it rather be forgotten?) when the present present is replaced (pushed aside, elbowed out, made obsolete, cast into oblivion) by some other, tomorrow's present.

And so nothing needs to be done forever. Nothing *can* be done forever. Knowledge I studiously master today will become thoroughly inadequate, if not a downright ignorance, tomorrow. The skills I learn today by the sweat of my brow will not carry me far in the brave new world of tomorrow's technology and know-how. The job I won yesterday in fierce competition will disappear tomorrow. The career whose steps I am negotiating will vanish – the stairs, the staircase, the building and all. My prize possessions, my today's pride, will tomorrow become yesterday's taste and my embarrassment. The union which I have sworn to cherish and preserve will fall apart and be dissolved tomorrow at the first sign of my partner's or my own disaffection. Perhaps there will be a string of 'life-long partners'. None is, none will be my partner 'till death us do part'; or at least nothing I do may assure me that she or he will.

With eternity decomposed into a Brownian movement of passing moments, nothing seems to be immortal any more. But nothing seems mortal either. Not in the old – supra-human, sinister, awesome – sense of 'once-for-allness', of irrevocability, of irreversibility.

Making history in a world without history

'Making history' means becoming immortal; be *made* immortal by being recorded; be, from now on, kept in the records, intended to be preserved forever, indestructible; be meant to be always ready to be dusted off, recovered, returned to the agenda of current living; be confirmed as 'of importance' for that living because of changing or preserving its form, its character. In the universe lived as a string of episodes, every event and every actor can 'make history'.

In the pre-modern world it was the kings and the warlords and the popes who 'made history'. They were the only ones to have the right to be recorded – and the exclusivity of that right was jealously guarded. History was, for all practical purposes, a chronicle of dynasties. As we saw in chapter 2, that concept of history was not so much contested, as sapped and eroded by the practice of chronicle-writers – the scribes. Not until the dawn of modernity, however, the monopoly of history-making had been broken in a decisive fashion and the right of events and actors to be recognized as 'making history' had become a matter of ferocious contest, known as the struggle for *historicity*. Modernity was marked by the relentless broadening of the contents of history. Not just crowned heads, but elected leaders; not just leaders, but assemblies of legislators; not just office-holders, but their popular contestants; not just the speakers and programme-makers, but the crowds of their followers – classes and mass movements as, metaphorically, collective *actors of history*.

Neither was 'history making' confined any more to the realm of politics – to the actual and the would-be rulers of actual and would-be states. Modernity brought a proliferation of histories. Whatever they meant otherwise – the modern separation of discourses, functional specialization, the institutional division of labour signified as well the new plurality of autonomous histories and with that the radical broadening of the occasions of history-making and the arsenal of the history-making tools.

Democratization of history-making (of the access to *historicity*) meant, first and foremost, relaxing of the limitations once constraining the chances to individual immortality. As in so many other areas of human life, the modern world also became the 'land of unlimited opportunity' for the immortality-seekers. And, like in so many other areas, the ever more lavish distribution of the opportunities led inexorably to the destruction of the very stakes in the name of which the access to opportunity had been sought. The more universally it was available, the more 'history-making' was losing its distinction-conferring capacity, the very foundation of its attraction and allurement. The meaning of history (as distinct from 'non-historicity': the anonymous mass, non-historical nations etc.) resided in its selectivity: 'making history' was a privilege one needed to inherit or at least earn with superhuman heroic effort. With the gates to history-making thrown wide open and admission tickets abolished, everything is 'historical' and therefore nothing is. Any act can acquire, in principle, instant immortality. All actors with all their deeds have become, in principle, immortal. Becoming part of the historical narrative has turned into the game of chance – though measures have been taken to ensure that some probabilities are high and that one knows in advance in what area and under what circumstances they are likely to be particularly high.

'Official records' are now run in countless areas of activity by countless agencies. Everything that has been recorded is recoverable, and can be reinstated as an element of some future present; it disappears from view only temporarily – it does not 'die', it is just put on a side shelf so that it remains constantly handy and within reach. Its invisibility is not allowed to remain too dense for too long. Its permanent, though invisible presence is periodically rehearsed and thereby solidified, officially endorsed, 'objectified', entrenched. The most postmodern of games, the great twentieth-century institution of the quiz, is a public spectacle of universal and instant 'recoverability' of past events, of the public ritual through which the being itself is turned into the state of perpetual resurrection. The democratization of immortality is manifested in the retrospective levelling up (or down) of the value of events and their performers. The same score is attached to recovery of any past event – a start of a new political universe counts for as much as the first performance of a hit song or running an Olympic race – and thus varieties of immortality are retrospectively accorded an equal status. 'Mastermind' is he or she who excels in the game of recovery; quality of intellect is measured by the resurrecting skill of competitors. Thus everyone is publicly encouraged to engage in the DIY resurrection rites, seduced by prestige attached to successful performance, and thus allured to aid and abet the resulting 'mundanization' of immortality.

Like in all other dimensions of equality, this new 'equality of immortality' is at best an equality of *opportunity*, not of the distribution of the good itself. Here, as in other dimensions of equality, allocation is managed; a new profession (or professions) of immortality-brokers, armed with skills geared to new, mundane form of immortality, has emerged to supervise the distribution. With immortality deconstructed into fame and immortality-earning virtue into the quantity of tied public attention, Madison Avenue has taken the place of the Papal See. Advertisers, publicity-promoting and image-grooming companies, critics, gallery owners, publishers, programmers of TV companies and editors of the press are the most prominent of the new professions whose function (and importance, and esteem) consists in the brokerage of immortality. Their clients may be given diverse names and assigned to diverse functions; they may be politicians or terrorists, writers or pop-singers, tycoons or criminals – but they all need their immortality-brokers, and it is in the end the skills of the latter who makes the difference between anonymity and prominence, the opposition which in the postmodern vanity fair has replaced that between mortality and immortality. It is not the great deeds which are immortalized; the deeds become great the moment they are 'immortalized' by having been forced – for a brief, elusive, but never fully erasable moment – into the centre of public attention.

Death's disappearing act

There is no more secure a place to hide than the crowd. The bigger and denser, the better.

The play called hide-and-seek-and-find-again is now played twenty-four hours a day, to full capacity, in the public arena. The stage is dazzlingly lit, so that the wings are barely visible and actors seem to emerge from nowhere only to melt back again into abstruse fuzziness (a singer in an obscure and shoddy night-club is 'discovered', a local lad makes it good with his guitar and a few clever verses, a school drop-out scores enough goals to break the transfer-price record). It seems, indeed, *childishly* easy to make one's way to the stage. It seems, on the other hand, damn difficult. nay impossible, to stay there for long. There must be many actors waiting in the wings, more than the stage is able to accommodate, and so each has been given short lines, They are, as Warhol observed, celebrities for fifteen minutes. Because the time they spend on the stage is so brief, many among the audience may expect also to be allowed, when their turn comes, to rehearse the easy accessibility, and the volatility, of immortality.

The terror of death may be exorcised in more than one way. Yet however varied and numerous, all ingenious techniques of exorcism may be roughly divided into two basic classes. One follows the principle of 'We'll cross that bridge once we come to it'; it admits that the bridge will have to be crossed sometime, but insists that the time of the crossing may be postponed – perhaps indefinitely (the current craze of *cryonics* represents this hope at its radical *privatized* extreme; the immortality of the nation or other 'causes' has long offered the extreme *collectivized* version). The second – one that seems to be increasingly favoured by the world we live in, by the increasingly *postmodern* world – makes the whole of life into a game of bridge-crossing: all bridges seem by and large alike, all are – comfortably – part of one's daily itinerary, so that no bridge seems to loom ominously as the 'ultimate' one (most importantly, none seems to be the bridge 'of no return'). Crossing the bridge becomes a habitual, sometimes even pleasurable activity – all the more so for the fact that each crossing practised thus far has been demonstrated to be reversible. None of the bridges has been shown to be a one way road. Nothing seems to vanish forever, 'for good' – so that it cannot reappear again; objects seem to go lingering on, even if for a time they stay invisible. Nothing that has been botched once cannot be done better next time. No loss is irretrievable.

This new experience has been captured well by Guy Debord:

> Media/police rumours acquire instantly – or at worst after three or four repetitions – the indisputable status of age-old historical evidence. By the legendary authority of the spectacle of the day, odd characters eliminated in silence can reappear as fictive survivors, whose return can always be conjured up or computed, and *proved* by the mere say-so of specialists. They exist somewhere between the Acheron and the Lethe, these dead whom the spectacle has not properly buried, supposedly slumbering while awaiting the summons which will awake them all . . .

It is immortality itself that becomes now mortal – but death ceased to be a one-off act, a single, unique event with irreparable consequences. The sting of finality has been pulled out from mortality, all mortality, including the mortality of immortality: things disappear from view for a time only; that time may last long, but the odds are that it will not last forever. Death is but a suspension, a transitional state . . . Only the suspension seems to be truly 'immortal' – permanent, assured to last forever (everything is securely stored on computer disks, anyway) – never to disintegrate, surreptitiously, into 'real' death. 'When the spectacle stops talking about something for three days, it is as if it did not exist. For it has gone on to talk about something else, and it is that which henceforth, in short, exists.' No need to worry, though:

> The manufacture of the present where fashion itself, from clothes to music, has come to a halt, which wants to forget the past and no longer seems to believe in future, is achieved by the ceaseless circularity of information, always returning to the same short list of trivialities.[7]

Objects come and go, but then come again, never overstaying the capacity of attention to concentrate. They are condemned to the nomadic existence of commercial travellers. Last year's rubbish becomes a cherished antique, the last generation's fallen stars turn into the idols of nostalgic dreams, abhorred killing fields of yore are invaded by awe-struck tourists searching for 'our glorious heritage' of industrial or military triumphs. Yesterday's obsolete becomes the rage of today, but is doomed to slip once more into oblivion even before it has forced its way, with drum-beating and fanfare, into the centre of today's attention. Mortality daily rehearsed turns into immortality; everything becomes immortal, and nothing is. Indeed, only the transience itself is durable.

'What has disappeared', says Baudrillard, 'has every chance of reappearing. For what dies is annihilated in linear time, but what disappears passes into the state of constellation. It becomes an event in a cycle which may bring it back many times.'[8] 'Nothing disappears any more through an end or death, but through proliferation, continuity, saturation and transparence...' 'No more *mode fatal* of disappearance, only *mode fractal* of dispersion.'[9]

Death and disappearance are two sharply distinct modes of 'ceasing to be'. As sharply distinct are the worlds, in which one or the other gains prevalence.

---

[7] Guy Debord, *Comments on the Society of the Spectacle*, trans. Malcom Imrie (London: Verso, 1990), pp. 55, 20, 13.

[8] Jean Baudrillard, *Cool Memories* (London: Verso, 1990), p. 92.

[9] Baudrillard, *Le Transparence de mal*, p. 12. Not for nothing the 'recycling' is the ideal of the day. Waste is to be reused; circulation between life and death ought to be kept in all areas – and the practices of culture suggest that, indeed, it is. As Iain Chambers observes, 'with electronic reproduction offering the spectacle of gestures, images, styles and cultures in a perpetual collage of disintegration and reintegration, the "new" disappears into a permanent present. And with the end of the "new" – a concept connected to linearity, to the social prospects of "progress", to "modernism" – we move into a perpetual recycling of quotations, styles and fashions; an uninterrupted montage of the "now" ...' (*Popular Culture: The Metropolitan Experience* (London: Methuen, 1986), p. 190).

One world (a world in which death looms large as the final horizon of being, in which time has not just a beginning, but a precise, clearly definable end) is a *succession* of beings. It is a world of *finality* – of scarcity of space. Space is at a premium. Beings must vacate the place they occupy if other beings are to appear. *All* beings have their point of emergence – they are born (that is, they were not in the world *before*, but they are *now*), and they have their *ends* – they die (that is, they are in the world now, but they will not be). Of these two events in the biography of beings, the first is reversible: a being which is here today may not be tomorrow. The second is irreversible: a being that ceased to be will not be again. It is only of the second event that one can say that it is 'final'. No birth contains a promise of durability, permanence, *immortality*. Only death does – and there is certainty attached to its promise of immortality.

The other world (that where death is reduced to the status of 'mere' suspension, temporary disappearance) is a *coexistence* of beings. It is a world in which space makes an impression of not being scarce. Or, rather, space has many levels, its living floors and its cellars, open stages and hidden limbos. To make room at one level, beings may, and do, just move to another. True, beings are born (though they try to hide it, presenting themselves as quotations, the past remembered, traditions restored); but once born, they stay – it is the event of birth, known or lost, admitted or denied, distant or recent, that is now irrevocable and irreversible.

True, beings still undergo transformations *superficially* similar to death; indeed, they vanish from sight and cease to communicate. Yet the resemblance to death is but superficial, since unlike death their departure is reversible and revocable; one can always 'recover' the vanished beings from the limbo where they reside. (Reversibility, says Baudrillard – 'cyclical reversal, annulment', 'puts an end to the linear time'.[10] Linear time is, as a matter of fact, a metaphor, or a visual representation, for the idea of 'no return'.) Unlike death, disappearance is not final, not 'forever'; there is no certainty of its permanence.

In this other world immortality is, so to speak, a birthright. By the same token, it has none of the attractions that used to surround it in the world it has replaced (or is about to replace). Immortality is not a challenge to be taken up, a task to be performed, a reward to be earned. Neither is it a project that can give meaning to the being-in-the-world. In the world in which *disappearing* has replaced the dying, immortality dissolves in the melancholy of presence, in the monotony of endless *repetition*.

---

[10] Jean Baudrillard, *Selected Writings*, ed. Mark Poster (Cambridge: Polity Press, 1988), p. 120.

Of repetition, the principal mode of production in our type of society (products are paid not according to their elusive quality or use value, but according to the number and frequency of repetitions, as avidly recorded and portrayed in the best-sellers or top-twenty lists), and of the difference between repetition and representation, the mode it replaced – Jacques Attali had the following to say:

> [representation] is that which arises from a singular act; repetition is that which is mass-produced. Thus, a concert is representation, but also a meal à la carte in a restaurant; a phonograph record or a can of food is repetition. Other examples of representation are a custom-made piece of furniture or a tailored dress; and of repetition, ready-made clothing and mass produced furniture. One provides a use-value tied to human quality of the production; the other allows for stockpiling, easy accessibility, and repetition. In representation, a work is generally heard only once – it is a unique moment; in repetition, potential hearings are stockpiled.[11]

Representation, we may say, belongs to the world of individuality, and thus also of individual immortality. In our world it is confined to the realm of wealth, luxury, distinction. Outside that realm there is only the mass-produced immortality, immortality for the masses; a widely accessible mass copy, a pastiche of the 'real thing', bearing a tinsel likeness to the precious-metal original. Repetition, we may say, is the poor man's representation; similarly, the disappearance which makes repetition possible is the poor man's immortality. But now, at least, each poor man is allowed to dream of partaking in the immortality (or the market version of it), once

---

[11] Jacques Attali, *Noise: The Political Economy of Music*, trans. Brian Massumi (Manchester: Manchester University Press, 1985), p. 41.

When he patented the phonograph on 19 December 1877, Thomas Alva Edison, one of the most insightful and forward-looking persons of his time, was convinced that the significance of his invention lay in stabilizing and preserving the representation, rather than multiplying it. 'The phonograph was thus conceived as a privileged vector for the dominant speech, as a tool reinforcing representative power and the entirety of its logic. No one foresaw the mass production of music: the dominant system only desired to preserve a recording of its representation of power, to preserve itself.' (p. 92) We may comment that at the time of Edison's invention still at stake was 'traditional' immortality – the death-defying individual achievement. Since Edison's display of a rather puzzling lack of foresight, however, technological and – more generally – cultural development brought not so much a replacement of representation by repetition, as the effacement of the distinction between the two. In Iain Chambers's poignant phrase (*Popular Culture*, p. 196), 'today, the metaphysical separation between ideas and material, between original and derivative, production and reproduction, taste and commerce, culture and identity, has collapsed'.

that immortality, in its mass version, has been translated as a never ending possibility of the repetition. The hauntingly elusive value of *quality*, once the impenetrable shield of privilege, is no more a secure defence against *quantity*.

It was in the arts that the gradual dissolution of representation in repetition was first explored, played with, brought to the surface, made ready for philosophical meditation. It was in Rodin's *Gates of Hell* and *Three Dancers* that the perceptive analyst of modernist and postmodernist art, Rosalind Kraus, spotted the disappearance of 'the original', the melting of the work's singularity in the series of its reassemblances.[12] But what in Rodin's *oeuvre* could be an exploration of the hidden possibilities of creation, later to transpire as the premonition of things to come, has been since built into the very process of artistic production. This is, for instance, how Stephen Struthers sums up the eviction of 'representation' from the practice of contemporary music:

> The concept of replicable art, art made for reproduction, is particularly apposite for sound recordings ... The idea of a contemporary musical recording as a reproduction of a real musical event is not tenable as, using multi-track magnetic tape recording, the final recording is assembled and 'reconstructed' from a number of fragments, and so there is no 'original' of which that published recording can be a reproduction. Indeed a significant amount of popular music has never existed in a prerecorded stage, being created as it was being recorded, or as a unique combination of previously recorded process first heard together during editing. Many recordings today are made with the circumstances of reproduction uppermost in mind, either on the radio or for domestic listening.[13]

One may say that in such and similar cases the work is born already in

---

[12] Cf. Rosalind Kraus, *The Originality of the Avant-Garde and Other Modernist Myths* (Cambridge, Mass.: MIT Press, 1985).

[13] Stephen Struthers, 'Recording Music: Technology in the Art of Recording', in *Lost in Music: Culture, Style and the Musical Event*, ed. Avron Levine White (London: Routledge, 1987), pp. 244–5.
What contemporary technology of recording made salient and self-conscious in case of popular music, the analysts of art come to consider as an endemic feature of all artistic production. Notably, Barthes on non-originality of any intended representation: to depict is to 'refer not from a language to a referent, but from one code to another. Thus realism consists not in copying the real but in copying a (depicted) copy.' 'Through secondary mimesis' the realist author 'copies what is already a copy'. (Roland Barthes, *S/Z* (New York: Hill & Wang, 1974), p. 55) – a usually unconscious process which, for instance, Sharon Levine made deliberately blatant when she signed with her own name prints she made of other photo-

a replicable form, as a potentially 'unlimited edition' of copies which are indistinguishable from each other; never for a moment such work of art is tied down to a single, perishable material object. But as one would expect, the submerging of uniqueness in the sea of replications does not go unopposed. One can see an opposite tendency – a desperate attempt to salvage the traditional, modern concept of artistic uniqueness. This may take only a form of art as an event, as a happening which is not meant for, and preferably not fit for, repetition: installations which are to be dismantled before the gallery opens the next show and will never be assembled again, or wrapping the Brooklyn Bridge in plastic sheets for a day, before the traffic resumes. Such attempts, by and large, are not, however, immune to the 'disease' of replication: one-off compositions may be (and, to have an impact, must be) recorded to be re-shown in countless copies on countless occasions, and the plastic-wrapped bridge may be 'preserved' in thousands of postcards. Worse still, the form which artistic work must take if it intends to resist the assault on originality, cannot but expose the transience, volatility, evanenescence of 'uniqueness' determined to remain 'unique'. Victory bears uncanny resemblance to suicide . . .

---

graphers' negatives; images endlessly reproduced before and by now familiar to anyone interested in photography.

Umberto Eco calls our historical period 'the era of repetition' – 'when iteration and repetition seem to dominate the whole world of artistic creativity, and in which it is difficult to distinguish between the repetition of the media and the repetition of the so-called major arts'. This new situation is quite a challenge to modern aesthetics, which was 'so severe apropos of the industrial-like products of the mass media' and considered all iteration as essentially inferior and non-artistic (Cf. *The Limits of Interpretation* (Bloomington: Indiana University Press, 1990), p. 84.) In fact, the 'radical, or "postmodern" aesthetic solution' consists, in Eco's view, in a virtual effacement of the once paramount division between seriality and innovation, repetition and originality. In postmodern drama as much as in music or visual art the focus of theoretical inquiry ought to be shifted: 'Before, mass mediologists tried to save the dignity of repetition by recognizing in it the possibility of a traditional dialectic between scheme and innovation (but it was still the innovation that accounted for the value, the way of rescuing the product from degeneration). Now, the emphasis must be placed on the inseparable scheme–variation knot, where the variation is no longer more appreciable than the scheme.' (pp. 97–8) The condition of enjoyment for both the ingenuous ('semantic') and the sophisticated ('semiotic') reader or viewer is previous intertextual knowledge of the plot or motif which are repeated, so that ingenuity of the infinite play of variations can be grasped (as Benjamin suggested, the message of mass media can only be received in a state of inattention). To look at this from the opposite angle, change and novelty have become aspects of 'sameness'; the new is nothing but the reiterated old – novelty resides in the very act of reiteration.

As in so many other areas of economy, so also in the economy of death and immortality does the Gresham's Law seem to be at work. In the immortality market inferior (counterfeit?) coins seem to oust and supplant the superior (prototype) ones. Singularity of skill, prowess, attainment becomes an offence – and a challenge. Unique achievement must confirm itself – acquire value – in leaving behind its vexing, baffling singularity and becoming available to repetition. Events acquire true importance, stand a chance of surviving a bit longer, only if they have been captured on the videotape and thus can be seen again and again, in straight or reverse order, in fast or slow motion. No skill, achievement or event is exempt from this test.

On new computer 'expert systems', which aim at encapsulating in computer software (and hence in something usable without end and by everyone and not perishing in the course of their use) what has been thus far unique know-how ensconced in the expert's brain, Anthony Stevens commented: '[I am] extremely curious to know what exactly will be considered valuable when the romance between society and human intelligence comes to an end because intelligence will be so cheap. Does anyone these days admire someone who can dig a hole or paint a car quickly? We shall soon feel the same dullness about the brainwork'.[14]

Contrary to the common tendency to demonize them, computers can hardly be held responsible for the tendency to dissolve 'singularity', to replace singularity with repetition, uniqueness with repetitiveness. Computers were avidly embraced because they chimed well with a tendency that was already well established and actively seeking better tools; they only, so to speak, answered an existing, though perhaps not fully articulated, demand – offered a technological means to finalize the process long under way. It is true, however, that only with the help of computers the process could have realized fully its inner tendency.

As Anthony Smith observes, knowledge and creativity, information as such, ceased to be an attribute of individuality, have been finally 'deprivatized', detached from all 'physical substance' and lost all 'fixed abode': 'It is foolish to build the value too completely upon the individual personality of the creator of the information, for the value is created through the perception of the value and through the specialists who work with the information months, years, decades, centuries after the act of "authorship"

---

[14] Quoted after *Expert Systems: Principles and Case Studies*, ed. Richard Forsyth (London: Chapman & Hall, 1984), p. 39.

which gave rise to it in the first place.'[15] Nothing can gain durability unless it finds its way to widespread popular use; but once the requirement has been met and mass use has become a fact, durability is no more attached to the individual name or deed. For obsessively portraying such a world which has no more room for the original, in which everything has the right to exist only as an infinitely multipliable copy, Robert Rosenblum proclaimed Andy Warhol the 'court painter to the 70s': Warhol's 'numb, voyeuristic view of contemporary life, in which the grave and the trivial, the fashionable and the horrifying, blandly coexist as passing spectacles, is a deadly accurate mirror of a commonplace experience in modern art and life'.[16]

Games and spectacles

Only finite objects – the irreversible events – have that indomitable, rock-steady solidity which we baptize 'reality'. They are serious and command respect. One may, perhaps, ward off or at least delay their arrival; once they had occurred, however, they cannot be undone. And as long as the events remain irreversible, 'unanticipated consequences' remain the most sinister of nightmares. 'The unpredicted' is viewed as the proof of a most ignoble of failures and 'the uncontrolled' appears to be the most unnerving of challenges. Descartes' *malin génie*, the patron of all deception and error, the sinister confuser of good sense, the conjurer of false appearances and the archpriest of delusion, is the most deadly of enemies. Irreversibility – as it were – favours foresight, meticulous examination, sobriety of judgement, calculation, planning. It enthrones the faculty of *reason*, trusted to possess all those skills, in the managing seat.

Reason is first and foremost the art of separating the real from the apparent – the 'truly real' from the 'pseudo-real', the real that is really what

---

[15] Anthony Smith, 'Telecommunication and the Fading of the Industrial Age: Information and the Post-Industrial Economy', in *Impact and Influences: Essays on Media Power in the Twentieth Century*, ed. James Curran, Anthony Smith and Pauline Wingate (London: Methuen, 1987), pp. 336–7. With value accrued mainly, perhaps even exclusively, from the frequency of repetition, 'the critic who helps to establish the reputation of a new writer or composer or film-maker is creating value . . .'. One may say that the production of consumer desire through the management of public attention has turned into the principal mode of value-creation.

[16] Robert Rosenblum, 'Andy Warhol, Court Painter to the 70s', in *Theories of Contemporary Art*, ed. Richard Hertz (Englewood Cliffs: Prentice-Hall, 1985), p. 58.

it claims to be, from the fraudulent and guileful pretence of reality. Reason is both the umpire and the trademark of the real; it is reason that determines and guarantees reality, the same way that all other producers determine and guarantee their respective products. The 'irreal', by opposition, stands for everything which reason does not control. Reason derives its *raison d'être* from keeping watertight the boundary separating the real – the genuine product, from the irreal – the counterfeit.

As long as the strict conceptual/practical distinction between reality and its representation is maintained (whether as satisfactory achievement or a task for the future), no beings can be taken at face value, and not taking them at face value is, literally, a matter of life and death. It is *vital* to trace every shred of deception, 'get the facts straight', to know exactly what the things are like, since being different from what they seem to be may prove *fatal in its consequences*. Prudence commands that all beings be suspected of hiding as much, if not more, as they are trusted with revealing. Hence the imperative of lie detectors, of truth testing, of the obsessive search for proofs and certificates of sincerity. Beings are just *signifiers* – appearances floating on the surface of solid reality. They may not be always deceitful, but they are always opaque. One needs an effort to pierce their opacity, to 'see through them' into that reliable reality that does not change – though its representations, signifiers, appearances, can and do. The world of irreversible events and realities distinct from their representations cannot but be obsessed with *interpretation*. Things are to be tested for the degree of dissimulation. The testing never stops. One needs to 'get down to the real thing', always prostrated at some distance from its sign. The road to the 'real thing' never seems to end – there is another depth beneath the one already reached. What the signifier points to, proves to be, at a closer look, just another signifier. A desperate plight. Reason bent on foreclosing, finalizing, completing, faces the mortal danger of *unlimited semiosis*;[17] more correctly, it cannot but view the unlimited

---

[17] Umberto Eco's expression (cf. *The Limits of Interpretation*, chap. 2). Unlimited semiosis conveys the idea of an infinite interpretative drift, of which Charles Peirce, for many the principal forerunner of postmodern criticism of the naive realism of modernity, argued in the following way: 'The meaning of representation can be nothing but a representation. In fact it is nothing but the representation itself conceived as stripped of irrelevant clothing. But this clothing never can be completely stripped off: it is only changed for something more diaphanous. So there is an infinite regression here. Finally the interpretant is nothing but another representation to which the torch of truth is handed along; and as representation, it has its interpretant again. Lo, another infinite series.' (*Collected Papers*, vol. I (Cambridge, Mass.: Harvard Univesrity Press, 1934), p. 339.) Of the spokesmen for

semiosis, the semiotic drift which never wind up in any steady harbour, as a mortal danger.

On the other side of the modern era, however, there seems to be no clear distinction between existence solid or soft, durable or elusive, more and less trustworthy. Everything that is, shares in the same modality of transience that at any moment, for reasons impossible to pinpoint in advance, may assume all the trappings of durability. What is seen and heard need not therefore be mistrusted (cannot be, realistically, mistrusted?). The modality of talking is not inferior to the modality of that which is being talked about. But a representation which is not a derivative, subordinate version of what is being represented, is no more a representation, with its past opprobrium of derivativeness, inferiority, untrustworthiness (a 'mere representation'): it need not be held under surveillance, put under the microscope as, possibly, 'mere appearance'. All beings beckon to each other, are beckoned back; there are loops between them instead of straight lines; exploration of each route returns ultimately to the starting point. After a number of detours, the signifiers fall upon themselves.

One may legitimately suspect *dissimulation* in any act of *simulation*; but on the other side of the modern era beings *do not* simulate any more. Simulation, like dis-simulation, connotes feigning and deception; deception, in its turn, invokes the presence of the 'real thing', as things must first be 'real' to be able to be feigned or mis-represented. (A suspicion of fraud is at all times an oblique tribute to the solidity and invincibility of truth, which – as is forever hoped – 'will out' in the end.) The worry about simulation is born, in other words, of the insistence on keeping the strict distinction between the signifiers and what they signify. But there is no such distinction if signification does not discrimate and thus does not degrade, if beings signify but each other in a closed circle, if signification is two-pronged and mutual, if all objects have the same solidity, or suffer the same dearth of solidity, if they are all engaged in the same never ending quadrille of disappearances and reappearances.

The other way of putting all this is to say that the modern world is prominent for its preoccupation with the *search* for meaning. Meaning is not what is seen, not what is seen directly, 'right away'. Meaning can only be grasped through pursuing the relation between elusive appearance and

---

the view Peirce has decomposed, Richard Rorty writes, critically: 'The intuitive realist thinks that there is such thing as Philosophical Truth because he thinks that, deep down beneath all the texts, there is something which is not just one more text but that to which various texts are trying to be "adequate".' (*Consequences of Pragmatism* (Minneapolis: University of Minnesota Press, 1982), p. xxxvii.)

solid, yet hidden, reality. Meaning is the hard, yet invisible core wrapped tightly in what offers itself to the senses, what can be seen and heard: the signifier. That core can be uncovered and repossessed if the carapace of the signifier is broken. The modern world needs detectives; Sherlock Holmes, who never trusted things to be what they seemed, is that world's archetypal hero. With all his notorious mistrust of appearances, the detective true to his name is not a postmodern sceptic. He never treats things lightly – however untrustworthy he suspects them to be. They may bear false evidence, but they are *evidence* all the same. Appearances lie; but to say that they *lie* is to corroborate the existence of *truth*. Mistrust of appearances sustains (and is sustained by) the unshakeable trust in 'real things'. However misleading they may be, the appearances are charged with *meanings*.

The postmodern world, on the other hand, seems to have no time for Sherlock Holmeses. Not that the postmodern world agrees to live at peace with a lie (whenever alerted to a lie, the residents of that world would feel pushed off course and react angrily and neurotically); but having been awarded immortality at birth, all things stand ultimately for nothing but themselves – there is no division between things that mean and things that are meant. More exactly, each such division is but momentary, protean and ultimately reversible. 'Il n'y a pas de hors-texte' (Derrida); there is no 'outside' in the game of signs. It is just by a sort of linguistic inertia that we still talk of signifiers bereaved of signifieds, as signifiers; and of signs which stand but for themselves and for other signs like them, as of 'appearances'.

Already in 1916, in the name of the avant-garde still in the hot pursuit of the absolute and final truth, sounded the sober voice of Man Ray, which preceded by no less than half a century what was to become the common wisdom of postmodern philosophy and art criticisms:

> The creative force and expressiveness of painting reside materially in the colour and texture of pigment, in the possibilities of form, invention and organization, and in the flat plane on which these elements are brought to play.
>
> The artist is concerned solely with linking these absolute qualities directly to his wit, imagination, and experience ... He uncovers the pure plane of expression that has so long been hidden by the glazings of nature imitation, anecdote and other popular subjects.[18]

---

[18] Man Ray, 'Statement', in *Dadas on Art*, ed. Lucy R. Lippard (Englewood Cliffs: Prentice-Hall, 1971), p. 156.

Man Ray owed his insight to the achievement of the avant-garde. That movement, which inscribed modernity on its banners and appropriated it as a task and a programme, was – naturally – the first to discover the futility of its promise. The most insightful among avant-garde artists could recognize the failure precisely because they were so spectacularly successful: they did manage to unmask, one by one, the inadequacy of all and any representation – until there were no more signifiers left whose assumed innocence one could still hope to test and confirm. At the end of the long march toward the ultimate and the absolute, the avant-garde discovered torn-up canvas, the empty art gallery, the blank page and the silent tape. The pool of the would-be representations of the 'truth out there' has been exhausted. What remained – as the only sensible (or the only 'realistic') programme – was the play of significations; a play aware of being a play, and not at all worried (or worried only privately) by this awareness.

We now live, says Jean-François Lyotard, in an *open space-time*, in which there are no more *identities*, only *transformations*. Self-consciously, this space-time is the blank, the emptiness, the nothingness 'in which the universe presented by a phrase is exposed and which explodes at the moment the phrase occurs and then disappears with it'. The one thing lost under that condition is being itself: it has no solid roots in time. Being, as it were, 'is always escaping determination and arriving both too soon and too late'.[19] This is a space-time of the perpetual present and ubiquitous 'here'. The waning of tough reality goes together with the decomposition of history into a flow of episodes, and together with the cancellation of resilient, 'objective distance', now made flexible, mutable and pliable thanks to the emancipation of the shifting attention from geographical constraints.

In open space-time, life can only be conducted in the *dramatic mode*. Drama may have a stiff scenario closely followed by the actors, but the stiffest of scenarios remains a scenario, a contrived text scripted in this rather than that way, and a text which could well have been scripted in that way rather than this; and even the most disciplined of actors remain actors, playing their parts, these part rather than some other which they could play instead with the same flourish and dedication.

Drama may not be entirely contingent, but it is taken as incomparably more contingent by its actors and viewers than the sought-after reality was ever taken by Rorty's 'naive realists' and their trainees. Drama may be tragic, it may cause the heart to beat and tears to flow; but then all this –

---

[19] Jean-François Lyotard, *Peregrinations* (New York: Columbia University Press, 1988), pp. 31, 32.

events, emotions and all – happens here, inside the theatre, during the performance; there is, perhaps, a candlelight dinner waiting for the final curtain to fall, and the curtain will surely fall on this story here and now, only to permit another to rise and another story to begin (or this one to be repeated). Drama may be a serious matter (one tries to be very serious indeed about drama one watches – otherwise there will be little fun in watching it), but the seriousness, like drama itself, is but a convention – the seriousness, like the drama itself, is 'but a play'; one knows all the time that disbelief is only suspended for the duration, that the trust invested may be at any moment withdrawn. There is nothing irrevocable, irreversible about the drama; the ostensible irrevocability of dramatic play is itself a play, a make-believe and thus a revocable event. Drama is a constant, never ending, perpetually repeated *rehearsal* of the mortality of things and people, of people's possessions and people's achievements; and it will remain forever a rehearsal, never the 'real thing'. In a world that remains permanently in the dramatic mode, how one would tell the 'for real' if one saw one? Ours is, as Michel Maffesoli suggested, a form of life of the theatre, and in the theatre each scene – serious, not very serious, and not at all serious – counts: 'in theatricality nothing is important, because everything is important'.[20]

The modern-type world, Baudrillard would say, is ruled by *law*; our own is, instead, guided by the *rule*. Laws prescribe, inhibit and prohibit. By the same token, they create the possibility of transgression or even their own abolition; they draw a benchmark for *liberation*, as well as for conspiracy, clandestinity, hidden transcripts and latent discourse. None of these is done by the rules. Rules are not a set of constraints imposed on the world: rules are the whale on which the world rests. Take the rules away, and the world shall capsize and vanish. 'It makes no sense to "transgress" a game's rules; within a cycle's recurrence, there is no line one can jump (instead, one simply leaves the game).' If all players leave, the game ceases to be (rules 'exist only when shared, while the Law floats above scattered individuals'). But in our world many games go on at the same time and each player has a wide choice of rules. If each set of rules conjures up and sustains their own game, a mini-world of their own – then one can enter and leave worlds at will, each stay being solely 'until further notice'. (As a matter of fact, the supposition that there is but one world, subject to the same set of invariable and logically apodeictic laws, does not ring true any more; one feels that there must be more worlds,

---

[20] Michel Maffesoli, *L'Ombre de Dionysos: contribution à une sociologie de l'orgie* (Paris: Méridiens, 1985), pp. 16–18.

perhaps even infinite multitude of universes, as both present-day cosmologists with their guesses about the awesome universe-devouring and universe-concealing capacity of 'black holes', and postmodern philosophers with their questions like 'what kinds of world are there, how are they constituted, and how do they differ?' (Brian McHale) and their knack for describing other possible, as well as impossible, worlds, would cordially agree.)

One thing the player cannot do is to opt out from playing altogether. There is no other world but many rule-guided games; no tough, resilient, stubborn world held in place by legal repression. Each game has another game for a neighbour (or other games for neighbours) – but together, the games leave nothing outside. They have no 'exteriority' still waiting to be invaded, conquered and colonized. No game aspires to universality, and 'there is no metaphysics looming on the horizon of the game's indefinitely reversible cycle'. Games are cyclical and recurrent; they 'reproduce a given arbitrary constellation in the same terms an indefinite number of times'. Games promise *eternal return*. Doing so, they deliver the players 'from the linearity of time and death'. Once more, everything is potentially immortal (is immortal-like), and so nothing is; nothing is *privileged* by its durability in the world that dissolved the durability of the game in the transience of every move.

Games (and thus the world made of games) are not a realm of chance, distinct from the orderly and determined sequences of the law-ruled world. The very notion of chance makes sense only within the law-guided world of determination. Chance is the abominable Other of the world governed by Law. Put the rule in place of Law, and *chance* vanishes, together with the *norm* in which it dwelled as its not-yet-fully-exorcised 'inner demon'. Games deny objective determination, but they deny also objective *contingency*: 'the basic assumption behind the game is that *chance does not exist*', 'that the world is built of networks of symbolic relations – not contingent connections, but webs of obligation, webs of seduction. One has only to play one's hand right . . .'[21]

---

[21] Jean Baudrillard, *Seduction*, trans. Brian Singer (London: Macmillan, 1990), pp. 132, 136, 147, 146, 143–4.

Baudrillard's analyses bear close affinity to Giani Vattimo's *il pensero debole* – the 'weak thought' opposed to the domineering, atemporal, militantly universalistic and intolerant 'modern metaphysics'; to Richard Rorty's conception of hermeneutics replacing in present-day thought modern epistemology which took seriously the trans-historical claims of theory; as well as to the idea, promoted by a number of writers, most prominently by Agnes Heller, that *phronesis* – soft,

No determination, no chance; just a soft, pliable game without set or predictable denouement, a game which exhausts itself fully in the aggregate of players and their moves. The player cannot determine the outcome; but the player's moves are not devoid of consequence either. As there is no Law that unambiguously links action to its outcome, there is no clear prescription of what one should do in order to attain the result one wishes. This world promises no security but no impotence either; it offers neither certainty nor despair; only the joy of a right move and the grief of a failed one.

Death daily rehearsed

None of the traditional ways of dabbling with timelessness (themselves timeless) have been abandoned under postmodern conditions. And yet those ways (including the ones in which the modern era excelled) have been, so to speak, relegated to the second league of public attention, elbowed out by a new, specifically postmodern, life strategy. The latter differs from other strategies by presenting itself, alluringly, as geared to a wide, nay universal, use. It also differs from other strategies in that it attempts to resolve (in fact, to dispose of) the haunting issue of survival by making it less haunting or not haunting at all ... Instead of trying (in vain) to colonize the future, it dissolves the future in the present. It does not allow the finality of time to worry the living; and it attempts to do it, mainly, by slicing time (all of it, every shred of it, without residue) into short-lived, evanescent episodes. It deprives mortality of its vile terror by taking it out of hiding, and tossing it into the realm of the familiar and the ordinary – to be practised there day in, day out. Daily life becomes a perpetual dress rehearsal of death. What is being rehearsed in the first place, is *ephemerality* and *evanescence* of things humans may acquire and bonds humans may weave. The impact of such daily rehearsal seems to

---

pragmatic, pliable, adaptable and adjustable wisdom, rather than absolutistically inclined *theoria*, offers the best model for knowledge fit for our contingent universe.

As Matei Calinescu has suggested, the modern deterministic model of the universe, spurning the chance and declaring it off limits, contributed to the famous phenomenon of the *disenchantment of the world*; whereas the newly fashionable science of the type put forward by Ilya Prigogine and Isabelle Strangers, which follows contemporary culture in restoring chance to its sovereign glory, promises a *re-enchantment of the world*. (Cf. *Five Faces of Modernity* (Durham: Duke University Press, 1987), pp. 70–1).

be similar to one achieved by some preventive inoculations: if taken in daily, in partly detoxicated and thus non-deadly doses, the awesome poison seem to lose its venom. Instead, it prompts immunity and indifference to the toxin in the inoculated organism.

Images on offer both reflect and reinforce this novel life strategy: 'aesthetic innovation is thus basically aesthetic ageing – [the image-makers] are not interested in the new as such. Their determining aim is the outdating of what exists, its denunciation, devaluation, and replacement' comments Wolfgang Fritz Haug.[22] As soon as they are acquired, the coveted and dreamt-of possessions are discredited and devalued by their 'new and improved', and so more prestigious, versions. Before they have time fully to enjoy their acquisitions (to use them up to the limits of their physical capacity), the proud owners of things are cajoled, blackmailed, ridiculed and shamed into shunning them, discarding them, disowning and wishing to replace them. A perfectly serviceable photo-camera ceases to satisfy because 'it cannot do' ingenious things newer cameras do, and lacks the gaudy gadgets newer cameras so impressively display. A many times enjoyed, dearly loved hi-fi tape recording ceases to satisfy once there are compact disc recordings now proclaimed to have reached new heights of fidelity, the only one acceptable for a *connoisseur* (and one is cajoled into *becoming* a connoisseur by acting on that assertion). Things do not die because of old age, metal fatigue, disintegrating beyond repair – not of 'natural causes'; not because death is inescapable. They disappear long before they reach the point of 'natural death'; indeed, well before they begin to show signs of 'senility'. Their removal from the life-world at such a trouble-free age would not undermine their 'principal' timelessness. They could be infinitely durable, nay immortal, if we wished them to be. But we *do not wish* them to be immortal.

The urge of mobility, built into the structure of contemporary life, prevents the arousal of strong affections for places; the places we occupy are no more than temporary stations. The progress in life is measured and marked by moving homes and offices. Addresses do not retain their prestige capacity for long; they move up and down the scale of respectability, attractiveness and pulling power. Nothing seems to be 'for life', and none of the things in life are approached and embraced and cherished as if they were. Skills, jobs, occupations, residences, marriage partners – they all come and go, and tend to annoy or bore or embarrass when they stay

---

[22] Wolfgang Fritz Haug, *Critique of Commodity Aesthetics: Appearance, Sexuality and Advertising in Capitalist Society*, trans. Tobert Bock (Cambridge: Polity Press, 1986), p. 42.

too long. Nothing is truly irreplaceable, and thus the tragedy is neither unbearable nor too shattering when things or partners disappear from view. Again, all too often the disappearance of things and persons alike comes before their 'natural death'. Modern society, with its insistence on the permanence of marriage bonds, on the 'till death us do part' type of marriage, 'created void around the widows';[23] widows exuded the scent of mortal destiny which everyone around did their best to deodorize. Ariès observation does not hold for our society, though. Before we have a chance of becoming widows, too many among us have rehearsed more than once the 'departure' of the putatively 'life-long' partner through divorce or separation. We have played and rehearsed that drama of mortality many times, and we cannot any more clearly see in what way, if any, the rehearsals differ from the 'real' performance.

The dramas we watch do not outlive the pressing of TV button; the books we buy and read last from one railway stop to another. The main function of the news is to chase yesterday news off, to force it out from attention and memory – and to agree in advance to be driven away in a similar way by tomorrow's news. The centre of public vision is permanently overcrowded, and the 'news' must fight, tooth and nail for a share of attention. Those selected 'public events' and celebrities who make it to the centre seem to appear from nowhere; soon they will return whence they came – they will fade into non-existence. As long as they manage to stay on the stage, however – their short-lived, but intense public cult, enhanced and magnified by being echoed in millions of synchronized and similarly patterned reactions, celebrates the birth *ab nihilo*, the painlessness of disappearance, the wonder of evanescence, the beauty of the fleeting moment, the glory of transience. Obliquely yet significantly, the cults proclaim durability to be boredom, and age to be obsolescence. They turn permanence into a word of ridicule. The cults self-annihilate as they self-reproduce: today's cults whet the appetite for tomorrow's cults and make them necessary.

There is in operation, as Thielicke suggested, a 'centrifugal tendency of a continually enhanced dissipation'. Skin-deep fascinations and commitments, never given enough time or enough attention 'to stick', leave a vacuum beneath. This void must be filled 'with ever new imports from outside'.[24] The game goes on. And there comes a point when the game needs no more reinforcement from outside. It self-perpetuates. It is naive to blame the merchandisers of the consumer products and particularly

---

[23] Philippe Ariès, *L'Homme devant la Mort* (Paris: Seuil, 1977), p. 576.
[24] Herbert Thielicke, *Living with Death* (Grand Rapids: Eydermans, 1983), p. 27.

their hired troubadours – the advertisers – with the responsibility for the curious 'thirst of vertigo' which afflicts the denizen of the postmodern universe. They merely take hold of the opportunity (the need, the demand) entailed in a society bent on deconstructing immortality. In such a society, nothing can grip attention for long; one skill which all but perished is the ability to concentrate one's mind and effort over long stretches of time. What the advertisers (for commercial products, for politicians, for 'causes') try hard to achieve is to keep the shifting attention in focus long enough to assure that the desirable conduct would follow. And so we read, for instance, in one of the most influential, best-selling handbook for the advertisers and other 'managers of consumer behaviour': 'Given the tremendous number of ads competing for the consumer's attention, an ad's attention-grabbing ability is often a critical determinant of its effectiveness . . . [A]n ad must dislodge the consumer's current thoughts so that the message can be processed'.[25]

Another rehearsed quality of things and events, closely related to that of transience, is their *inconsequentiality*. 'No strings attached' is the sought-after ideal and the measure of value. Events are kept strictly separate and their autonomy is closely guarded; they should not, they do not affect the events of tomorrow and the deeds committed next door. Episodes may be stopped in the middle of the action, started again, watched once more in slow motion. They are what they are: episodes, occurrences with no history and no follow-up; one-off happenings. Skills acquired today are useful for today and bear no relation to the skills called for by tomorrow's challenges. Enjoyment does not lend itself to moral scrutiny and does not impeach moral conscience. Sex does not result in social duty; preferably, in emotional attachment either. Life is not a novel with a finite set of characters, a plot and a denouement; it is instead a railway-station bookstand packed to overflowing with the latest best-sellers. And the shelf life of a best-seller, as one of their authors observed, is somewhere between milk and yogurt.

With the transience and ephemerality re-forged into daily practice, glorified and ritualistically celebrated, the strategy of survival came full circle. It is now immortality, not mortality, which is deconstructed; but deconstructed in such a way as to show that permanence is nothing but the sequence of evanescences, time is nothing but a succession of episodes without consequence, immortality is nothing but an ongoing sequence of mortal beings. Deconstructed, immortality reveals mortality as its

[25] James F. Engel, Roger D. Blackwell, Paul W. Miniard, *Consumer Behaviour*, 5th edn (Chicago: Dryden Press, 1986), pp. 196, 202.

only secret. Mortality need not be deconstructed: it ought to be lived. The consumer bliss is the final, long solicited and expected, yet slow to come, stage of secularization, that trademark and self-eulogized triumph of modernity. Now, at last, truly, *everything* is in human hands. But the meaning of 'everything' is not what it was expected to be.

Beneficiaries and victims

Like many other policies of survival, the postmodern strategy has a stratifying potency. The richness, volume and fast pace of the impressions in which it aims to dissolve mortality do not come to all with the same facility and in the same measure. Their uneven availability sets apart those who can reasonably hope for free access from those who have little chance of passing through the entry gate. Access and non-access are not separate conditions; they depend on each other, they limit each other in what is best described as the zero-sum game of freedom.

At all times, survival strategies reflected and bred social inequality. In the previous chapter, we have looked at the stratifying impact of the modern strategy of deconstructing mortality. The attempts to follow modern strategy of survival (i.e. deconstructing death) go on in our days unabated, and thus the stratifying consequences of that strategy, if anything, deepen. Most recent advances in the traditional modern effort of deconstructing *mortality* (of translating the issue of preserving life into the problem of resisting and conquering the identified causes of death) seem to promise no more a universal extension of time-span and certainly not the improvement in general quality of extended life. 'The cruel irony of history', writes Kenneth L. Vaux, 'is that as man learns how to increase human well-being through science, the number of persons who profit from these gifts is fewer and fewer.' He also offers an insight into what may be the cause of this irony: 'Reducing deaths from sudden causes like accidents and infections necessitates endurance of more costly deaths. While sudden coronary or cerebral death may be a blessing in terms of expense, cancer and the other degenerative disorders often devastate one's personal finances.'[26] 'There is a tendency', writes Nicholas Garnham, 'towards a two-tier market structure in which choice, being increasingly expensive, is offered to upper-income groups – while an increasingly

---

[26] Kenneth L. Vaux, *Will to Live – Will to Die* (Minneapolis: Augsburg Publishing House, 1978), pp. 48, 43.

impoverished, homogenized service is offered to the rest.'[27] Ostensibly, the offer is extended to a fairly large chunk of the population; but in every case it remains an offer to *contract out* 'from the rest'.[28]

The effort to push back the frontiers of 'natural life' is ever more evidently subject to the law of diminishing return. Every next 'disease', every next 'identified cause of death' requires more exorbitant resources to be staved off or defeated. As in Aldous Huxley's dystopia of consumer bliss, each new medical gadget (like all gadgets, meant to excite the hope-fed imagination and trigger consumers' desires) differs from the ones it comes to replace above all by its higher costs. The allurements of survival offered by advancing medicine – survival itself, as defined by the medical 'state of art' – become more and more selective – *socially* selective. The condition of survival offered by contemporary medicine is an explicit or implicit refusal of solidarity. When translated into life policy, it results in the deconstruction of sociality.

The inequalities brought into relief by the advances of modern medicine make an excellent stuff for electoral manifestos of opposition parties; spectacular, nay miraculous accomplishments of the gallant conquerors of diseases inspire popular imagination and – when denied access to – inflame popular wrath. Yet the promise to make medical advances available to all – to do unto all what the medical expert can do unto a selected few – has little practical value, whatever its political potential and its impact as a propaganda slogan. (Its greatest practical impact, as a matter of fact, has been so far adding further to the prestige and social stature of the medical 'new frontiers breakers'.) If the present trend of medical art demonstrates anything, it is, rather, that the life-enhancing potential once carried by the 'deconstructing mortality' strategy is close to being exhausted. Little mileage has been left today in the old hope of pushing back the frontiers of death. For most people, the passage beyond the

---

[27] Nicholas Garnham, 'The Information Society is also a Class Structure', in *Information Technology*, p. 289.

A.E. Cawkell has quoted a poignant rendition of the same problem by Jo Grimond: 'The new technology has not been used to make services cheaper and better for ordinary people. Big business, the better professional firms and such like have been able to contract out of deteriorating services. When I complained of the postal services to a fellow sufferer she replied: "Of course my husband's firm send anything urgent by motor-bicycle or telex." This is not an option open to most of us.' (Cf. *Evolution of an Information Society*, ed. A.E. Cawkell (London: Aslib, 1987), pp. 2–3.)

[28] On freedom as social relation and a stratifying factor, see my *Freedom* (Milton Keynes: Open University Press, 1987), particularly chap. 3.

present frontiers is not a practical proposition; for sober minds, it is downright unimaginable.

All the more room is left for the novel strategy of deconstructing immortality, in line with one of the most common expedients drawn upon when a cognitive dissonance is encountered: if you cannot beat them, declare them unworthy of beating . . . Life energy untapped (and untappable) by old worries is harnessed to other concerns. In a roundabout way, these new concerns are manifested in the unprecedented value attached to the 'quality of life'. With immortality (standing for all transcendent aims) no more on the cards, no unsatisfying moment, however brief, may be justified in terms of the service it renders to some future accomplishments. Calls to sacrifice for the sake of future generations would have cut some ice with the pilgrims, but hardly any with the nomads of the *Jetztzeit*. 'Now' is the site of happiness – its only site. Life duration is split into succession of such 'nows', none less significant than any other, each equally deserving to be lived to the full, enjoyed to the full, squeezed to the full of all its pleasure-giving juices. One may say that inequality of life chances, no more attacked point-blank, no more challenged directly, seeks its compensation in the new spirit of egalitarianism of life moments.

This splitting of the duration into endless series of transient moments, this breakdown of linear (project-oriented) time resulting in the sovereignty-cum-inconsequentiality of each and any present, has – as we have seen before – a far-reaching impact on the business of self-identity. Either identity is imposed by a social position which offers little or no freedom of choice – and then it feels like a cage one dreams of escaping – less a home than a prison. Or identity is something to be sought, evaluated, freely chosen and appropriated – and then, in our immortality-deconstructing universe, it is rendered fragile and lacking in confidence; the frailty of any identity they may desire or (always for a time) acquire denies their bearers a moment of rest, prompting them instead to shift, with neurotic compulsion, between aggressive and depressive postures. As identity cannot be established 'forever', and as no successful self-assertion, however spectacular and celebrated at the moment, can vouch for the permanence of identity it warrants or augurs – the anguish about identity saturates each of the 'presents' into which the life-process has been split. Life is transformed into endless and never-likely-to-be-satisfied chase after individual or (if individual identity cannot be afforded for the lack of resources) shared, collective identity. As Richard Sennett profoundly observed, people tend to experience today all interpersonal and intergroup conflicts as 'contests for personal legitimation':

> Just as individuals framing a conflict in terms of legitimacy are *struggling over who they are rather than specifically what they want*, modern collective

units in conflict gradually come to substitute for questions of power, entitlement, and flexibility of action more abstruse, amorphous, and asocial assertions of the moral legitimacy of the group. It has an identity, a collective self, and therefore it deserves to be fed and its demands met ... When a crisis escalates to the question of legitimacy of self, a destructive gemein-schaft is created.[29]

Paradoxically, the only content of 'identity' allowed in the universe of shifting 'nows' is the *right to choose* an identity; the right to renounce an unfashionable or otherwise unappetizing identity, to don a currently recommended one, to distinguish oneself (oneselves) not necessarily by being autonomous, but by having – and practising, and above all demon-strating – the right to be autonomous, in case one wished to be. The agonizing hopelessness of the struggle for self-identity so moulded derives from the fact that victory is impossible; or, rather, that victory, if won, would bring more agony instead of succour. What would one do with freedom to choose identity at will, were the will not authoritatively guided? How would one know that freedom has been truly won, if the choice of identity were not authoritatively preset and fixed?

Again, it would be preposterous to blame the conspiracy of commercial advertisers for the paradox of freedom expressed in the frantic search of heteronomous authority; the apparent paradox of freedom rebounding as a new dependence. The advertisers can claim with a clear conscience that they are merely rendering the public a service the public badly needs and yearns for. True, many a commercial expert holds an unflattering (though sober) view of the intended objects of his or her 'opinion-management': we read, for instance, in another handbook for advertisers, that 'consum-ers are like chickens. They are much more comfortable with a pecking order that everybody knows about and accepts.'[30] And yet the commercial experts did no more than fill the void left by crushed prefabricated identities and the now discredited and rejected as impracticable 'life-projects' once meant to deputize for them. Advertisers answer to an acute

---

[29] Richard Sennett, 'Destructive Gemeinschaft', in *Beyond the Crisis*, ed. Norman Birnbaum (London: Oxford University Press, 1977), pp. 183–5. The conflict aimed at 'identity legitimation' is, as Sennett suggests, unresolvable: 'collective change cannot occur as long as the fantasy exists that collective life can instantly change its essence' (p. 182). But 'instantly changing its essence' is the only thing identity may do in a universe which emphatically (and effectively) refuses it having an essence ...

[30] Al Ries and Jack Trout, *Positioning: The Battle for Your Mind* (New York: McGraw Hill, 1981), p. 53.

pain-inflicting need, and had better be as persuasive as they can if that pain is to be assuaged. In the curt yet precise summary of Michel Parenti, 'in order to live well and live properly, consumers need corporate producers to guide them'.[31] Whoever committed the original sin, the descendants can no longer do without a stern parental figure of a life-style guide. They do not trust themselves – not as individuals, not as autonomous decision-makers. They need reassurance that what they do makes sense, is worth doing, is not a waste of any of the precious moments which succeed each other in the flow of their individual lives. In the poignant phrase of E. Allemand, 'it is not Big Brother who watches us, it is we who watch Big Brother'.[32]

Whence the reassurance may come? From experts in reassurance, the professional sellers of meanings, of course. But what arguments could they use to make their message truly reassuring? The predicament in which the free-floating nomads of the post-linear-time, post-life-project universe have found themselves, is burdened with anxiety mostly because the structures of authority which could be perceived as 'natural', 'just there', unproblematic, have been all but dissembled, or, to put it the other way – because such structures of authority as do retain their hold on various segments of social life have found their hold over people weakened, as individuals emancipated from all but a few basic and residual, mostly impersonal, ties may now escape the grip of one structure while 'choosing'

---

[31] Michel Parenti, *Inventing Reality: The Politics of Mass Media* (New York: St Martin Press, 1986), p. 65.

[32] E. Allemand, *Pouvoir et télévision* (Paris: Anthropos, 1980), p. 44. Commenting on this phrase, Michèle Mattelert ('Education, Television and Mass Culture', in *Television in Transition*, ed. Phillip Drummond and Richard Paterson (London: British Film Institute, 1985), p. 168) suggests the name of *telepanopticon* for the form presently taken by Bentham's surveillance machine; fascination and seduction have undermined, so to speak, the once uncompromisingly asymmetrical nature of the supervising gaze, but the effect remains much the same: it is Big Brother who makes the decisions and stays firmly in control. The orphans of linear, meaning-allocating time have all the urge to seek reassurance; the merchandisers of sense have all the profit accruing from reassuring them. The outcome, in the memorable description of Aldous Huxley, is as follows: 'Find some common desire, some widespread unconscious fear or anxiety, think out some way to relate this wish or fear to the product you have to sell, then build a bridge of verbal or pictorial symbols over which your customer can pass from fact to compensating dream, and from the dream to the illusion that your product, when purchased, will make the dream come true.' (Cf. the interesting discussion of Huxley's formula in Frank Whitehead, 'Advertising', in *Discrimination and Popular Culture*, ed. Denys Thompson (London: Heinemann, 1973), pp. 53ff).

the domain of another. No single structure may impose its authority unconditionally – and to make the picture still more confusing, no authority may demand obedience by invoking explicitly its putative right to command. Commanding as such has been discredited as oppression, and felt as unbearable. Authority may only be effective if it does not demand obedience in its own name; if it does not seem to demand obedience at all, when it disguises the command as allurement. An effective authority must not appear to be an authority – but a helpful hand, a well-wisher, a friend. Authority must not be seen as seeking and choosing – but as sought and chosen. Its future subjects should be seduced to scramble for the right to hide under its protective shelter.

Under the postmodern condition, authority is not given matter-of-factly. It must be *construed* – and it is construed daily, from one *Jetztzeit* to another – by the seekers of reassurance. For their construction job, the seekers of authority have but one building material at their disposal: *trust*, which Anthony Giddens defined as 'confidence in the reliability of a person or system, regarding a given set of outcomes or events, where that confidence expresses a faith in the probity or love of another, or in the correctness of abstract principles (technical knowledge).'[33] The function of the objects of trust is to persuade that, for the reassurance-seekers, they are a secure investment. The volume of trust invested in such objects provides the ultimate evidence that the job of persuasion has been well done. We may say that trust emanates from the need for reassurance; it actively seeks anchoring, and the reassurance-seekers are eager to embrace any credible offer: they are eager to be seduced and persuaded. The construction of authority under present conditions may be compared to the working of a stock exchange; a certain amount of capital in frantic search of secure and profitable investment; running in panic from unsafe havens (thereby making them unsafer still) and crowding into those not yet discredited and promising.

Confidence in the capacity of the beneficiaries of trust to deliver on their promise is fickle – and bound to remain so, given the nature of services expected. Once the trust has been invested, yesterday's free choice smells – more pungently by the day – of dependence. The unhinged present which has replaced the project-oriented life is bur-

---

[33] Anthony Giddens, *The Consequences of Modernity* (Cambridge: Polity Press, 1990), p. 34. Giddens distinguishes later between trust in persons ('facework commitments'), and in symbolic tokens or expert systems ('faceless commitments') – stressing that faceless commitments are 'linked in an ambiguous way with those demanding facework' (p. 80).

dened, as it were, with a task it can hardly perform: it has to justify itself by its own resources – provide its own satisfying interpretation complete with the code that makes the interpretation trustworthy. But a genuinely *self*-interpretation is almost as incongruous an idea as that of a private language. Interpretatively grounded identity can come to be and live only in a network of interactions; it can be only a collective achievement and shared operation. Yet it will cease to meet its own conditions if it lodges its authority openly in the power of collectivity. Hence the incessant play of autonomy and heteronomy, the first proudly displayed, the other self-ashamedly let in through the back door; a mind-boggling *virement* of freedom and dependence, of heroic choice and surrender to socially prompted 'musts'; a hysterical protest against any outer-directed moves, in which the dreaded oppression is invariably sniffed – combined with the horror of loneliness, abandonment and of the unwillingness of others to listen and to confirm the truth of what they hear.

Life after the deconstruction of immortality is filled with efforts to construct collectivities as the last shelters of reassurance. Postmodernity is the age of *communities*. Not Tönnies-style *Gemeinschaften*, of course; not those human pincers, forged of supervised rituals and neighbourly sur-veillance, in which the 'iron hand of history' was once seen to hold its posterity. Postmodern communities must do without police and friendly spics. They are works of the imagination; and they derive all their confidence-donating power from the stamina and devotion of those who imagine them. Postmodern communities have no councils of elders, no clergy, no army. And yet they are powerful – if imagined as such.

Reassuring capacity of communities comes all from one source: belief that they are more solid, more durable, more lasting than the fleeting moment which they are expected to stamp with a more-than-ephemeral, more-than-mortal significance – and are thus imbued, indeed, with that 'stamping power'. They suck in and incarnate the transcendence which has been all but extirpated from the *Jetztzeit*; or, rather, they compensate, in a typically postmodern, *immortality*-deconstructing style, for the loss of temporal transcendence. (On an ever growing scale, they take over this replacement function from science, which was called to provide the surrogate reassurance throughout the era of modernity. Science per-formed that function in a specifically modern, *mortality*-deconstructing fashion; it rested its authority on the linear accumulation of wisdom, on the accretion of ever less fatality-prone knowledge and know-how. No such argument is available to postmodern communities, suspended in de-immortalized space.) In their very existential mode, postmodern com-munities are resonant and isomorphic with the omnivorous present they are called to serve. They derive their authority neither from the past nor the guaranteed future, but from their current notoriety. Being in fashion, sitting in the centre of public attention, counting more devotees than any of the competitors, is all the power they have, and all the power they need.

Hence postmodern communities would hardly survive the demise of public opinion polls. Public support (or just the fact that the public 'takes note') is their life juice – and they do not need any other source of strength. They claim authority, as Michel de Certeau suggested, not in the name of 'doctrines that have become unbearable', but 'in the name of the others';[34] of the many others unknown to me, faceless at a distance, yet – like me – residents of the present, struggling to make the best of it and find the best way of making it. Most of them do not know, and in all likelihood will never know, of my existence – except in a form in which I am aware of theirs: as a digit in a statistical table.

Postmodern community differs also radically from one experimented with by the hippies – those precursors and first explorers of the postmodern condition. The hippies tried to make their community real, fleshy, tangible – make it an product of mutuality, hold it together through intercourse, through an emotional embrace which is meant to be reciprocated and cemented by the sentiment of shared belonging. 'The hippies' sense of community', in Paul E. Willis's perceptive assessment, 'came from a collective conspiracy to hold their world as "real" '[35] – but at least the hippies, unlike many community-conscious denizens of the postmodern world, attempted to act on the faith they professed. Collective conspiracy sustains the postmodern communities of tribesmen or fashion-followers as well – but now each 'member' of the tribe or fan-crowd can only *believe* them to be collective; he or she has no way to make that collectivity anything more than a phantom of sedimented urge. The *sociality* of the postmodern community does not require *sociability*. Its togetherness does not require interaction. Its unity does not require integration. The life of

---

[34] Michel de Certeau, *The Practice of Everyday Life*, trans. Steven F. Rendell (Berkeley: University of California Press, 1984), p. 189. 'We are all inclined to feel safer if we know we are only doing what other people do', observes Frank Whitehead (*Discrimination and Popular Culture*, p. 56).

[35] Paul E. Willis, *Profane Culture* (London: Routledge, 1978), p. 114. Hippy communities were fictions from the start, and hopelessly so. 'How could the notion of something beyond be kept alive when it could never actually be possessed?' asks Willis, and answers: the hippie 'resolution of this paradox took the form of the playing out of an interminable and symbolic game ... The *game forever holds the possibility of resolution*, the starkness of failure need never be faced: existentially the game is a solution.' (p. 86)

postmodern community is itself a daily rehearsal of mortality; or of the irrelevance of immortality for the business of life – which amounts, as it were, to the same.

With its arch-enemy, immortality, safely out of the way – in the geriatric ward, if not yet in the coffin – mortality creeps back uninvited. Its face blinks in each ephemeric moment which promises more than it can deliver and vanishes before it can be taken to court. One cannot erase this face. One can only blot it out with a thick layer of lurid paint. No moment is eternal! But perhaps one can try to do what the romantics clamoured for *in vain* through high modernity (remember Faust, that archetypal hero of modernity, who went to hell for demanding that the enchanting moment should last forever?): to 'open up' the moment so that it can accommodate eternity: to make it *feel* like the eternal: to force it to expand, by inflating it to the limits of endurance, or perhaps beyond the limits of its capacity – with excitement, intoxicating emotions, vertiguous feelings? Baudrillard's post-orgiastic era is still a time of the orgy. After the modern orgy of liberation came the postmodern orgy of community-chasing: of tribalism, of rock-festivals and football crowds. Tribes, fashions, cults are to repair the damage done to security by the victorious battle against constraints. The deconstructing of mortality made the presence of death more ubiquitous than ever: it made survival into the meaning of life, and anti-death magic into life's pattern. The deconstructing of immortality, on the other hand, seems to subvert the meaning and deny the need of a pattern. The paradoxical outcome of modernity's project is that the work of modernity is being undone. Death is back – un-deconstructed, unreconstructed. Even immortality has now come under its spell and rule. The price of exorcising the spectre of mortality proved to be a collective incapacity to construct life as reality, to take life seriously.

Postscript: 'To die for . . .', or Death and Morality

> I have seldom, very seldom crossed this borderland between loneliness and fellowship. I have been settled there longer than in loneliness itself. What a fine bustling place was Robinson Crusoe's island in comparison!
>
> Franz Kafka

The greatest gift one human being can offer another is the gift of one's life. 'To die for another' is the ultimate ethical act; one by which all morality is measured, one of which all morality is but an allegory. It is, simultaneously, the beginning (as *readiness* to die), and the horizon (as the *act* of dying) of ethical attitude.

'In the last account' (as one is immediately prompted to quibble by the calculating, computing spirit of our age) this gift may prove useless. Indeed, my death will not make the other immortal. My sacrifice will not conquer death. My sacrifice will not improve on the final score, and in most cases would not do so on the current one. It will not make the statistics of mortality look any better. Where survival is the goal and the criterion of rationality, the greatest of human gifts is abominably irrational. For the 'realists', 'the human' is 'a scandal, a "disease" of being.'[1] No wonder that the legal and political order, which founds the only human togetherness recognized by the Law and serviced by Politics, has neither time nor place for it. Burdened with the greatest of gifts, 'the human' stands outside the Law and Politics; in the legal and political sense, the human (the truly human, the *moral* human) stands outside *society*.

Dying for anOther is the most individual (arguably, the only truly individual) of human acts. Indeed, the readiness to die for anOther is the constitutive act of human individuality and uniqueness. Yet, simulta-

---

[1] Emmanuel Levinas, 'Philosophie, justice et amour', in *Entre-Nous: Essais sur le penser-à-l'Autre* (Paris: Grasset, 1991), p. 133.

neously, it is also the constitutive act of inter-human communion. According to Levinas, 'in its ethical position, the self differs from both the citizen arising of the City, and the individual who in his natural egoism precedes all order, and from whom all political philosophy since Hobbes attempted to derive, or succeeded to derive, the social and political order of the City.'[2] The City confers equality: equality of the citizens. The Citizen is he who is like anyone else. He has the same rights and the same duties all others enjoy or suffer, and in this all-distinction-suspending similarity of citizens he is 'no matter who'. He may rightfully demand for himself everything the others receive, and for the same reason he may not name any duty, any task, any mission, any responsibility as *exclusively* his. As Citizen, he is eminently replaceable in whatever he does, may do and may wish to do. 'The citizenship' in the Citizen is that which is shared, copied, non-unique; the unity of the citizens is one of similarity, monotony, uniformity. Whatever stands out from that monotony, stands out from the City and from that part of the human which the City has appropriated, made its own domain, proclaimed its concern and charge and subjected to its management. As for the imaginary pre-City egoist (whom Aristotle dubbed, because of his ego-centred loneliness, an 'idiot'), he would find no escape from his solitude, and for this reason he would have never known of his individuality. For that egoist, no 'significant other' exists through whom he could fathom his own uniqueness, in whom he could seek its confirmation, as well as its eventual dissolution. His is a prospectless, hopeless solitude, a solitude which will never articulate itself as individuality, let alone give birth to the union with the Other – that union in which individuality finds both its transcendence and fulfilment.

Only in the shape of the ethical self is humanity complete. Only in that shape does it attain the subtle blend and sought-for reconciliation of uniqueness and togetherness. Only when raised to the level of the ethical self, individuality does not mean loneliness, and togetherness does not mean oppression. 'Concern for the other, up to the sacrifice, up to the possibility of dying for him; responsibility for the other' – this is, as Levinas insists, the 'otherwise than being', the only exit from what otherwise would be a self-enclosed, selfish, lonely, void (and ultimately meaningless) existence.

> It is the break in indifference..., the possibility of one-for-another, which is the ethical event. In human existence that interrupts and transcends its effort to be – its Spinozian *conatus essendi* – the vocation to exist-for-the-

---

[2] Levinas, 'La souffrance inutile', in *Entre-Nous*, p. 119.

other which is stronger than the threat of death; the existential adventure of the neighbour which matters to me more than my own, that posits myself from the beginning as one responsible for the being of anOther – responsible, so to speak, as unique and chosen, as an 'I' which is no more no-matter-which individual of the human kind.[1]

In this break of difference, in this readiness for self-sacrifice, in this decision (or is it just a pre-reflexive urge, never decided upon, never considered as an option?) to put the other's survival above one's own, the liberation from the tyranny of self-preservation is won and the individual sovereignty proudly proclaimed. The readiness for self-sacrifice, which is begotten of an existence lived as being-for-anOther (and not of the Heideggerian *Mitsein*, which – as Levinas commented, means no much more than being all in the same spot, at best *zusammenmarschieren*)[4] and stretches as far as the preference to die rather than see the Other dying, is what prises the self off the series of faceless, exchangeable specimens of the species and grounds the self's uniqueness and irreplacability. Now no one else can fulfil the self's vocation, now that destiny is mine and mine only, now no one can deputize for me, to do the job only I am qualified to perform. Now my being-in-the-world acquires the significance it would otherwise sorely lack, now it fills what otherwise would stay forever a gaping hole in-what-is. My responsibility for the Other is my importance – all the importance I have, I may have and may dream of having.

My responsibility means that the fate of the other depends now on what I do. My existence matters, it has consequences, it is more than just another episode in the monotony of the species' self-reproduction. In her version of the Kantian categorical imperative, Agnes Heller demands that I should act as if the alleviation of suffering of every being depended upon my action.[5] Only when dedicated to such action, my *life* counts; its termination, its being-no-more, my *death*, is no more a senseless, absurd, unjustifiable occurrence: not that sinking into the emptiness of non-existence it once was – that vanishing which changes nothing in the world. Through making myself for-the-other, I make myself for-myself, I pour meaning into my being-in-the-world, I refuse the world the licence to disdain and dismiss my presence; I force the world to note, and to dread in advance my passing away, and to bewail it when it comes. In the words

---

[3] Levinas, 'Avant-propos' in *Entre-Nous*, p. 10.

[4] Levinas, 'Philosophie, justice et amour', p. 135.

[5] Agnes Heller, 'The Legacy of Marxian ethics', in Agnes Heller and Ferenc Feher, *The Grandeur and Twilight of Radical Universalism* (New Brunswick: Transactions Publishers, 1987), p. 140.

of Mikhail Bakhtin,

> that I see the Other from the place which only I occupy; that I see Him,
> think of Him, do not forget Him; that He is also for me – this is what only
> I can do for Him at this very moment and in all existence, this is an act
> which completes His being, an enriching act, a new one and such as only I
> can perform.

If I know of this, if I remember this, and only then, am I 'real, irreplaceable, and thus bound to fulfil my uniqueness'.[6] The absurdity of my being-in-the-world has been annulled; an accomplishment which the 'for-itself' of both the Hobbesian egoist and the departicularized, abstract citizen, stripped to bare universality, would forever find beyond their reach.

The for-itself of the ethical self is, simultaneously, the discovery of my uniqueness and of our togetherness. This kind of transcendence establishes in one swoop my own significance and the bond which ties together human community. To repeat after Levinas: the in itself of being is transcended 'in the gratuity of beyond-myself-for-the-Other, in the sacrifice and the possibility of a sacrifice, in the perspective of saintliness'.[7] Or after György Lukács, who penned down these words seventy years before Levinas:

> Such dedication puts an end to solitude. Perhaps the greatest life-value of
> ethics is precisely that it is a sphere where a certain kind of communion
> can exist, a sphere where the eternal loneliness stops. The ethical man is
> no longer the beginning and the end of all things, his moods are no longer
> the measure of the significance of everything that happens in the world.
> Ethics forces a sense of community upon all men.[8]

These are the benefits of living-for-the-Other; this is what the readiness to sacrifice one's life, to die-for-the-Other, may accomplish.

And yet, why should one wish to die for the other, or for that matter *instead* of the other, or – admittedly failing that – simply *before* the other? The existential significance of such a death does not necessarily supply the motive for my readiness to die; hardly is it a motive itself. Existential significance rests, and can be found, away from the realm of quotidianity, on the territory which only poets and philosophers explore. That territory

---

[6] Mikhail Bakhtin, *K filosofii postupka* [Towards a Philosophy of the Deed] (Moscow: Progress, 1986), p. 112.

[7] Levinas 'Avant-propos', p. 11.

[8] György Lukács, 'The bourgeois Way of Life and Art for Art's Sake', in *Soul and Form*, trans. Anna Bostock (Cambridge: Mass.: MIT Press, 1974), p. 57.

is not likely to be visited by others; certainly it is not easy, and again not very likely, to be sighted from the vast, flat space where living is done. Few but certain science fiction heroes copulate and make children in order to assure the continuation of the human species; but virtually all of us find enough pressing urges and down-to-earth, very private needs, to prompt us to do just the kind of things which, directly or obliquely, accomplish what the survival of the species demands. Few but the heroes of romantic poems and *Bildungsromane* are willing to die-for-the-other in order to cut the harrowing tangles of individuality and loneliness, or of togetherness and oppression. But many would find enough forceful reasons to will exactly this, and so, in a serendipitous way, resolve the conflict others struggle with but in vain.

One may, for instance, wish to die for the Other in order to set the Other, this particular Other, free; this is what Søren Kierkegaard had ostensibly done for Regine Olsen, the woman he loved. To love, as young Lukács observed, is 'to try never to be proved right'. As it happens, most human bonds prove to be so appallingly brittle and fissiparous, and most human emotions so volatile, because in the human encounter the elusive yet hotly desired quality of 'being in the right' shifts, like a pendulum, once to one side, then to the other, staying nowhere for long. Love is a hostage to drifting domination; togetherness is a plaything of the argument. There is but one way of rendering love, and the love-saturated relationship, secure: 'to love in such a way that the object of love will not stand in the way of my love'.[9] To prise asunder love from the possession;

---

[9] Lukács, 'The Foundering of Form against Life', in *Soul and Form*, p. 34.

Lev Shestov (in *Athens and Jerusalem*; here quoted after *A Shestov Anthology*, ed. Bernard Martin (Athens: Ohio University Press, 1970)) contests the version of the Kierkegaard–Olsen affair which Lukács, following virtually any other author, accepts. According to Shestov, Kierkegaard 'did everything in his power to make people believe that he had broken with Regina Olsen voluntarily, that it was on his part a freely offered sacrifice . . . Even more, not only did he succeed in making others believe this, he almost succeeded in persuading himself.' (p. 295) In fact, Kierkegaard was deprived of his love by the most mundane, unheroic and morally numb 'external events': Regine was betrothed to another man. If Shestov's hypothesis is true, however, it does not necessarily change the significance of the case. Insisting on the voluntarity of the tragic ending of his love, Kierkegaard paid obliquely a tribute to the limitless demand all true love makes; not making such a demand, and not forcing the lover to obey it, hurts perhaps the lover's *amour propre*; but it also puts in question the viridity of love itself. Shestov in the end admits as much: 'What can be more shameful, what can be more outrageous than the necessity to think and say not what we desire to say . . .?' The act of sacrifice is the ultimate confirmation that the demand of love – one that calls for freedom of sacrifice – has been heard and followed. Otherwise, Kierkegaards's agony would have no meaning.

not to ask the object of love to prove worthy of the loving emotion; not to expect the object of admiration to provide the certificate of admirable qualities; and, above all, not to demand this humility to be reciprocated. My dedication is safe and wholesome only if the object of my dedication is free.

Rightly or wrongly, Kierkegaard came to the conclusion that a permanent match with Regine would destroy both partners. He loved Regine too much to see her destroyed; too much to allow her to see himself, the man she loved, to be destroyed. Opting out from the match before it reveals itself as a mismatch was the only solution such love permitted. Yet the opting out could be, for Regine, as destructive as staying in. Regine *needed* him; and so the task, *his* task, was to make her cease needing him, so that the end of the liaison would bring but a momentary, easy-to-heal pain – that brief shock of sudden deprivation which usually precedes liberation. To fulfil the task, he had to destroy himself. First as an image: stripping himself of all that made him attractive, endearing, desirable in the eyes of Regine. Ultimately, as a person: disappearing forever from Regine's vision and lingering in her memory as no more than one among many wasted or missed or rejected options of a meaningful life. Kierkegaard's eagerly embraced death was the accolade, and the fulfilment, of his love for Regine. She was married to another man, and now – set free – she could reconcile herself to that other marriage. Freedom – the greatest of gifts love can offer the beloved.

Or one may wish to die because love – all love, love as such – cannot be fulfilled, not in this world of the passing and the transitory; because the union at which love aims is doomed to remain forever a goal, never to be reached. There is more than a touch of egoism in this kind of death-for-anOther; perhaps one should speak here of dying *because*-of-another, rather-than *for*-anOther, this death-wish looking suspiciously like an escape rather than a sacrifice. Like all hope, the love union lives but in the future, and it stays alive, enticing and haunting, as long as there is a future left. Death – my death – is the radical annulment of the future. By the same token, death is the radical emancipation from hope lived as a nightmare.

> Someone has died. And the survivors are faced with the painful, forever fruitless question of the eternal distance, the unbridgeable void between one human being and another. Nothing remains they might cling to. For the illusion of understanding another person is fed only by the renewed miracles, the anticipated surprises of constant companionship; these alone are capable of giving something like reality to illusion, which is directionless – like air. The sense of belonging together is kept alive only by continuity, and once this is destroyed, even the past disappears; everything

one person may know about another is only expectation, only potentiality, only wish or fear, acquiring reality only as a result of what happens later; and this reality, too, dissolves straightaway into potentialities . . .

The truth, the finality of death, is dazzlingly clear, clearer than anything else, only, perhaps, because death alone, with the blind face of truth, snatches loneliness from the arms of possible closeness – those arms which are always open for a new embrace.[10]

Death destroys the possibility – the only place where closeness, that dream-horizon of love, feels at home. Death is, in this sense, the ultimate bankruptcy of love, insolvency which will never be redeemed. But, at the same time, it is eternal suspension, and thus a perverse victory over bankruptcy; it freezes the hope at a point just short of ultimate frustration and surrender. To die, in order not to live to be frustrated; but to die so that the loved one be not allowed to be frustrated. To 'cryonize', so to speak, the illusion and the hope. To die myself, rather than permit the Other's hope to die the shameful death of ignominy and rejection. One dies, so that the hope which keeps the Other alive could live, or that it might die no sooner that it turns unneeded, detoxicated, forgotten, unable to hurt. Thanks to the finality of death, all proofs to the contrary, however potentially frustrating, are certain to stay forever inconclusive. The hope would survive – in that illusion which will be never put to a test, and thus never be dashed.

Or one may die, or wish to die, of the fullness of love, as did Goethe's Werther and generations of romantic lovers after him. In James D. Wilson's reading, 'Werther kills himself not because his love is barren but because it is so full of intensity that he cannot bear life without it . . . All love on earth is by its nature incomplete as it is ephemeral; love is sustainable only in the transcendent realm it foreshadows.'[11] Werther's love for Lotte is too big for the pettiness of earthly concerns; it could only be soiled and degraded by the mediocrity and meanness of daily life. Werther's love lifted Lotte to the heights where neither the poisoned arrows nor depraving temptations of quotidianity could reach her. At that distance, however, Lotte lost all connection with life concerns. She can be reached, if at all, in the 'nether world' in which such concerns grind to a halt. Love, truly fulfilled and victorious, reaching the ultimate it is capable of reaching, is ready for the end (and for nothing else): there is nothing left to be sought, less still to be found, on earth. Death, on the other hand, becomes a

---

[10] Lukács, 'The Moment and Form', in *Soul and Form*, pp. 107–8, 109.

[11] James D. Wilson, *The Romantic Heroic Ideal* (Baton Rouge: Louisiana State University Press, 1982), p. 46.

gateway leading into the company of the immortal – if only in the enchanted kingdom of romantic imagination which the realist would deride. Death, this emphatic denial of immortality, is the only way to make immortality feel, sound, look true.

And so one can *wish to die* for the Other in order to set the Other free; in order to save the Other a life-destroying frustration; or in order to believe in a communion so complete and perfect that it is no more thinkable in the world where life is lived. In all three incarnations, this is a fixated wish, targeted on the Other picked up and set side from the rest of the otherhood densely populated with people who do not deserve and cannot be offered a similar self-sacrifice. The act of picking up and setting aside fuses the self-sacrifice with the obsession of mastery. These kinds of 'dying for the Other' are, perhaps, the supreme and extreme manifestations of moral drive – yet they are, simultaneously, desperate attempts to possess the Other, if not in the personhood, then in her destiny, to possess completely, radically, and irrevocably. This Other here, chosen by me, appropriated by me, made into the object of my decisions, of my setting of preferences, of my evaluation of values. The most altruistic of loves is also the most selfish.

But one can also be *ready to die* for the Other not 'in order to', not at all as a means to an end, not as a trade-off of a lesser good for a more precious one; as a matter of fact, not in the result of any calculation at all and not out of desire for any achievement. Without thinking. Without justifying. Without rationalizing. Without arguing – with others, or with oneself. Without the gratifying belief in the 'effectiveness' of one's death. Without hoping to 'accomplish' anything or even as little as embellish one's life record or adorn the memory of one's death. And without *wishing* to die. One can be ready to die for anOther just because one is ready to see one's responsibility for the Other through to its end, whatever the end may be – and if that responsibility has a price tag of death attached to it, so be it. The devastating irony (but one that makes such a death truly, self-deprecatingly disinterested) is that the death, if and when it comes, may not save the Other for whom the sacrifice has been made. It may not assure her survival, or extend her life. It may not even make the Other's life any easier and any more wholesome than it otherwise would have been. Yet it does not matter. When the responsibility for anOther speaks, the calculating reason keeps respectful silence. It has nothing to say; being reason, it also knows that it would not be heard.

Such a readiness-to-die-for-anOther is the sign of moral awakening from the egotistic somnolence in which life is for most people, most of the time enveloped. Egoism and egotism of quotidianity blurs the moral sense and makes the Other invisible as an object of my responsibility. It takes a shock of which only the Other as the Face, as the command to help and to care, is capable, to 'sober up' from egological intoxication, to wake up from the proto-moral, egotistic nap.[12] Such a shock, and the de-intoxication that follows, goes beyond the self-awareness, the lucidity of being-for-itself, that 'inauthentic authenticity', or 'identity of non-identity'; it founds the Self as that what is from the start exceeded, rescued from its solitude, fulfilled in being-for-anOther.

That responsibility for the Other which is the starting point of all morality is not a conditional responsibility, not a contractual responsibility, not a responsibility 'from here to there', 'from this moment to that'. It is a total responsibility, a no-excuse and no-limits responsibility, which at no point of space or time can rest and celebrate itself as done and fulfilled. The care for the Other lives as long as the Other lives (and, as Benjamin insisted, the dead are not safe either: they also need protection); it never dies first, it survives its object. That care, and that care only, makes life worth living; but it may so happen that it demands that life is sacrificed. Death may be the price of caring life, but it is a price which caring life, being caring life, cannot and would not refuse to pay. Such death comes not as an outcome of a decision – heroic or romantic, carefully calculated or off the cuff, rational or foolish. It comes uninvited and unwelcome. It comes because it cannot be avoided. It comes because one cannot go on caring while trying to escape it.

It is a moral world in which the responsibility for anOther goes as far as the readiness to die. It is a cruel, inhuman and immoral world in which that readiness is called, and required, to be acted upon. Such is the world at war. Such was, more than any other world, the world of the Holocaust, of the Gulag, of the genocide. The moral actors of those worlds were not heroes at all. Or, rather, they acted heroically because they were moral – it was not the act of heroism that grounded their morality. They were, purely and simply, the 'morally awakened', caring people. People who just could not make themselves live at the expense of their responsibility for Others, and hence were ready to make their lives – even their lives – the price of that responsibility. They did not see themselves as heroes. And they would not be heroes, if the circumstances had not put an equals sign between being human and acting heroically. Being (and staying) human comes to mean being a hero in an inhuman world, like the world of the

---

[12] Cf. Levinas, 'Philosophie et l'éveil', in *Entre-Nous*, pp. 102–4.

Holocaust or the Gulag. This is not a heroism by choice. Wishing to be human, and wishing to be a hero, are not the same wishes; and they should not be. More often than not, they differ sharply. In an important way they are mutually incompatible: one justifies deeds which the other condemns.

Heroes and moral people are both called to sacrifice their lives; to die for, for a cause which is nobler, loftier, more worthy that their own self-preservation. For a moral person, however, that cause is the life or well-being or dignity of another human being. For a hero, that cause is the continuation or promotion or triumph of an idea: that of a nation, of a race, of a class, of progress, of a 'way of life', of God, sometimes of 'man as such'. There is a moral abyss stretching between the two causes. The first cause cannot justify any death but one's own (in the words of Jean Guehenno, one cannot deny that there are reasons for which one should be ready to die, but there are no reasons for which one could claim a right to demand that the others die).[13] In the name of the second cause, one may, one should, one is exhorted and encouraged to kill. ('It is possible to sacrifice an indeterminate number of human lives in the name of the defence of Man', observes Tsvetan Todorov.)[14] The first cause is about saving people. The second – about saving values. Values often gain when people die. Like vampires, values need blood to replenish their life juices. And the greater the number of dead, the more splendid and divine grow the values on whose altar the lives had been burned. In the end it is death, rather than lives it claimed to preserve, which turns into the supreme value. Death itself becomes the cause for the hero of a cause.

The 'ethics of responsibility' of the kind which Weber recommended as the virtue of the politicians, comes from the same stable in which the heroes of causes have been trained and groomed. Like the mythology of heroism, that ethic turns the preservation of life into an excuse for the death of others. ('Observing the norms of the ethics of responsibility does

---

[13] Cf. Jean Guehenno, *La Mort des autres* (Paris: Grasset, 1968), pp. 169–70.

The distinction, so sharply drawn by Guehenno, is, as it were, a time honoured one. The French philosophical tradition, while known for the eulogizing of heroic life, contains a profound critique of heroism as a service to domination or a demand of the tyrant or a tyrannical idea. As Robert Favre has found after a thorough study of the legacy of Enlightenment, 'Les philosophes n'ont aucune estime particulière pour le "héros" ni pour le "martyr", mais c'est qu'ils dénoncent à travers eux la guerre et la fanatisme et non pas du tout les valeurs héroïques.' (*La Mort dans la littérature et la pensée françaises au siècle des Lumières* (Presses Universitaires de Lyon, 1978), p. 482).

[14] Tsvetan Todorov, *Face à l'extrême* (Paris: Seuil, 1991). p. 14.

not prevent any hero from becoming a murderer on *moral* grounds if he considers the consequences of the murder *beneficial*, as Agnes Heller comments.[15]) For this reason, Weber's ethics of responsibility, exactly like heroism 'for a cause', fails the test of morality, ignorant or neglectful as it is of morality's most fundamental precept. No principle or norm can claim to be moral as long as it justifies the death of anOther, let alone the murder of anOther – in the same way as no principle or norm may claim to be moral, if it implies that my responsibility for the Other stops short of the gift of my life.

---

[15] Heller, 'The Legacy of Marxian ethics', p. 137.

Index

211